Clwyd Limestone

Mark Glaister

Lee Proctor

Text, topos and crag photography
by Mark Glaister and Lee Proctor.
Action photography by Mark Glaister or as credited.
Edited by Alan James.
Printed in Europe on behalf of Latitude Press Ltd.
(ISO 14001 and EMAS certified printers).
Distributed by Cordee (cordee.co.uk).

All maps by ROCKFAX
Some maps based on original source data
from openstreetmap.org.

Published by ROCKFAX in December 2015
© ROCKFAX 2015
rockfax.com

All rights reserved. No part of this publication may be reproduced, stored in
a retrieval system, or transmitted in any form or by any means, electronic,
mechanical, photocopying or otherwise without prior written permission of the
copyright owner. A CIP catalogue record is available from the British Library.

This book is printed on FSC certified paper
made from 100% virgin fibre sourced
FSC from sustainable forestry

ISBN 978 1 873341 03 2

Cover: Julian Heath on the immaculate vertical face climbing of
Traction Trauma (6c+) - *page 171* - at Dinbren, Clwyd's most popular
venue for high-standard sport climbing.
Photo: Keith Sharples

This page: Mark Glaister setting off up the final exposed groove of
Delta Force (6c+) - *page 104* - at the magnificently situated Craig Arthur.
Photo: Phil Black

Contents: Clwyd Limestone

Introduction 4
   The Rockfax App 8
   Symbol, Map and Topo Key... 9
   Previous Guidebooks 10
   Acknowledgements 12

Clwyd Limestone Logistics   16
   Getting Around and Maps ... 18
   Accommodation 20
   Pubs and Climbing Shops... 22
   Climbing Walls and Cafes ... 24

Clwyd Limestone Climbing .. 26
   Access 28
   Gear and Bolting 30
   Grades 32
   Sport Graded List 34
   Trad Graded List 36
   Destination Planner 38

Ruthin and Mold Area 40
   Denbigh Castle Quarry 42
   Ruthin Escarpment 44
   Devil's Gorge 52
   Maeshafn Quarry 58
   Pot Hole Quarry 70
   Minera Quarry 76

Eglwyseg Valley 80
   World's End 82
   Craig Arthur 96
   Twilight Area 116
   Pinfold 128
   Monk's Buttress 154
   Dinbren 160

Trevor Area 196
   Trevor Quarry 198
   Independence Quarry 215
   Ruabon Quarry 221

Outlying Areas 222
   Pandy Outcrop 224
   Llanymynech Quarry 230
   Pontesford Rocks 252

Route Index 258
Crag Index 263
Map and General Index 264

Mark Pretty on the Devil's Gorge classic *Grand Canyon* (7b+) - *page 55*. The Devil's Gorge is an impressive gash in the hillside with its 25m overhanging east wall with a set of tough sport climbs on it. Once dry it provides an option for a rainy day and plenty of shade. Photo: Tim Glasby

Clwyd Limestone — Introduction

The long moorland covered spine of the Clwydian hills runs down the Welsh side of the northern borders of Wales and England and is dotted with picturesque villages and beautiful isolated valleys. Lurking toward the southern end of the range is the Eglwyseg valley - a spectacular layered escarpment of limestone that provides the centrepiece of climbing in the region and this guidebook.

The Eglwyseg valley is set high above the tourist trap of Llangollen and its magnificent frontage can only be fleetingly glimpsed from the main A5 road that rushes people on toward Snowdonia. However, for those that make the surprisingly short diversion up into the valley a revelation of fine limestone crags and climbing awaits. The line of natural cliffs has four main sections that begin in the narrowing head of the valley at World's End and conclude at the unbroken strip of Dinbren. Both traditional and sport climbs are numerous in the valley with the easily-accessed Dinbren now firmly established on the destination list of must-visit sport crags. Its concentration of high quality and well equipped lines and wonderful outlook are guaranteed to maintain the crag's popularity, and even though new routes have been steadily added over the last decade there is still some space left for more. Moving up the valley is the long Pinfold escarpment, and the towering rampart of Craig Arthur. These tend to be quieter but are both excellent destinations plastered with superb sport and trad climbs. Finally, just as the valley pinches and opens out onto the moors, is World's End - an enduring traditional venue that still attracts those after some good amenable trad routes.

As the Eglwyseg valley fans out opposite the hilltop ruin of Castell Dinas the escarpment has been quarried in the distant past. The string of quarried faces have now been fully developed into a very popular sport climbing area known collectively as Trevor Area. The plethora of routes and stunning outlook are just two of many reasons to visit.

To the north of Eglwyseg Valley are several limestone quarries. Some are quaint trad spots such as Pot Hole and Maeshafn quarries. For the harder climber, the narrow defile of Devil's Gorge, once dried out, has some good stamina sport routes.

The low quarried walls of the Trevor Area are home to some great sport routes in the 4 to 6 grade range. The climbing in this area has become very popular offering plenty of options, an easy approach and stunning views out over Castell Dinas to the Berwyn mountains and beyond. In this photo of the Suspect Wall a climber is surmounting the overhang of *No Remittal* (6a) - *page 211*.

Clwyd Limestone Introduction

South of the Clwydian range and very sheltered from poor weather coming from the west is the massive quarry of Llanymynech. The quarry is a nature reserve and has a number of huge walls that provide plenty of excellent sport and trad climbs. Given reasonable weather many of the best climbs can be climbed year round. Here a climber is just about to make a rightward traverse to finish the fine *Black Wall* (E1 5b) - *page 246*.

Introduction Clwyd Limestone

South of the Clwyd are three outlying crags very different in character. Llanymynech Quarry is a vast abandoned working that has been developed to give a major sport climbing destination - its huge walls span the grades from 6a to 7b attracting ever more interest as news of its quality of climbing and sheltered aspect have spread. The final two outliers are long-established easier non-limestone trad cliffs that have not appeared in a guidebook for well over two decades. Both Pandy Outcrop and Pontesford Rocks have delightful climbing in some of the finest locations in the Welsh and Shropshire hills.

This Clwyd Limestone Rockfax covers virtually all of the sport and trad climbing available in the area. The book builds on the previous Clwyd Limestone Rockfax with many more routes, bigger topos and more crags. The book covers a wide grade span in both the trad and sport styles - it will have something to entice the vast majority of climbers of all abilities.

Mark Glaister, November 2015

Introduction **Clwyd Limestone**

Coverage
This edition of the Clwyd Limestone Rockfax guide covers a similar area to the previous Rockfax book published in 2005. New additions include Pandy Outcrop and Pontesford Rocks which, although formed of igneous rock, are geographically not too distant and have not been featured in any guidebook for well over two decades.

Even in the relatively short 10 year period since the last edition, guidebook production has moved on apace with larger photo topos, cutting-edge action photography, GPS navigation and QR codes now standard. Our fundamental aim hasn't changed though and that is that you should never have to turn more than a few pages to first get to the crag, then get to the buttress and finally locate the start of your chosen route. All route descriptions are on the same page as their topo and listed from left-to-right. There are many other features to help choose suitable routes and crags depending on specific weather conditions or your ability level. You can select a crag from the crag tables on page 38. Each topo also has crag symbols for a quick glance check - see key on page 9.

This book is also the first Rockfax to be brought out at the same time as the Rockfax App version - see page 8 for more information.

Clwyd Limestone — The Rockfax App

The Rockfax App brings together all the Rockfax climbing information with UKC Logbooks and presents it in a user-friendly package for use on Apple iOS devices (Android version to follow in 2016).

The heart of the App is the Rockfax crag and route information which is downloaded by way of paid in-App purchases for individual crags, or bundles of crags, in 'Areas' which correspond roughly to printed guidebooks. You can purchase each crag individually, or the whole book.
The main data on the App is downloaded and stored on your device so you don't need any signal to be able to read the descriptions and see the topos and maps. There is a free sample crag for each area and some of these are quite extensive enabling you to get a really good impression of what the App is like, without shelling out any money.

The Rockfax App itself is a free download and incredibly useful in its own right. It contains a detailed crag map linked to the UKClimbing crags database (currently with basic information and routes lists for around 20,000 crags worldwide). The map also displays all the 4,000+ listings from the UKClimbing Directory of climbing walls, outdoor shops, climbing clubs, outdoor-specific accommodation and instructors and guides amongst others.

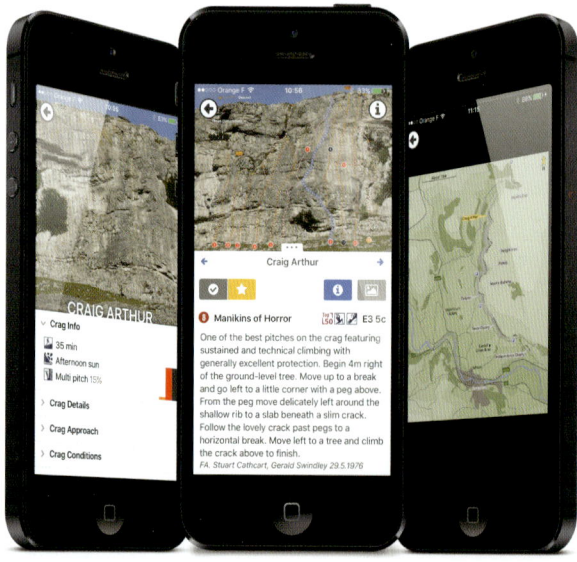

To find the App, search for 'Rockfax App' in Google or on the appropriate store.
The current Rockfax books with App versions are shown on the inside back cover flap.

UKC Logbooks

An incredibly popular method of logging your climbing is to use the **UKClimbing.com** logbooks system. This database lists more than 338,000 routes, over 19,800 crags and, so far, more than 28,000 users have recorded over 4.2 million ascents! To set up your own logbook all you need to do is register at **UKClimbing.com** and click on the logbook tab. Once set up you will be able to record every ascent you make, when you did it, what style you climbed it in and who you did it with. Each entry has a place for your own notes. You can also add your vote to the grade/star system linked to a database on the Rockfax site used by the guidebook writers. The logbook can be private, public or restricted to your own climbing partners only.
The Rockfax App can be linked to your **UKClimbing.com** user account and logbook so that you can record your activity while at the crag and look at photos, comments and votes on the routes. To do this you will need a 3G/4G data connection. You can also look at the UKC logbooks to see if anyone has climbed your chosen route recently to check on conditions.

Symbol, Map and Topo Key — Clwyd Limestone

Route Symbols

 A good route which is well worth the effort.

 A very good route, one of the best on the crag.

 A brilliant route, one of the best in the Clwyd area.

 Top 50 A significant route which is one of the best of its type and grade in the book.

 Technical climbing requiring good balance and technique, or complex and tricky moves.

 Powerful climbing; roofs, steep rock, low lock-offs or long moves off small holds.

 Sustained climbing; either lots of hard moves or steep rock giving pumpy climbing.

 Fingery climbing with significant small holds on the hard sections.

 Fluttery climbing with big fall potential and scary run-outs.

 A long reach is helpful, or even essential, for one or more of the moves.

 Some loose rock may be encountered.

Crag Symbols

 Angle of the approach walk to the crag with approximate time.

 Approximate time that the crag is in the direct sun (when it is shining).

 The crag is exposed to bad weather and will catch the wind if it is blowing.

 The crag can offer shelter from cold winds and it may be a good suntrap in colder weather.

 The crag suffers from seepage. It may well be wet and unclimbable in winter and early spring.

 The crag is steep and may well offer some dry rock to climb when it is raining.

 Some or all of the routes have a restriction due to nesting birds. Details in the crag information.

 Some or all of the routes are affected by an access problem. Details in the crag information.

 Deserted - Currently under-used and usually quiet. Fewer good routes or remote and smaller areas.

 Quiet - Less popular sections on major crags, or good buttresses with awkward approaches.

Busy - Places you will seldom be alone, especially at weekends. Good routes and easy access.

Crowded - The most popular sections of the most popular crags which are always busy.

Topo Key

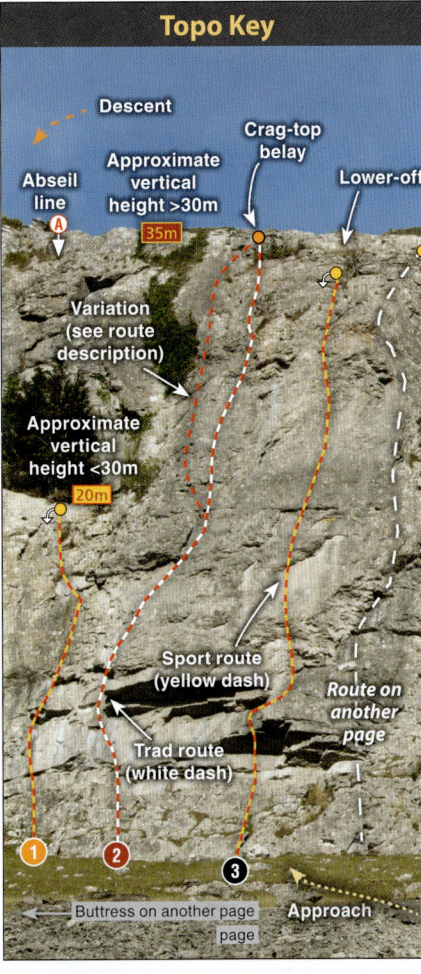

Map Key

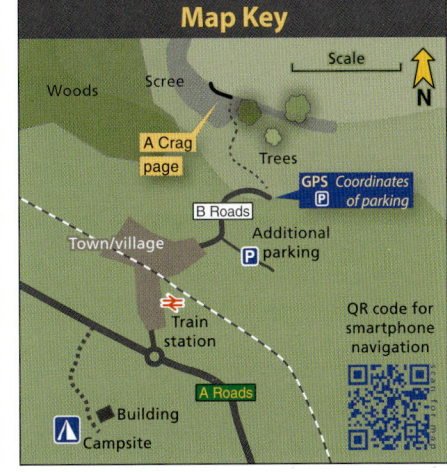

Key Previous Guidebooks and Route Information

The climbing on the limestone crags of Clwyd and its outlying neighbours has been documented since the 1970s. We are very grateful to all those who have worked on previous guidebooks. The key books are listed below.

Clwyd Limestone
Stuart Cathcart (Cicerone Press 1983)

West Midlands Rock
Doug Kerr (Cicerone Press 1988)

Clwyd Rock
Gary Dickinson (Cicerone Press 1993)

Clwyd Limestone
Lee Proctor, Mark Glaister (Rockfax 2005)

Non Rockfax/UKC Website route information:
sportsclimbs.co.uk - Topos and new route developments on Gary Gibson's web site.

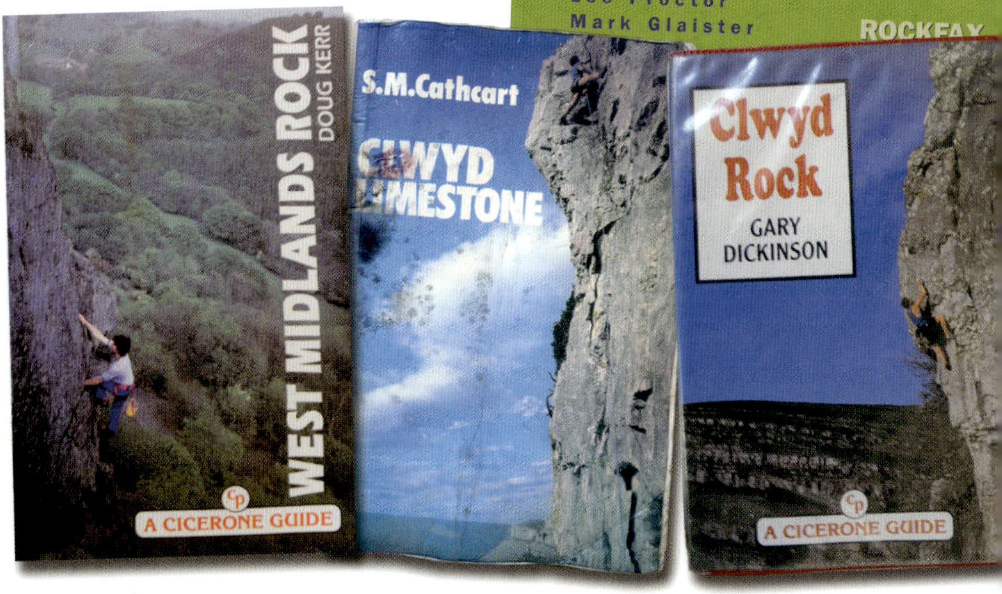

Guidebook Footnote

The inclusion of a climbing area in this guidebook does not mean that you have a right of access or the right to climb upon it. The descriptions of routes within this guide are recorded for historical reasons only and no reliance should be placed on the accuracy of the description. The grades set in this guide are a fair assessment of the difficulty of the climbs. Climbers who attempt a route of a particular standard should use their own judgment as to whether they are proficient enough to tackle that route. This book is not a substitute for experience and proper judgment. The authors, publisher and distributors of this book do not recognise any liability for injury or damage caused to, or by, climbers, third parties, or property arising from such persons seeking reliance on this guidebook as an assurance for their own safety.

Clare Reading perched on the headwall of the long and varied Top 50 sport pitch *These Foolish Things* (7a+) - *page 114* - at the Sunnyside Area, Craig Arthur. Craig Arthur is a large and exposed wall of limestone, which has a mix of trad and sport routes up to 40m in length. Photo: Keith Sharples

Clwyd Limestone — Acknowledgements

Acknowledgements — Clwyd Limestone

We would like to thank all those listed below who have helped in some way to put together this edition of Clwyd Limestone - Gary Gibson, Rob Watt, Gary Morgan, Allister McNeil - Wrekin MC, Karl Smith, Nick Dixon, Ryan McConnell, Luke Owens, Luke Clarke, Ed Booth, Patricia Novelli, Elfyn Jones, Rob Mirfin, Dave Rose, Phil Black, Alison Martindale, Stuart Cathcart, Ally Smith, Marti Hallett, Debbie Roberts, Paul Cox, Mr Guy Kennaway, Mr Thomas, Lucy Creamer, Craig Bailey, Steve Mattock, Ellie Morgan, John Stringfellow, Bridget Collier and Sarah Braithwaite.

A massive thank you to all those who have taken and been the subjects of the superb portfolio of shots that make such a huge contribution to the appeal of this guidebook - Mike Hutton, Tim Glasby, Keith Sharples, Sophie Baring, Phil Black, Paul Cox, John Stringfellow, Craig Bailey, Patricia Novelli, Dave Rose, Ryan McConnell, Rob Mirfin, John Warner.

It has as ever been a pleasure to work with Alan James and the Rockfax/UKC team on the production of this guidebook.

Mark Glaister and Lee Proctor, November 2015

Rockfax is very grateful to the following advertisers who have supported this guidebook:

Awesome Walls - *Page 2*
awesomewalls.co.uk

Berghaus - *Inside front cover*
berghaus.com

DMM - *Outside back cover*
dmmclimbing.com

High Sports - *Inside back cover*
highsports.co.uk

Plas y Brenin - *Page 23*
pyb.co.uk

Plas Power - *Page 25*
plaspoweradventure.com

The Boardroom - *Back cover flap*
theboardroomclimbing.com

Sue Hazel in the upper corner of the tricky trad pitch *Alison* (E1 5b) - *page 171* - at Dinbren. Although the majority of visitors now tackle the sport climbs on this crag, there are many classic trad routes scattered all along the Clwyd crags that are worthy of attention. Photo: Patricia Novelli

Clwyd Limestone Logistics

Immaculate limestone is the big draw on the Left Wing of Dinbren, its long low wall providing a mix of powerful and fingery climbing. In this picture the subtle grooves and pockets of the classic *Climb High* (7a) - *page 171* - are linked by Craig Bailey prior to unlocking the puzzling rockover that provides the route's memorable crux. Photo: Keith Sharples

Clwyd Limestone Logistics

Mountain Rescue
In the event of an accident requiring the assistance of Mountain Rescue:

Dial 112 and ask for 'POLICE - MOUNTAIN RESCUE'

This is very important since just asking for 'Police' will redirect you to a switchboard which could be a long way from your current location. This can cause delays in the rescue procedure as the authorities try and track down where the injured party is. Asking for 'Mountain Rescue' will immediately redirect you to people who know the area well.

Mobile Phones
All of the crags featured in this guide have mobile coverage although the quality of signal varies dependant upon provider.

Tourist Information Centres
If you are short of ideas about what to do on a wet day or need some accommodation, take a look at the Tourist Information Centres. They contain a lot more useful information than it is possible to include in these pages.

Llangollen - Y Chapel, Castle Street, Llangollen. Tel: 01978 860828
Mold - Earl Road, Mold. Tel: 01352 759331
Wrexham - Lambpit Street, Wrexham. Tel: 01978 292015
Shrewsbury - The Music Hall, The Square, Shrewsbury. Tel: 01743 258888
More information and other travel tips are at **information-britain.co.uk**

Temperature °C	Jan	Feb	Mar	Apr	May	Jun	Jul	Aug	Sep	Oct	Nov	Dec
Average Max Temp (°C)	8	8	10	13	16	19	21	21	18	14	10	7
Average Min Temp (°C)	2	2	3	5	8	10	12	12	10	7	4	2
Approx. Rain Days/Month	18	14	17	11	11	10	10	11	11	16	15	18

When to Go
The best time to visit the higher crags in the Eglwyseg valley is from early spring to late autumn when the air temperature is warm and seepage will be less of an issue, but keep away if there is a wind blowing from the west. Cold stable weather in winter does allow for some pleasant days out of the wind and in the sun.

Maeshafn and Pot Hole Quarrries are year-round venues as long as the sun is out during the colder months. The Devil's Gorge has a climate of its own and even in summer can be out of condition in humid weather, although it is rainproof once the seepage has dried up.

Llanymynech is a great choice when gales are roaring from the west and can be excellent during the colder months as it takes little seepage and gets the sun early in the day.

The trad crags of Pandy Outcrop and Pontesford Rocks are usually out of condition in the winter months and are exposed to rain and wind, but once in condition, have little seepage.

Clwyd Limestone Logistics

Leon Bowen on one of the very popular sport routes on Dinbren's Right Wing *Trailer Trash* (6b) - *page 183*.
Photo: Ryan McConnell

Clwyd Limestone Logistics — Getting Around and Maps

Getting Around

The starting points for approaches to the crags are all easily reached by car and the approach descriptions are written assuming you have access to a car.

For those travelling to the area on public transport a good number of the crags can be reached without too much walking. Maeshafn, Pot Hole Quarry and The Devil's Gorge are within easy walking distance of buses from Mold. The lower Eglwyseg Valley (Trevor Area and Dinbren) is walkable from Llangollen in about half an hour. Both Chester and Shrewsbury are serviced by fast train services but trains are less useful for penetrating the area more deeply. There are local trains to Buckley, Wrexham, Chirk and Gobowen. Llangollen can be reached by bus from Chester or Shrewsbury. Llanymynech and Pontesford Rocks can also be reached by bus from Shrewsbury.

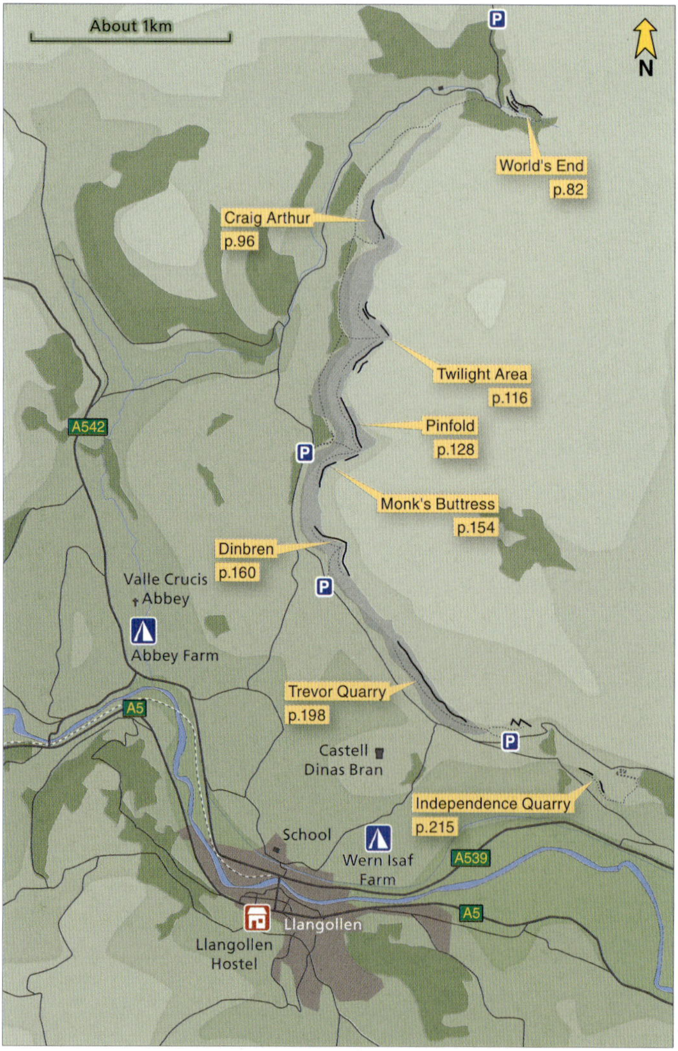

Buses - The website **traveline.info** is an excellent place to get a quick idea of links and times of bus services. The tourist information centres are also useful for travel information.
Trains - For timetable information go to **thetrainline.com**

Satellite Navigation

GPS 54.060178 / -2.154509 — All the parking spots are indicated with a precise GPS location. This is in the form of two decimal numbers as in the sample blue box. Different GPS devices accept these numbers in alternative formats.

QR codes (right) have also been included. You can scan the QR code using an app such as **Scan** (for iOS) or **Google Goggles** (for Android) and choose to open the result direct into the **Google Maps** navigation app on your phone.

Getting Around and Maps Clwyd Limestone Logistics

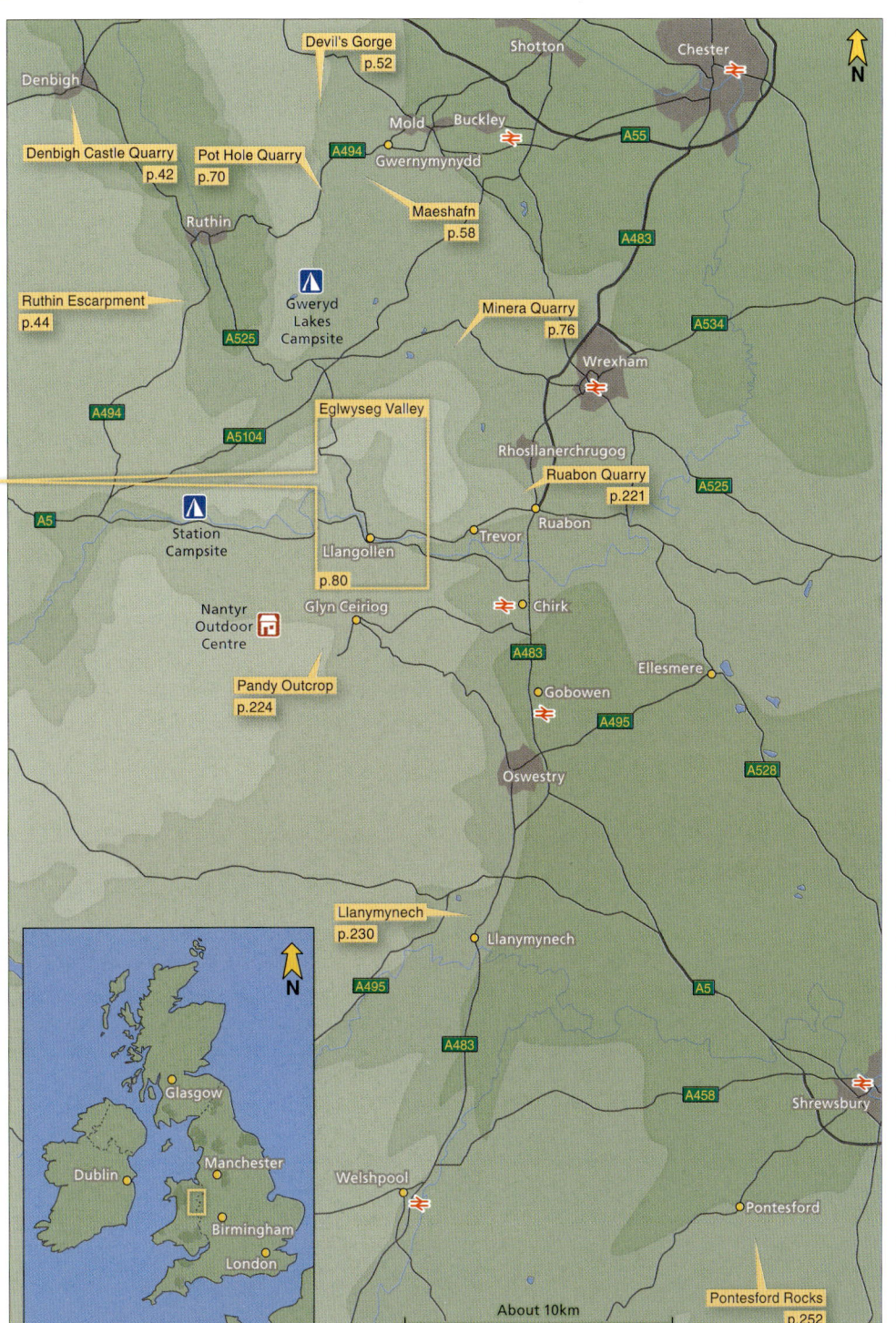

Clwyd Limestone Logistics — Accommodation

Camping and Hostels   See map on page 18/19 for locations

There are a number of campsites and hostels within easy reach of the crags but those listed below are the best for reaching the crags from.

Wern Isaf Farm, Llangollen - wernisaf.co.uk
The best option for those without a car. It is only 1km from Llangollen and within walking distance of the Eglwyseg crags. Tel: 01978 860632

Station Campsite, Carrog - stationcampsite.com
A nice site 10km west of Llangollen. Tel: 01490 430237

Abbey Farm Caravan Park, Llangollen - abbeyfarmcaravans.co.uk
Large tent and caravan site just north of Llangollen and close to pubs that serve food. Can be very busy at weekends and Bank Holidays. Tel: 01978 861297

Gweryd Lakes Camping, Llanarmon-yn-lal - gwerydlakes.co.uk
Site midway between Maeshafn/Pot Hole Quarries and the main Eglwyseg valley cliffs. Tel: 01824 780230

Llangollen Hostel - Convenient for crags and evenings in town - llangollenhostel.co.uk

Nantyr Outdoor Centre - Close to Pandy Outcrop. Good for groups - www.nantyr.co.uk

Not Camping

The Clwyd area is popular with tourists and accommodation plentiful. There are many bed and breakfasts in Llangollen, Mold, Ruthin and in the surrounding villages and farms. Contact local tourist information offices for more details - see page 16.

Accommodation **Clwyd Limestone Logistics**

Phil Black on the three star *Extreme Ways* (7c) - *page 168* - at the Climb High Area, Dinbren. This route, along with many others, have been put up at Dinbren since the previous guidebook. Photo: Phil Black Collection

Clwyd Limestone Logistics — Pubs and Climbing Shops

Pubs

There are many pubs in the area covered by this book, but those listed below are some of the best for those seeking out a good après-climb drink and food.

The Sun - Trevor
On the A539 between Llangollen and Trevor. Popular with climbers and close to the Trevor Quarries and Dinbren.

The Corn Mill - Llangollen
Lively riverside pub and restaurant in the centre of Llangollen.

Nag's Head - Pontesbury
Nearest pub for Pontesford Rocks. On the main road to the east of Pontesbury.

The Oak - Glyn Ceiriog
Community-owned pub in the village closest to Pandy Outcrop.

The Dolphin Inn - Llanymynech
Good little spot in the village near to quarry.

Druid Inn - Llanferres
Good pub that is very convenient for Pot Hole Quarry.

The Miners Arms - Maeshafn
In the village close to Maeshafn Quarry.

We Three Loggerheads
Roadside pub in Loggerheads Country Park not far from Maeshafn Quarry, Pot Hole Quarry and Devil's Gorge.

Climbing Shop

High Sports
51/52, Wyle Cop,
Shrewsbury.
Tel: 01743 231649
highsports.co.uk
See advert inside back cover

The Sun Inn at Trevor is a popular choice of climbers looking for a good après-climb pint and food.

IMPROVE YOUR CLIMBING WITH US

Here at the National Mountain Sports Centre we have a course that's perfect to help you develop, whatever standard you climb at. From complete beginner to performance climber, our coaches will help you take the next step, and help you get more out of your climbing. For more details, visit our website.

PLAS Y BRENIN
www.pyb.co.uk

Plas y Brenin The National Mountain Sports Centre Capel Curig Conwy LL24 OET   Tel: 01690 720214   Email: info@pyb.co.uk

 www.plus.google.com/+plasybrenin   www.facebook.com/plasybrenin   www.twitter.com/plasybrenin

Clwyd Limestone Logistics — Climbing Walls and Cafes

Climbing Walls
For those times of year when climbing outside isn't possible, the following climbing walls are well worth considering.
More information at **ukclimbing.com/walls/**

Awesome Walls - Liverpool
St Albans Church, Athol Street,
Liverpool, L5 9TN.
Tel: 0151 2982422
awesomewalls.co.uk
See advert on page 2

The Boardroom
Rectors Lane Ind. Est.,
Pentre, Queensferry,
CH5 2DH.
Tel: 01244 537476
theboardroomclimbing.com
See advert on back cover flap

Wrexham Climbing Centre
Plas Power Road, Southsea,
(near Wrexham), LL11 5SZ.
Tel: 01978 754747
plaspoweradventure.com
See advert opposite

North West Face
St Anns Church, Warrington.
northwestface.com

Shropshire Climbing Centre
Newport, Shropshire.
newportrock.com

Oswestry Climbing Centre
Maesbury Road, Oswestry.
oswestryclimbingcentre.co.uk

Cafes

Trevor and Eglwyseg Valley
Prospect Garden Tea Rooms is excellent. It is signed from the road that runs below Trevor Quarry.

Devil's Gorge, Maeshafn, Pot Hole Quarry
Loggerheads Park Cafe. Nice seating outside.

Llanymynech - Village Pantry Cafe.

Pontesford Rocks
Cafe in shop in nearby village of Pontesbury.

Llangollen
Has lots of cafes. The Dee Side Cafe next to the bridge over the river is good.

One of many cafes in Llangollen - a few minutes from many of the popular Eglwyseg Valley crags.

Wrexham climbing centre @ Plas Power Adventure

plas power adventure

The closest thing to rock
and closest to the rock
20 mins from Llangollen
Much more than just a wall

plaspoweradventure.com

Visit us on Facebook

01978 754747

Plas Power road
Southsea
Nr Wrexham
ll115sz

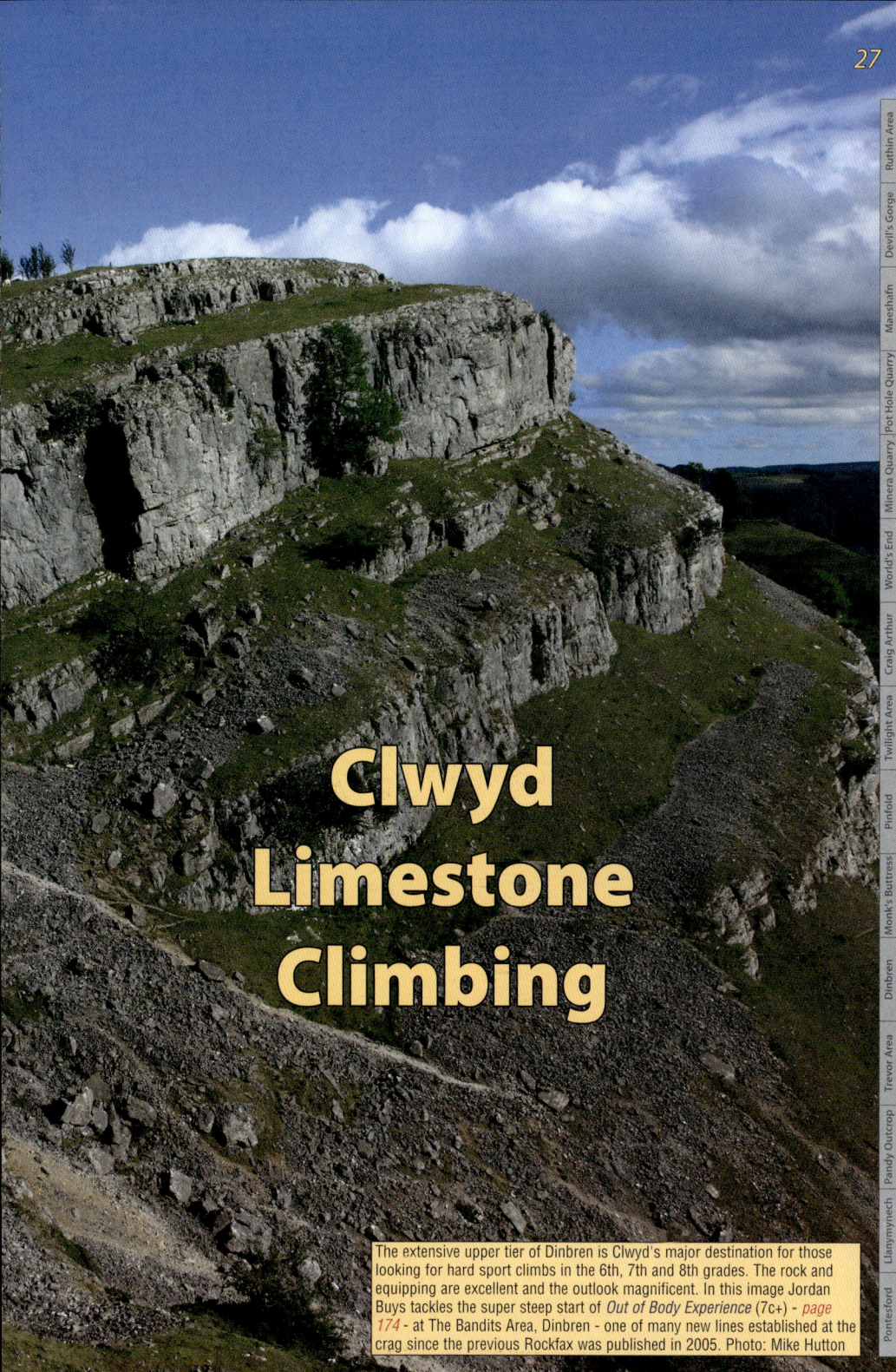

Clwyd Limestone Climbing

The extensive upper tier of Dinbren is Clwyd's major destination for those looking for hard sport climbs in the 6th, 7th and 8th grades. The rock and equipping are excellent and the outlook magnificent. In this image Jordan Buys tackles the super steep start of *Out of Body Experience* (7c+) - *page 174* - at The Bandits Area, Dinbren - one of many new lines established at the crag since the previous Rockfax was published in 2005. Photo: Mike Hutton

Access

As with most climbing areas in the UK there have always been access issues on the various crags covered in this edition of Clwyd Limestone. Nesting birds, flora, historical sites, land ownership, gardening and dogs have all been causes for disagreements in the past. Despite this, and thanks to the great work of the BMC and its volunteers, most of the crags in this book currently have good access arrangements.

Bird restriction marker. Climbing only to be undertaken between the green arrows when restriction is in place.

There are some restrictions at certain times of year so please keep a look out for the red symbols. The restrictions are usually because of nesting birds and the dates generally range from the beginning of February to the end of July.

Where a bird restriction applies to a section of the crag rather than the whole crag markers at the base of the crag like the one shown above are usually in place and climbing should only take place between the green arrows. Birds do nest in previously unrestricted areas and the absence of an agreed restriction does not mean that there are no nesting birds. Check UKC or BMC RAD if you are unsure. If you see agitated birds (lots of screeching and taking off and landing in the same spot, as well as aggressive flying in circles) then it is best to avoid that area even if there is no agreed restriction and report to the BMC.

Other crags have very precise parking and approach requirements. You will need to seek permission before you visit Maeshafn Quarry.

Individual crag access is covered in the respective chapters. Please read this information carefully and take great care not to infringe these necessary restrictions. If in any doubt contact the BMC (Tel: 0161 445 6111), or check the access section of the BMC website - thebmc.co.uk/modules/RAD/

Climbing access information sign at Trevor Quarry.

Climb it, Walk it, protect it

BMC ACCESS AND CONSERVATION TRUST

The **BMC Access & Conservation Trust** funds projects to protect your cliffs and mountains

ACT helps to fund:

1. Practical crag and footpath restoration
2. Mountain recreation and conservation research
3. Sustainable transport and rural initiatives
4. Campaigns for your countryside rights
5. Crag and mountain information and guidance

← Fix the Fells path repairs:
supported 2 projects to help repair paths in the Lake District mountains.

← The Three Peaks Partnership website:
a collaborative project to promote responsible behaviour on 3 Peaks challenge events
www.threepeakspartnership.co.uk

ACT is the charitable trust of the British Mountaineering Council (BMC).
ACT relies on your donations to turn climbing and walking conservation projects into reality.

You can donate online at www.thebmc.co.uk/donate-to-act or call 0161 445 6111
Or fundraise for us at **JustGiving** www.justgiving.com

ACT is a charitable trust (1089516), established by the British Mountaineering Council.

Gear

Most of the sport routes described in this book have good solid bolts and lower-offs in place. For the vast majority of routes a 60m rope and 14 quickdraws is sufficient to climb them. However, there are a number of lines that will require a longer rope to get down (and probably more quickdraws). **To avoid any doubt, always tie a stopper knot in the dead end of the rope to ensure that it will not pass through the belay device.**

The trad routes are best climbed on double ropes and are protected with a standard rack of wires, cams and slings. Many of the harder trad climbs also rely on fixed threads and pegs. All fixed gear should be treated with caution because many of the pegs and threads are old and at times might be the only protection available.

Bolting

The work of maintaining the bolts has been carried out by many people and has been a huge task. If you come across any routes that need re-equipping then please submit your comments to the databases on - **rockfax.com** or **sportsclimbs.co.uk**

Gary Gibson Bolt Fund

Gary Gibson is by far the most prolific bolter in the Clwyd area. Many of the routes on crags like Llanymynech, Trevor and Independence Quarry plus the Eglwyseg crags owe their existence to the bolting efforts of Gary. If you enjoy the sport climbing in the area then please consider making a donation to this effort. You can find the links to the PayPal page via **UKBoltFund.org**. Proceeds from some of the sales of this guidebook will go towards the Gary Gibson Bolt Fund.

Mark Glaister climbing *Subterranean Sidewalk* (6c+) - *page 249* - at Llanymynech Quarry, one of many routes featured in this book climbed and equipped by Gary Gibson. Photo: John Warner

UKBoltFund.org
Support local bolting volunteers

Lucy Creamer getting the gear in on *Survival of the Fastest* (E5 6a) - *page 107* - at Craig Arthur. Fantastic trad climbing is on offer throughout Clwyd ranging from the hard and adventurous, as pictured here, to more friendly venues such as Pot Hole and Maeshafn Quarry. Photo: Tim Glasby

Clwyd Limestone Climbing — Grades

The routes in this book are given one of two different grades depending on whether they are a trad route or a sport route. The table to the right roughly compares the sport and trad grade with two other international grading systems. On trad routes the majority of the gear is carried by the lead climber and is hand-placed.

A sport route is defined as one where all the major protection comes from gear fixed in the rock (bolts).

British Trad Grade
1) Adjectival grade (Diff, VDiff, Severe, Hard Severe (HS), Very Severe (VS), Hard Very Severe (HVS), E1, E2 ... to E10).
An overall picture of the route including how well protected it is, how sustained and a general indication of the level of difficulty of the whole route.

2) Technical grade (4a, 4b, 4c ... to 7b). The difficulty of the hardest single move, or short section.

Sport Grade
The sport grade is a measure of how hard it is going to be to get up a certain section of rock. It makes no attempt to tell you how hard the hardest move is, nor how scary a route is.

Sport Grade	British Trad Grade	UIAA	USA
1	Mod (Moderate)	I	5.1
2	Diff (Difficult)	II	5.2
2+		III	5.3
3	VDiff (Very Difficult)	III+	5.4
3+	HVD (Hard Very Difficult)	IV-	5.5
4a	Sev (Severe)	IV	5.6
4b	HS (Hard Severe)	IV+	5.7
4c	VS (Very Severe)	V-	5.8
5a		V	5.9
5b	HVS (Hard Very Severe)	V+	5.10a
5c	E1	VI-	5.10b
6a	E2	VI	5.10c
6a+		VI+	5.10d
6b	E3	VII-	5.11a
6b+		VII	5.11b
6c	E4	VII+	5.11c
6c+		VIII-	5.11d
7a	E5	VIII	5.12a
7a+		VIII+	5.12b
7b	E6	IX-	5.12c
7b+		IX	5.12d
7c	E7	IX+	5.13a
7c+		X-	5.13b
8a	E8	X	5.13c
8a+		X+	5.13d
8b	E9	XI-	5.14a
8b+		XI	5.14b
8c	E10	XI+	5.14c
8c+			5.14d
9a			5.15a
9a+			

Colour Coding
The routes are all given a colour-coded dot corresponding to a grade band. The colour represents a level that a climber should be happy at, hence sport routes tend to be technically harder than the equivalent coloured trad routes because the climber doesn't need to worry about the protection.

❶ Up to Severe / Up to 4c
Mostly these should be good for beginners and those wanting an easy life.

❷ HS to HVS / 5a to 6a+
General ticking routes for those with more experience.

❸ E1 to E3 / 6b to 7a
Routes for the experienced and keen climber. A grade band which includes many of the area's great classics.

❹ E4 or 7a+ and above
The really hard stuff including some of the top sport routes in the country.

Clwyd Limestone Climbing

Dave Rose making the crucial moves on the headwall of *Highway* (8a) - *page 175* - at The Bandits Area, Dinbren. Dinbren is the destination of choice for climbers looking for hard and powerful sport climbing. Photo: Rob Mirfin

Clwyd Limestone Climbing — Sport Graded List

8 b +
- Leftism — 168

8 b
- The Sound and the Fury — 164
- Binary Finary — 174
- El Zapatistas — 175
- Insomnia — 170

8 a +
- Hades — 55
- Counting Sheep — 169
- No Kneed — 174
- The Orgasmatron — 175

8 a
- El Rincon — 175
- Pi — 102
- Cerberus — 55
- Canyonlands — 55
- Elite Syncopations — 164
- Back-Bee Tubin — 237
- Highway — 175

7 c +
- The Final Solution — 86
- Broken Flowers — 170
- Statement of Ewes — 165
- Out of Body Experience — 174
- Train to Hell — 165
- Born Slippy — 55

7 c
- Underworld — 55
- When Saturday Comes — 170
- Broken Dreams — 170
- Dyperspace — 180
- Flowers are for the Dead — 169
- People Give Me The Eyes — 152
- Little Weed — 237

7 b +
- Ten — 105
- Brainbox — 139
- Generation of Swine — 139
- Back in Black — 165
- The Bandits — 174
- Fine Feathered Fink — 167
- Relentless — 105
- Grand Canyon — 55
- I Punched Judy First — 170

7 b
- Alpha Track Etch — 104
- Broccoli and Ice-Cream — 55
- The Butterfly Collector — 49
- The Screaming Skull — 238
- Sunnyside Up Mix — 115
- Through the Grapevine — 140
- Ice — 181
- Planet Claire — 138
- Dance of the Puppets — 101
- Walking with Barrence — 170
- Strawberry Tubin — 241

7 a +
- Fat Boys — 180
- Fire — 180
- Killer Gorilla — 138
- Nomad — 238
- Dreadlocks — 171
- Incy Wincy Spider — 242
- Bananas and Coffee — 57
- Mussel Bound — 251
- Echoes — 55
- Technicolour Yawn — 170
- These Foolish Things — 114
- In Search of Someone Silly — 170

7 a
- Prickly Heat — 135
- CCR — 46
- Hickory Dickory Dock — 242
- Jack the Smuggler — 241
- Lobster on the Loose — 249
- Rapture of the Deep — 249
- Unbroken — 238
- Hot Stuff — 181
- What's Goin' On — 140
- Dead Man's Fingers — 249
- Long John Codling — 251
- This Won't Hurt — 238
- Atmospheres — 138
- Climb High — 171

6 c +
- Subterranean Sidewalk — 249
- Delta Force — 104
- Inaugural Goose Flesh — 182
- Traction Trauma — 171
- Humpty Dumpty — 242
- I Saw Three Ships — 251
- Jaspers — 169
- Stupid School Boyz — 43
- Eddie Waring Lives On — 140
- Crash Diet — 122
- Ship Dip — 251
- Line of Fire — 165
- Runner Bean — 46
- The Deep — 251
- Trabucco — 213

6 c
- Cold Turkey — 169
- Grid Iron — 242
- Traction Control — 206
- Gemma's World Direct — 171
- A Night Torchlight Parade — 241
- Margin of Error — 206
- Dead Man's Creek — 107
- Just Another Route Name — 183
- Clevor Trevor — 213
- Mud Slide Slim — 213
- Crab Stick — 249
- This Way to Clitheroe — 213

6 b +
- Rabble Rouser — 238
- Curfew — 241
- Green Bean — 46
- The Dinbren Sanction — 168
- Clematis — 251

6 b
- Gaza Strippers — 241
- The Calch — 78
- Smack the Juggler — 241
- Where's the President's Brain — 176

6 b
- Crime Scene — 210
- Checkpoint Charlie — 206
- Day of the Triffids — 251
- Snakes in the Grass — 205
- Suspect Criminal — 210
- Resist and Exist — 176
- Lost Control — 206
- The Fuddites — 204
- Quartz Wall — 71
- Impact Imminent — 208
- Under Suspicion — 210
- Fudd Off — 204

6 a +
- Suspect Device — 210
- Borderline — 206
- Forever the Suspect — 210
- Super Furry Frogs — 205
- The Great Escape — 206
- Over the Wall — 206
- Suspectus — 210

6 a
- The Quartz Slab — 79
- Long-legged Lizard.... — 205
- Dogmatic — 204
- Slow, Araf, Slow — 205
- No Reptiles — 205
- All Fudd Up — 204
- About a Bay — 234

5 c
- Bay Leaf — 234
- Sgrech yr Hebog — 200
- Cluedo — 210
- Canal Canol — 202
- Innocence — 210

5 a
- Ogre in the Ogof — 200
- Dai Laughing — 202
- Disappearing Act — 210
- K9 — 205
- Co-ed in the Coed — 200

4 c
- Catch the Pigeon (Trevor Q) — 207
- Easy Grooves — 79
- Clue, So? — 211
- Deputy Dog — 205
- The Welsh Wizard — 202

4 b
- Merlin Magic — 201

4 a
- The Open Grey Groove — 79
- Hot Dog — 205
- Sudden Impact — 208
- Dim Parcio — 201

Clwyd Limestone Climbing

Sport Graded List

Having overcome the hard lower bulges the climber is moving up the slightly less demanding upper section of *Hot Stuff* (7a) - *page 181* - at the Fire and Ice Area, Dinbren. Powerful undercut starts followed by technical and fingery upper walls are typical of many of the sport lines to be found at Dinbren. Photo: Keith Sharples

Clwyd Limestone Climbing — Trad Graded List

E 7
- ** Shoot to Thrill — 151

E 6
- ** Bolt from the Blue — 165
- * The Fog — 167
- *** Shootin' Blanks — 110
- *** Manic Mechanic — 110

E 5
- ** Tres Hombres — 110
- *** Heaven or Hell — 103
- ** Black is Beautiful — 246
- ** Dangermouse — 144
- ** Punch and Judy — 107
- *** Eliminator — 102
- 4 Survival of the Fastest — 107

E 4
- 4 Mental Transition — 140
- *** Shooting Star — 86
- *** Another Red Line — 157
- *** Waltz in Black — 188
- ** While the Cat's Away — 246
- ** Flash Dance — 85
- * Pussyfooting — 60
- ** World's Edge — 84
- * Calculus — 64

E 3
- * Titanium Man — 87
- *** Sir Cathcart D'Eath — 157
- * Vertical Games — 84
- *** Suicide Crack — 88
- *** The Royal Arch — 186
- * Crystal Ship — 89
- ** Raging Storm — 192
- ** Combat Zone — 191
- * A Different Kind of Hypertension — 178
- *** Solo in Soho — 151
- *** Mathematical Workout — 64
- ** Butter Arete — 88
- ** The Fall and Decline — 99
- * Hydrogen — 193
- ** Hyperdrive — 178
- 4 Manikins of Horror — 101
- * Le Chacal — 99
- * Vetta Variation — 75
- * Ego — 75
- * Ego Beaver — 87

E 2
- * Royal Plume — 64
- ** Unknown Feelings — 134
- ** Bitter Entry — 122
- * Stratagem — 101
- 4 Digitron — 103
- * A Touch of Class — 99
- * Sentinel — 132
- 4 Tearg Wall — 85
- 4 Black Bastard — 246
- * Right Wall — 74
- 4 Black Wall Direct — 246
- ** Any Which Way — 213
- ** Vacances Verticales — 150
- ** Windhover — 88
- ** Go-a-Go-Go — 118

- * Running with the Wolf — 60
- * Tito — 102
- 4 A World of Harmony — 187

E 1
- * Charlain — 106
- 4 The Minstrel — 64
- ** Black Wall — 246
- * Crystal — 87
- * Life — 158
- *** Jibber — 158
- ** Close to the Edge — 86
- * Flying Block — 64
- * The Corner — 64
- * Cornucopia — 90
- * Alison — 171
- * Cathcart's Got a Brand New Brodrie — 84
- *** Ceba — 74
- * Colour Games — 192
- * Vetta — 75
- * Talking Legs — 74
- *** Fall Out — 89
- * Warp Commander — 84
- * Last Fandango — 142
- * Knotty Problem — 65
- * Marander — 151
- * German for Art Historians — 189
- * Jocca — 63

HVS
- * Talking Fingers — 74
- ** Intensity — 86
- * Big Splat — 212
- 4 The Dog — 74
- * Marnie — 150
- ** Finer Feelings — 84
- * Insecure — 89
- ** Whim — 88
- * The Bulger — 68
- * Tosa — 72
- * Mitsuki Groove — 134
- * Crypt Tick — 146
- * Coltsfoot Crack — 91
- ** Major — 75
- * Mitsuki Groove — 134
- * Epitaph — 72
- * The Silver Line — 212
- * Yale — 176
- * The Trick — 84
- * Big Youth — 188
- * Grizzly — 75

VS
- ** Toccata — 151
- * Penetration Factor — 117
- * Gerald's Dilemma — 149
- * Chutney — 72
- ** Atlantic Traveller — 134
- *** Kinberg — 134
- * Recession Blues — 91
- * Ashgrove Prelims — 90
- * Quill — 84
- * Cristallo — 75
- 4 Face Value — 227
- * The Watzmann — 75
- * Sunday Driver — 118
- * Un-Aided — 75

- * Layback on Me — 63
- ** E.C.V — 149
- * The Arete — 68
- * Long John Silver — 212
- * Dino — 212
- * Gold Phlash — 212
- * Wilkinson Sword Edge — 61
- * Blue Flash — 212
- * Elmer J. Fudd — 204
- * Skullion — 118
- ** Puppy Power — 63
- ** Finale Groove — 255
- ** Sally in Pink — 192
- * Right Edge — 91
- * Ivy Groove — 88
- * Big Phlash — 212

HS
- * Wanderer — 68
- ** Jennifer Crack — 84
- * Yobo — 63
- * Sting — 84
- * Coltsfoot Corner — 91
- ** Funeral Corner — 117
- * Inspiration — 89
- * Murren — 75
- ** Shattered Crack — 68
- * Owl Wall — 72
- * Mango — 72
- ** Cannon Arete — 226
- * Obelisks Fly High — 144
- * Straight Edge — 91
- * Puffing Billy — 208
- * Twisting Corner — 90
- ** Shattered Crack — 68

S
- * Rambler — 63
- * Loran — 117
- ** Open Book — 88
- 4 Schmutzig — 228
- * Babbling Arete — 194
- * Ivy Crack — 85
- * As Yew Like It — 90
- * Thomas the Tank Engine — 208
- * The Fat Controller — 208

HVD
- ** Incompetence — 89
- ** Oak Tree Wall Direct — 255
- * Sesto — 75

VD
- ** Inelegance — 89
- * Wall End Climb — 255
- * Sloth — 119

M
- * Stoats Chimney — 255
- * West Crack — 254
- * West Wall — 254
- * Hell Hole — 164

Trad Graded List **Clwyd Limestone Climbing** 37

Leanne Callaghan embarking on the finely-positioned upper crack of *Manikins of Horror* (E3 5c) - *page 101* - at Craig Arthur. This is one of a trio of trad classics at Craig Arthur - the other two being *Digitron* (E2 5c) and *Survival of the Fastest* (E5 6a). Photo: Keith Sharples

Destination Planner

| Area | Crag | Routes | SPORT ROUTES |||| TRAD ROUTES ||||
			up to 4c	5a to 6a+	6b to 7a	7a+ and up	Mod to S	HS to HVS	E1 to E3	E4 and up
Ruthin and Mold Area	Denbigh Castle Quarry	11	–	1	4	2	–	–	3	1
Ruthin and Mold Area	Ruthin Escarpment	35	1	6	17	6	–	2	3	–
Ruthin and Mold Area	Devil's Gorge	34	–	–	1	22	–	7	3	1
Ruthin and Mold Area	Maeshafn Quarry	60	–	–	–	–	3	18	28	11
Ruthin and Mold Area	Pot Hole Quarry	39	–	–	–	–	3	23	13	–
Ruthin and Mold Area	Minera Quarry	10	2	4	3	–	–	–	–	1
Eglwyseg Valley	World's End	136	–	–	–	2	31	40	44	19
Eglwyseg Valley	Craig Arthur	100	–	4	24	23	–	4	25	20
Eglwyseg Valley	Twilight Area	108	–	5	11	5	23	36	25	2
Eglwyseg Valley	Pinfold	188	–	3	25	25	3	48	61	23
Eglwyseg Valley	Monk's Buttress	55	–	–	–	1	3	15	23	13
Eglwyseg Valley	Dinbren	200	–	–	35	52	10	35	46	22
Trevor Area	Trevor Quarry	132	15	56	24	–	6	23	6	1
Trevor Area	Independence Quarry	38	–	14	24	–	–	–	–	–
Trevor Area	Ruabon Quarry	2	–	–	1	1	–	–	–	–
Outlying Areas	Pandy Outcrop	21	–	–	–	–	8	7	5	1
Outlying Areas	Llanymynech Quarry	113	–	39	45	14	3	2	4	5
Outlying Areas	Pontesford Rocks	26	1	–	–	–	13	7	5	–

More colour density means more routes and more quality.

Approach	Sun	Sheltered	Dry in Rain	Restrictions	Summary	Page	
5 min	Not much sun	Sheltered			Hidden in dense woodland below Denbigh Castle, the crag offers a number of mid-grade sport routes. Conditions are variable and the face can get dirty.	42	Ruthin Area
10 - 20 min	Afternoon	Sheltered	Dry in the rain		A little-visited escarpment of excellent rock that has some intense short sport climbs. Butterfly Buttress has also been developed as a good bouldering venue. Sensitive access.	44	Devil's Gorge
5 min	Not much sun	Sheltered	Dry in the rain		An impressive gash in the hillside that has a large overhanging face which offers excellent high grade stamina routes. Conditions are crucial and the base is often muddy.	52	Maeshafn
5 - 6 min	Afternoon	Sheltered			A long, low line of vertical walls on a sheltered hillside. Good quality rock and plenty of low- to mid-grade trad routes. A great evening crag in a beautiful rural setting.	58	Pot Hole Quarry
6 min	Afternoon	Sheltered			In a lovely setting, these quarried walls are cut by numerous cracks that give lots of low- to mid-grade trad lines. Easy access and a good pub close by add to its appeal.	70	
5 - 10 min	Lots of sun	Sheltered			Only a minor venue but worth a look if in the area. The limited selection of sport routes are deceptive being more difficult than first appearances might suggest.	76	Minera Quarry
12 - 14 min	Afternoon				A series of tiered cliffs set in a stunning location at the end of the Eglwyseg Valley. Lots of testing trad routes throughout the grades on generally good limestone.	82	World's End
35 min	Afternoon	Windy		Restrictions	One of the region's biggest cliffs that has lots of mid- to high-grade sport lines as well as plenty of adventurous trad routes. Very exposed to the elements but dries quickly.	96	Craig Arthur
17 - 25 min	Afternoon	Windy			Rarely visited and a good place to avoid the crowds. The escarpment has a mix of sport and trad climbs mainly in the mid grades.	116	Twilight Area
13 - 20 min	Lots of sun	Windy			The extensive line of cliff has something for all - sport, trad and multi-pitch. Some of the area's classic climbs are hereabouts. A good destination for teams of varying ability.	128	Pinfold
20 min	Afternoon	Windy		Restrictions	A little-visited and shady cliff. Lots of interesting pitches for the enthusiast and a handful of good harder lines and trad cracks worth travelling for. Some climbs will need cleaning.	154	Monk's Buttress
7 - 10 min	Afternoon	Windy		Restrictions	One of the region's major mid- to high-grade sport climbing destinations. The long low escarpment is composed of high quality bulging limestone and also has good trad climbs.	160	
2 - 13 min	Afternoon	Sheltered		Restrictions	Very popular venue that has a huge number of low- to mid-grade sport routes along its length. The quarry itself has a few trad climbs. It can be reached on foot from Llangollen.	198	Dinbren
10 min	From mid morning	Sheltered		Restrictions	Large quarry set below Trevor Quarry and offering a similar type of climbing at a slightly higher grade. The climbs are fairly new and the rock needs handling with care in places.	215	Trevor Area
10 min	Not much sun	Sheltered	Dry in the rain		An extremely steep venue with just two routes. Of local interest only as good conditions are difficult to find but, once dry, climbing in the rain is possible. Not limestone.	221	Pandy Outcrop
25 min	Afternoon	Windy		Restrictions	Set deep in a remote and beautiful valley, the crag is a great place for low- to mid-grade trad climbing. Exposed to the elements so only visit in good weather. Not limestone.	224	Llanymynech
5 - 10 min	To mid afternoon	Sheltered	Dry in the rain	Restrictions	A huge quarry with some massive (35m) single pitch sport climbs and number of fine trad pitches. A popular spot as conditions are often excellent and the climbing superb.	230	
15 min	Morning			Restrictions	A charming venue set in a gorgeous landscape with great views. Low- to mid-grade trad climbing both single and multi-pitch. Not limestone.	252	Pontesford

Faded symbol means that only some of the routes are: sheltered / dry in the rain / restricted

Mold and Ruthin Area

Denbigh Castle Quarry, Ruthin Escarpment, Devil's Gorge, Maeshafn Quarry, Pot Hole Quarry, Minera Quarry

Marti Hallett making the final moves to attain the steep headwall of the Pot Hole Quarry classic *Ceba* (E1 5b) - *page 74* - while Debbie Roberts belays. Pot Hole Quarry is an excellent crag which is packed with testing thin crack-lines that dry very quickly, are sheltered and close to a decent pub.

Denbigh Castle Quarry

	No star	★	★★	★★★
Mod to S / 4+	-	-	-	-
HS-HVS / 5-6a+	1	-	-	-
E1-E3 / 6b-7a	3	2	2	-
E4 / 7a+ and up	-	2	1	-

Denbigh Castle Quarry is a small, well-concealed crag that has a number of sport climbs and a few older trad lines. When the rock is clean the climbing is good, however good conditions are unreliable and when wet and or muddy the experience is not to be recommended.

Approach   Also see map on page 40
When entering Denbigh look for signs to the castle and park on the road nearby. From here, walk up the track to the castle car park itself and locate a gap in the wall to the left of the entrance. Walk down the path to a road, continue down a further path on the opposite side of the road to the base of the cliff-line and walk back right to the climbing.

Conditions
The crag is very shady and is hidden in dense woodland, though this means it can be a good place on warmer days. The crag can get dirty and the base can be muddy.

Sam Cattell moving up the initial wall of *Stupid Schoolboyz* (6c+) - *opposite* - at the steep quarried face of Denbigh Castle Quarry. Photo: Ryan McConnell (on a phone, hence the quality)

Denbigh Castle Quarry

① Dick Turpin .... 6a+
Climb to, and through, the bulge.
FA. Ryan McConnell 5.6.2013

② Meat Head 6b
Climb up to a long move just before the small roof.
FA. Ryan McConnell 22.5.2013

③ Force Majeure 7b
Access the groove via a crozzly crack and undercut. Escape the groove to gain a ramp and finish up the checkerboard slots.
FA. Luke Owens 9.3.2013

④ Freedom Fighters .... 7a+
The line of the crag. Climb to and past the scoop before a tricky move up and right gains a horizontal break. The meat of the climb is lurking a little higher.
FA. Luke Clarke 11.11.2012

⑤ King of the Castle 7a
Good climbing right of the scooped groove of *Freedom Fighters* to a large undercut shield. Passing this and gaining the lower-off provides the crux.
FA. Ryan McConnell 4.2.2012

⑥ Stupid Schoolboyz .... 6c+
The right-hand line of bolts has a difficult start moving on to the wall from the earthy corner. *Photo opposite.*
FA. Ryan McConnell 17.3.2012

⑦ Sam's Arete E1 5b
The stepped arete in the centre of the quarry. Steady climbing leads to more technical moves higher up.
FA. Sam Cattell 1999

⑧ Acer 6c
The long wall right of *Sam's Arete*. Technical face climbing up to the diagonal crack where a move leftwards gains a finger-ledge.
FA. Ryan McConnell 20.10.2012

The following three lines are on a shorter blank-looking wall 30m to the right of the topo.

⑨ The Fat and the Filthy E3 5c
The far left-hand crack on the wall - dirty.
FA. Jason Porter, Chris Silverstone 2004

⑩ Having a Crack E3 5c
The right-hand crack.
FA. Sam Cattell 1998

⑪ Howelling for Beaver E4 6a
A diagonal line right of the crack of *Having a Crack*.
FA. Sam Cattell 1998

Ruthin Escarpment

	No star	★	★★	★★★
Mod to S / 4+	-	-	-	-
HS-HVS / 5-6a+	7	1	-	-
E1-E3 / 6b-7a	5	9	6	-
E4 / 7a+ and up	2	3	1	-

(Craig Adwy Gwynt - Crag of the gate of the wind)
The climbing at Ruthin Escarpment has undergone a complete makeover since the last guide was published. Most of the existing routes have been cleaned, bolted and equipped with good lower-offs. Several new routes have been added and some new buttresses have been developed. The recently developed Butterfly Buttress in particular contains some high quality sport routes. All of this makes Ruthin Escarpment a little less esoteric and certainly worthy of attention if you are in the area. The climbing at Ruthin tends to be short, power-packed and very technical. The rock along the whole escarpment is exceptional and takes almost no drainage. There is some good bouldering along the base of Butterfly Buttress - see **UKClimbing.com** and **northwalesbouldering.com**

Approach   Also see map on page 40
From Ruthin, take the A494 south to Bala and Corwen. After around 3 miles the village of Pwll Glas is entered. Park immediately in a large lay-by on the left. Walk about 100m back along the road and take the smaller track/road on the right. Drop down along the side of the river and over a bridge, then climb uphill around a couple of bends that end at a large house. Just before the large house, take a footpath on the right and, after 30m, go right again on another path. The crag can now be seen up on the left. Various paths lead up to the cliff.
The Quarry Wall is situated on the right-hand side of the road when approaching from Ruthin and is around 200m from the Pwll Glas sign at the beginning of the village. Although this is a roadside crag it takes 5 minutes to walk to from the parking due to where you need to park. Park either at the large lay-by on the left-hand side in the village itself or just the other side of the bridge that leads to Llanfair DC.

Conditions
The crag receives plenty of sun in the afternoon, although parts of the wall are shaded by trees. There is little seepage and the rock on the whole is very good.

Access
The crag has two landowners and neither accept any liability for climbers' safety or for the reliability of any fixed gear. All of the escarpment is an SSSI and no vegetation removal, tree cutting or modification of the rock features is allowed. No new bolting or new routing are allowed. The left-hand side is owned by the Butterfly Conservation Trust and managed as a nature reserve and regarded as one of the most important locations of this type in the UK.

Ruthin Escarpment is made up of series of isolated buttresses that are composed of compact and leaning limestone. These provide some difficult, but thankfully short, well-equipped sport routes. Here Phil Black takes on *Chrysalis* (6c+) - *page 49* - on Butterfly Buttress. In the background the buttress steepens up and has some harder pitches as well as plenty of difficult boulder problems along its base.

Ruthin Escarpment — Beast Wall

Beast Wall
A steep section of crag that has some very powerful short pitches on good rock.
Approach - 110m from the split in the path behind the house head up a very faint path to the crag.

The main buttress has a line of bulges at mid height.

① Beastie Boys 7a
A hard bouldery pull through the bulge. Reachy!
FA. Lee Proctor 29.1.2011

② The Bloopers and Production No No's
.... 8a
Very difficult moves past the bulge and up the wall. Originally graded E4 6b, the route climbed through the lower bulge and then moved left to join *Beastie Boys* - it subsequently lost holds.
FA. (moving left to join Beastie Boys) Matt Jones 1991
FA. (direct after hold loss) Chris Doyle 6.2014

③ The Wee Beastie ... 7c
A bouldery pitch that tackles the centre of the bulging wall. A heel-hook works on the crux but only if you're the right height.
FA. R.Williams 14.9.1986

④ Green Bean .... 6b+
A start on good holds gains the base of the vague groove in the upper bulge. The groove provides the meat of the route and is a stubborn barrier to success.

⑤ The Route .... VS 4c
The flake and corner system to the right of *Green Bean* is now overgrown.
FA. Ruthin School Mountaineering Club 1976

Middle Wall

⑥ CCR 7a
A brilliant and demanding route on immaculate limestone with sustained difficulties throughout. One of Ruthin's best.
FA. R.Williams, M.Brennan 20.7.1985

⑦ Old Gunk's Grandad's Pastime
.... 6c+
A good climb with some challenging moves in its lower half. Finish at the *CCR* lower-off.
FA. Matt Jones 30.7.1990

⑧ Runner Bean ... 6c+
A great little pitch. Start beneath a juggy flake and, from its top, make a long move to a second flake and then another long reach into a rounded break. Traverse left then climb the difficult smooth wall to the lower-off.
FA. R.Williams, M.Brennan 29.7.1985

Middle Wall — Ruthin Escarpment

Middle Wall
A wall of excellent rock that has a limited selection of technical and fingery lines. This is a good place for those looking for some quality lines in the 6c+/7a grade range.
Approach - From the The Beast Wall walk along the path under the cliff-line for a further 140m - passing a scree slope - to arrive at the Middle Wall. The Middle Wall can also be easily reached from The Butterfly Buttress via the cliff base path.

9 Summertime Blues 7a
Excellent climbing with a difficult upper half. Climb the shallow groove and slight bulge to reach the mid height break. Either climb directly above the break via a long reach to gain holds on slightly poorer rock above, or step left to *Runner Bean* and make a hard move straight up to reach the next bolt. A final awkward move reaches the *Runner Bean* lower-off.

10 Eating Words 6c+
A good steep pitch with some excellent moves.
FA. Lee Proctor 8.10.2006

70m right is a short wall containing two sport routes.

11 Smooth Wall Left 5c
The short smooth wall leads to a thorny exit.

12 Smooth Wall Right 6a
A couple of interesting moves lead to a break by the second bolt. Move right past a small sawn-off tree stump to finish.

Ruthin Escarpment — Peg Wall

Peg Wall
A steep section of wall with some old trad lines that have a smattering of fixed gear in the form of pegs and a bolt.
Approach - Walk 150m further along the path from Middle Wall. There is a small wall just to the left with an old bolt in it but no recorded routes.
Descent - Walk off to the left for 100m looking out.

1 Ego Maniac .... HVS 5a
Climb up the wall to reach a shallow groove and peg, then move leftwards through the overlap on good jugs to the top.
FA. R.Williams 12.6.1985

2 Return to the Trees E1 5b
Climb the bulging wall keeping to the right of a yew tree near the top.
FA. Alan Hill 1.9.1986

3 Deuce Coupe E1 5b
Climb the wall with a tricky finish past two high pegs.
FA. R.Williams, M.Brennan 20.7.1985

4 The Nerd E1 5b
Climb the wall past a low bolt to an overlap. Surmount this - peg - and continue to the top.
FA. R.Williams, M.Brennan 4.6.1985

Butterfly Buttress
A short but excellent wall of leaning limestone that contains some of Ruthin's hardest lines. The buttress has also been developed into a first class bouldering spot - see crag introduction for details. The first four routes are on a small vertical wall of clean compact smooth rock.
Approach - From where the path splits behind the house, walk 400m until the path starts to rise towards a stile and the wall is just off the path on the left.

5 Vlinder 3
The easy ramp at the left end of the wall.

6 Papillon 5c
The wall connecting two flakes and exiting slightly leftwards.

7 Mariposa 6a
Direct up the wall with a tricky move above the bolt.

8 Farfalla 6a
An awkward start on small smooth holds reaches a better hold and twin bolts. Climb slightly left to reach the lower-off.

Butterfly Buttress — Ruthin Escarpment

The next routes lie on an excellent short leaning wall of perfect limestone. All routes are equipped with lower-offs that are set back from the top and can be hard to spot from below.

9 Fritillary Flake........ 6c
A boulder problem start gains the flake and good holds. Climb up and slightly left taking care with the rock higher up.
FA. Lee Proctor, Jamie Skates 2.1.2011

**10 The Butterfly Collector
.... 7b**
Three hard bouldery sections with the crux at the top.
FA. Lee Proctor, Jamie Skates 2.1.2011

11 Sting like a Bee.... 7c
A ferocious boulder problem tackling the blunt rib to the right of The Butterfly Collector.
FA. Jamie Skates, Lee Proctor 7.1.2011

**12 Float Like a Butterfly
.... 7a**
One of the best routes on the buttress that involves a big floaty dyno midway.
FA. Lee Proctor, Jamie Skates 2.1.2011

13 Metamorphosis.......... 6b
A steep blocky start leads to a more delicate finish.
FA. Lee Proctor, Jamie Skates 2.1.2011

14 Metamorphosis Direct 6b
Climb direct to join *Metamorphosis* by its second bolt. Beware - poor rock and no bolts until this point!.
FA. Matthew West 12.7.2011

15 Chrysalis .... 6c+
The route on the right side of the buttress packs in a few tricky moves. *Photo on page 45*.
FA. Lee Proctor, Jamie Skates 8.1.2011

Ruthin Escarpment — Lost Wall

① Lost Cause — 6c+
An easy start leads to a very fingery and slightly dynamic finish.
FA. Lee Proctor, Jamie Skates 22.1.2011

② Lost Arrow — 6b+
Cool moves up the blunt nose with a tricky last move.
FA. Lee Proctor, Jamie Skates 8.5.2011

③ Lost Innocence — 6c
A nice addition with a tough finish.
FA. Lee Proctor, Jamie Skates 8.5.2011

④ Lost Boys — 6b+
One of the best routes at Ruthin Escarpment. Climb the layback flake pulling right to reach the bulge from where a hard pull gains wonderful juggy pockets leading to the belay.
FA. Lee Proctor, Jamie Skates 22.1.2011

Lost Wall
A steep wall with one very good pitch, that is on private land. See access.

Approach - Walk 200m further along the cliff-base path from where the main footpath starts to rise just beyond Butterfly Buttress. The wall is about 50m above the path.

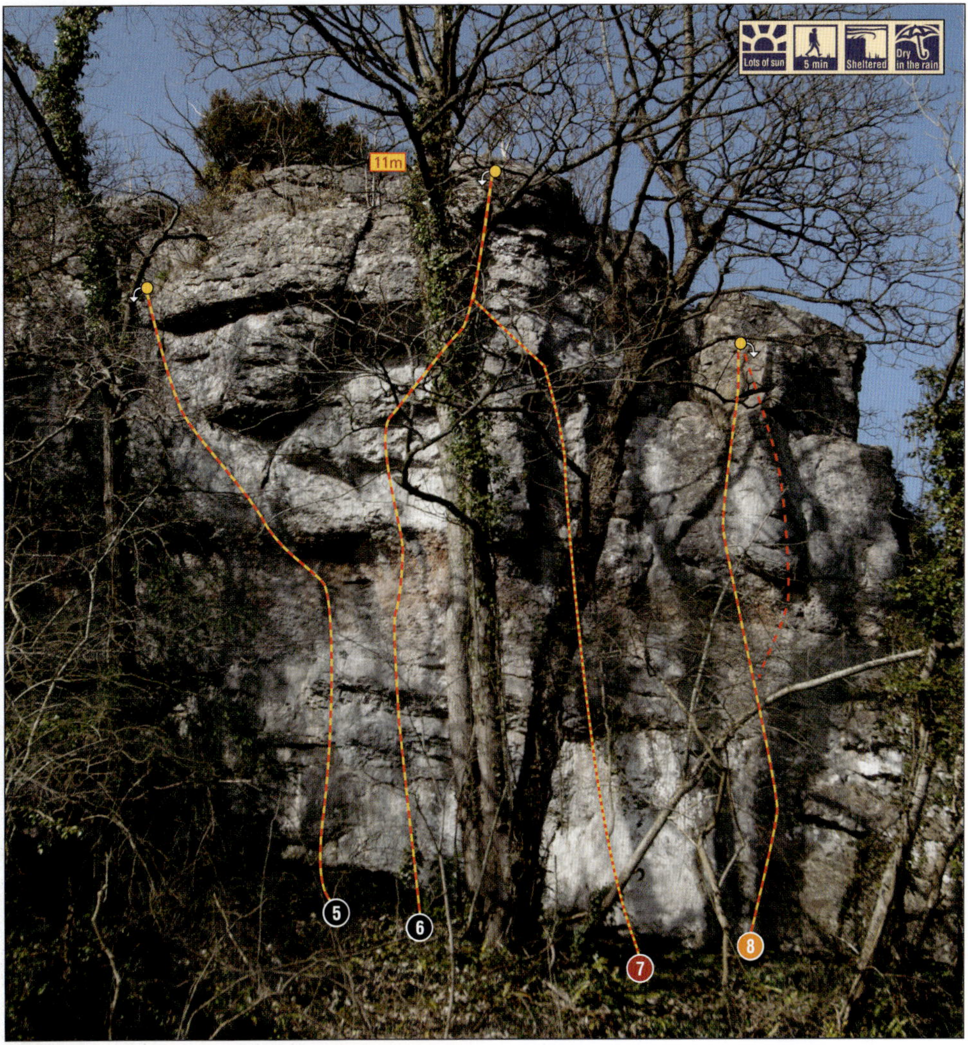

Quarry Wall **Ruthin Escarpment**

Quarry Wall
A roadside wall of bulging rock that has some crumbly sections. It is sheltered and sometimes dry in the rain. Hangers go missing from time to time.

Approach - Although this is a roadside crag it takes 5 minutes to walk to from the parking due to where you need to park. Park either at the large lay-by on the left-hand side in the village itself or just the other side of the bridge that leads to Llanfair DC.

5 Fraxinus Excelsior  **7c**
Starting on the big flat hold in the middle of the wall at head height, climb up and leftwards on small holds to finish up the groove. Bouldery.
FA. Ryan McConnell 25.9.2011

6 Apple Crumble **7b**
Start at two crimps. Make a dynamic move to the ledge before trending right into *21 Steps to Pigeon Street* to finish.
FA. Danny Cattell 3.9.2010

7 21 Steps to Pigeon Street  **6b**
Climb up and left keeping just right of the roof.
FA. Ryan McConnell 5.6.2009

8 Catch the Pigeon . . . . . . 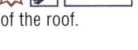 **6a**
This tackles the right-hand side of the crag before trending left around the bulge. It has also been climbed direct from the second bolt.
FA. Ryan McConnell 25.5.2009

Devil's Gorge

	No star	⭐	⭐⭐	⭐⭐⭐
Mod to S / 4+	-	-	-	-
HS-HVS / 5-6a+	7	-	-	-
E1-E3 / 6b-7a	2	2	-	-
E4 / 7a+ and up	4	8	4	7

The Devil's Gorge is a huge narrow limestone slit in the hillside, that on first viewing, is bound to impress. Closer inspection reveals that the gorge's steep side leans out over the sunless base and holds a clutch of very good stamina sport pitches in the 7th and 8th grades. The rock is generally reasonable but has sections of crystalline formations that are crumbly, so care is needed where routes come into contact with these areas. The Gorge has seen plenty of attention and development in recent times and the majority of the gear is now in excellent condition. There is also a lot of higher-end quality bouldering to be found just outside the gorge entrance - details at **UKClimbing.com** and **northwalesbouldering.com**.

Approach

Follow the A494 ring road around Mold following directions for Ruthin. Once on the south side of Mold, the road climbs through the village of Gwernymynydd. After 1 mile the road bends right and flattens out. Continue for another 0.5 mile and turn right, signposted Gwernaffield and Pantymwyn. Follow this road for 1 mile to a cross-roads and turn left. Go 0.8 miles and, at a sharp right-hand bend, go straight on and park immediately on the right. Please park with consideration. Walk straight on a short distance and take the tarmac track ahead as the road bends left.

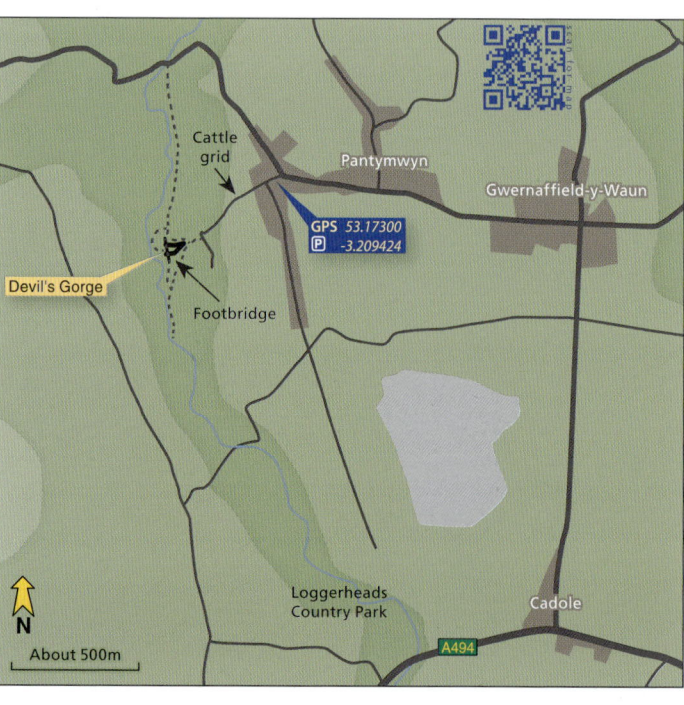

Cross a cattle grid and continue downhill to a sharp left bend in the track. Go straight on via a path over a stile and the edge of the gorge is reached. The bridge over the gorge is best reached via the right rim. To gain the base of the gorge walk 20m right (looking out) from the bridge to a good track that drops steeply to the river and the mouth of the gorge.

Conditions

The Devil's Gorge receives very little sun and can remain wet throughout the winter and into late spring. Seepage is persistent on the steep side but once dry, the wall provides sheltered climbing in heavy rain. The base of the gorge can be very muddy and a rope bag is recommended in anything but drought conditions. Many of the lower sections of the routes will need cleaning before an ascent. The slabby wall has some good sections of rock that would give some reasonable pitches if cleaned up.

Access

Do not lower off or abseil from the bridge.

Lucy Creamer contemplating the upper section of *Bananas and Coffee* (7a+) - *page 57* - at the atmospheric Devil's Gorge. Many of the sport lines allow climbing in the rain once the gorge has dried out. Photo: Tim Glasby

Main Wall Devil's Gorge

Main Wall
The left-hand side of the Main Wall is its steepest section and home to the best routes. The majority of the lines are worthwhile and once in condition offer some of the best stamina sport pitches in the region. However, the gorge is a damp spot requiring time for the seepage streaks to dry out. The base is often muddy. If on a first visit it is worth spending sometime checking out which route is which. The right-hand side of the Main Wall has more good long sport pitches that require care with the rock in places. The gorge is very enclosed and sees little sun. The wall seeps badly but once dry stays dry and climbing during rainfall is possible. The bottom of the gorge is often muddy and a rope bag is a good idea.

There is a single route on the wall above the vast cave at the far end of the gorge.

❶ Cave Wall E4 6a
A strange climb. Start up *Where We Going* (page 57) but then move right past a bolt to gain the steep wall above the cave. Continue up the wall, passing two iron spikes and several bolts, to a lower-off. Serious, especially if you hit the iron bars!
FA. John Codling, John Moulding 1990s

The rest of the routes all start on the steep side of the gorge.

❷ Echoes . . . . 7a+
A good and popular route when dry. An awkward and often greasy start just left of a tiny ground-level cave leads to a good handrail. Move left to a dirty niche, then pull awkwardly up to some massive holds that unfortunately run out when you need them most! A hard lunge left gains the lip of the cave and an ungainly grovel to gain the cave and lower-off.
The extension is an open project above the lower-off to the roof which then makes a traverse right to join *Hades*.
FA. John Elcock 17.8.1992

❸ Underworld 7c
Start at a tiny ground-level cave. Climb up to reach good holds and take a deep breath before tackling a taxing sequence of thin moves to reach a good hold beneath the bulge. Make a hard lunge through the bulge to better holds then sprint left to the belay before the pump takes over.
FA. Pete Harrison 13.7.2013

❹ Hades . . . . . . 8a+
The extension of *Underworld* is a classy piece of climbing. Make the most of a poor rest at the *Underworld* lower-off before embarking on a technical sequence of moves to gain reasonable holds underneath the roof. A spectacular sequence through the roof gains respite in the groove above and the lower-off.
FA. Owen Davies 31.8.2013

❺ Grand Canyon . . . . . Top 50   7b+
The best route in the gorge. Start at a diagonal borehole strike at head height. The climbing varies from dynamic lunges between jugs to sustained technical crimping and pocket pulling with a lactic-infused crux high up. Low in the grade. *Photo on page 3.*
FA. Gary Gibson 16.8.1992

❻ Canyonlands . . . 8a
The extension to *Grand Canyon* is a tremendous power endurance testpiece that features some very taxing moves on the impressively positioned headwall.
FA. Lee Proctor (1pt) 8.2013. FFA. Ally Smith 11.7.2015

❼ Devil's Haircut . . 7c
A brilliant route with some great moves. Start right of *Grand Canyon* beneath a shallow rounded depression. Climb easily into the depression before a hard and reachy sequence gains good holds above. Continue upwards to steeper ground and smaller holds. A fantastic move through the bulge gains good holds and the pumpy finale of *Broccoli and Ice-Cream*.
FA. Jamie Skates, Lee Proctor 24.9.2014

❽ Broccoli and Ice-Cream . 7b
A good route that is only marginally easier than *Grand Canyon*. Start just right of *Devil's Haircut*. A tricky initial 'slabby' pull is followed by a steep sequence of moves to reach good holds. Yard up jugs with a tricky pull through the mid height bulge to reach more jugs. Continue quickly, making a final energy-sapping move to reach the lower-off just beneath the roof. The extension is a project rumoured to be around 8b.
FAA. Stuart Cathcart, Gerald Swindley 1976. FA. John Codling 1990s

❾ Born Slippy . . . . 7c+
A good link-up that covers all the hard climbing on *Underworld* and *Grand Canyon*. Climb *Underworld* to reach the holds above the bulge then traverse rightwards via a tricky sequence of moves to join *Grand Canyon* just before its crux. Finish up *Grand Canyon*. Low in the grade.
FA. Ally Smith 28.8.2013

❿ The Mark of Zorro 7b
A link-up that covers some impressive ground mainly on very good holds. Climb past the first couple of bolts on *Underworld* then move right to join the rail of *Grand Canyon*. Climb a couple of moves up *Grand Canyon* then move rightwards to join *Devil's Haircut* and continue in the same line to join and finish up *Broccoli and Ice-Cream* - all very pumpy!
FA. Lee Proctor 25.9.2011

⓫ Cerberus 8a
A superb counter diagonal to *Born Slippy*. Climb the first half of *Grand Canyon* and then break leftwards using the *Born Slippy* hand holds for feet to reach a big pocket, use this to gain the crux sequence of *Hades* beneath its roof.
FA. Ally Smith 10.9.2013

⓬ Beetroot and Creatine 8a
Climb *Devil's Haircut* to just below its lower-off and then move left to join and finish up *Canyonlands*. At the upper end of the grade.
FA. Ally Smith 2.8.2015

Main Wall and Left Wall — Devil's Gorge

15 An Ivory Smile ... 7c
This is a very good route but it is rarely climbed and may need a bit of a clean first. The first bolt is old so clip-stick the second. The grubby lower wall leads to a hard and dynamic sequence to reach a good jug above the bulge. Continue up a vague technical groove that leads to a blind finishing move to reach the lower-off next to a couple of old iron bars.
FA. Gary Gibson 12.8.1992

16 The Ten Year Fog ... 7c
A good route with a wild finish. Start just right of *An Ivory Smile* beneath a groove in the bulge above. Another grubby start reaches good holds below and left of the groove line. A hard press move gains the groove which is followed with difficulty to better holds. Climb the ever steepening smooth wall to a crazy campus-board finish to reach the lip of the gorge. A heel hook can make clipping the lower-off easier. Low in the grade.
FA. (to a lower belay at 7b+) Gary Gibson 12.8.1992
FA. (as described) Lee Proctor 20.9.2012

17 The Ten Year Banana ... 7b+
A good logical link-up that covers the best climbing of the parent routes. From the good holds above the groove on *The Ten Year Fog* continue and finish up *Bananas and Coffee*.
FA. David Flux 9. 2012

18 Bananas and Coffee ... 7a+
A good route, unfortunately spoilt by some crumbly calcite holds midway up. An often dirty start past a couple of resin 'P' bolts reaches the bottom of a calcite groove. Climb the groove and trend leftwards at its top to reach a good handrail in the smooth wall. Continue upwards on flat holds to the belay - hopefully just before strength runs out. *Photo on page 53.*
FA. Carl Dawson, Nadim Siddiqui pre 1992

19 Fair Trade ... 7b+
A tough and fingery route that tackles the headwall right of *Bananas and Coffee*. Climb *Bananas and Coffee* to its fifth bolt. Move up and right to a good hold then make a hard pull to reach another good hold. Move leftwards using small crimps and tiny footholds to join *Bananas and Coffee* just before the lower-off.
FA. Lee Proctor 16.10.2011

20 Trade Fair ... 7b+
Climb *Fair Trade* to its penultimate bolt and move right via a hard press move to a lower-off next to the bridge.
FA. Owen Davies 29.9.2013

21 What's in a Word ... 7a+
An alternative right-hand finish to *Bananas and Coffee*.
FA. Gary Gibson 31.8.1992

22 Uhu ... 6b
Dirty. Start up *Bananas and Coffee* and then move rightwards following the flake-line to a lower-off under the bridge.
FA. Nick Thomas and S.Taylor 30.7.1991. An older and similar line, Communique E4 5c, is now unclimbable. FA.Stuart Cathcart, Gerald Swindley 11.8.1978

23 La Porte de l'Enfer ... 7b+
An extended boulder problem that climbs plumb centre up the steep entrance wall to the gorge.
FA. Lee Proctor 21.3.2012

24 Comfortably Numb ... 7a+
A worthwhile micro-route. Boulder out the start to reach a good hold. Pull up and move around onto the steep face to reach the belay of *La Porte de l'Enfer*.
FA. Nick Thomas 4.9.1991

Left Wall

The Left Wall of the gorge has some long slabby trad lines that see little traffic and are usually vegetated.
Approach - Walk down to the base of the gorge. The gorge is very enclosed and sees little sun. The bottom of the gorge is often muddy and a rope bag is a good idea. The starts are now heavily vegetated.
Descent - Walk off.

25 Ladywriter ... HS
A vegetated excursion. Start just left of a deep groove below the bridge. Climb the left wall of the groove to reach a leftwards traverse line which is followed to the edge of the wall.
FA. Frank Bennett, Mike Hughes 6.7.1980

26 Portobello Belle ... HS
From the top of the *Ladywriter* groove, continue direct up the slab, to finish just left of the bridge.

27 A Brown Shade of Lime ... VS 4c
The right-hand version of *Portobello Belle* is harder but just as unpleasant. From the top of the groove move right then climb the slab to finish just to the right of the bridge.
FA. John Elcock, Nick Thomas 3.1991

28 Single-handed Sailor ... HVS 4c
The mossy wall and slab, keeping to the left of a bush.
FA. Stuart Cathcart, Gerald Swindley 16.11.1976

29 Follow Me Home ... E1 5a
When clean and dry this is an excellent and memorable route that is worth two stars. Climb the mossy lower wall, between two bushes, to reach a bent iron bar at the bottom of a left-trending overlap. Follow the overlap to the top of the wall.
FA. Stuart Cathcart, Mike Hughes 6.7.1980

30 Angel of Mercy ... E2 5a
An excellent pitch that is worth two stars when clean. From the iron bar on *Follow Me Home*, pull around the overlap then take a direct line up the smooth bold slab to the top.
FA. Stuart Cathcart, Mike Hughes 6.7.1980

31 Grey Tripper ... E2 5a
A poor route. Climb direct past the lowest bush to reach a second bush by an overlap. Pull over this and ascend the bold slab to a grassy finish over a slight bulge.
FA. Greg Griffith, C.O'Keefe 1984

32 News ... HVS 4c
Start at a mossy rightward-trending ramp. Climb the ramp then follow the clean slab boldly to the top of the wall.

33 Where We Going ... HS
The corner bounding the right edge of the slab. Poor.

34 Great Slab Girdle ... HVS 5a
Start up *Portobello Belle* then traverse rightwards on good clean rock, to join the poor finish of *Where We Going*.
FA. Stuart Cathcart 21.8.1980

Maeshafn Quarry

Maeshafn Quarry is a very quaint spot with great views and plenty of trad routes in the severe to mid extreme grade range. The routes at Maeshafn Quarry are mostly on good compact limestone and although not long pack in the moves from the off. Here Paul Cox heads up towards the finishing crux moves of *Yobo* (HS 4b) - *page 63*.

Maeshafn Quarry

	No star	☆	☆☆	☆☆☆
Mod to S	2	1	-	-
HS to HVS	9	7	2	-
E1 to E3	17	8	1	2
E4 and up	5	6	-	-

Set in beautiful countryside Maeshafn Quarry is a smart little crag that catches lots of sun and is packed with shortish but sustained traditionally protected climbing on some excellent rock. The crag is split into around half a dozen buttresses, each with its own character, ranging from some fine thin crack-lines to a good number of fingery wall and slab climbs on perfect rock. The grade range is wide, with much to keep the lower and mid-grade climber happy. Access to the top of the crag is simple where many stakes are in place for belaying. Maeshafn makes a great place for an evenings climbing after work or for a day or weekend visit from further away, especially if combined with a visit to the nearby Pot Hole Quarry. There is a small amount of bouldering available - details at UKClimbing.com and northwalesbouldering.com.

Access

Maeshafn Quarry is on private land and climbing here is by permission of the landowner, Mr W. Thomas, at the Bryn Gwyn Farm opposite the parking. Mr Thomas is happy for climbers to use the crag but has requested that climbers ask permission to climb from the farm before approaching the crag. No camping or fires are permitted. Dogs must be kept on a lead and all gates closed as the quarry and the fields around it have cattle in at all times.

Approach   Also see map on page 40

From the A494 ring road around Mold follow directions for Ruthin. Once on the south side of Mold a wide road climbs through the village of Gwernymynydd. After 1 mile the road bends right and flattens out. Continue for another 0.1 mile and turn left signposted Maeshafn. Follow the road for 1 mile and turn left (just before the village of Maeshafn itself). Continue for a further 0.8 miles to a farm. Just beyond the farm park on the left verge before a track and bungalow on the left. Under no circumstances should cars park in the lay-by directly opposite the bungalow. Please park with consideration to allow for farm traffic that uses the track leading to the crag. Take the track on the left just before the bungalow, passing through two gates until the quarry is easily seen up on the right across the field.

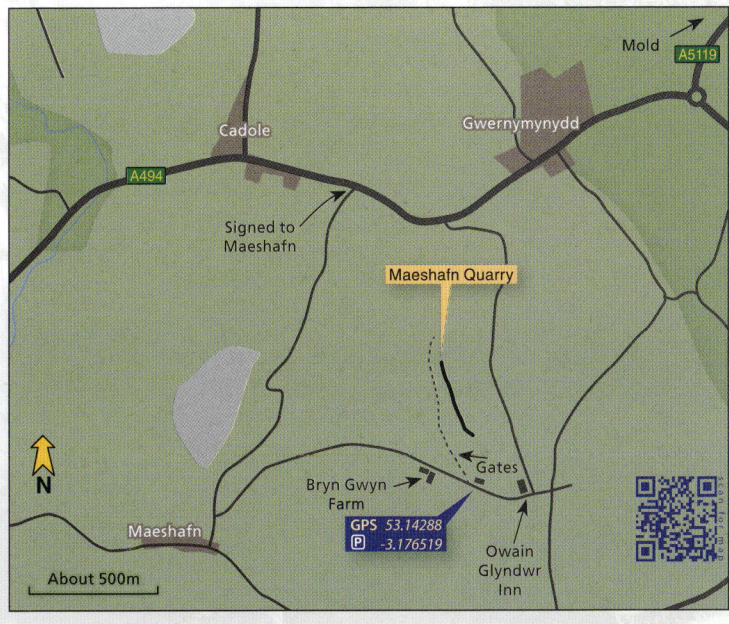

Conditions

Fairly sheltered and west facing, Maeshafn Quarry is an afternoon suntrap and is often in condition, although there is no opportunity for climbing in the rain.

Maeshafn Quarry — The White Wall

The White Wall

The left-hand end of the quarry has a clean wall of fine rock. It is less popular than the other areas but worth checking out especially if the Main Wall is busy. The routes in general are poorly protected. The top-outs have given concern to some climbers and a rope down to the top of the rock might be required by some. Holly Buttress is a narrow spire of rock just above the path.

Approach - From below the Main Wall walk right along a track at the base of the escarpment for 150m to the wall. Holly Buttress is around 50m before the the White Wall just above the track

Descent - Walk off to the left.

❶ Hot Tin Roof E4 6a
The thin crack right of the overgrown corner is also at risk of becoming overgrown.
FA. Stuart Cathcart, Gerald Swindley 7.10.1975

❷ Pant-y-Gyrdl Wall E1 5c
A nice route, with a difficult start, up the thin crack and short wall using some strange stuck-on holds. A few small wires protect.
FA. Gary Dickinson, P.Lockett 29.9.1991

❸ Haco E3 5b
Boldly solo leftwards across the wall, using stuck-on holds, before moving back right and over the vague bulge, finishing just left of a small yew tree.
FA. Stuart Cathcart, Gerald Swindley 16.8.1975

❹ Cyclops E2 5b
Poorly-protected climbing, following the super-thin crack immediately left of the arete.
FA. Stuart Cathcart, Gerald Swindley 18.8.1975

❺ Flotta Arete .... HS 4a
A committing route for the grade. Climb onto the arete from the left and then follow the easiest line to the top. There are some small wires halfway up.

❻ Rama .... HS 4b
Climb a crack to a ledge then finish leftwards up the slab.

❼ Muslim E1 5a
Follow *Rama* to the ledge but continue boldly up the wall above, finishing just left of the upper overlap.
FA. Stuart Cathcart, Gerald Swindley 15.8.1975

❽ Running with the Wolf .. E2 5c
The best route on The White Wall. Climb up and leftwards, using a variety of stuck-on holds, to a foot-ledge and good thread placement in the wall above. Move up to the slim overlap, then traverse right past a peg, before making a final pull around the overlap to jugs and the top.
FA. Stuart Cathcart, Tom Curtis 27.6.1976

❾ Pussyfooting E4 5c
An exciting technical pitch, directly up the centre of the wall, to join the finish of *Running with the Wolf*.

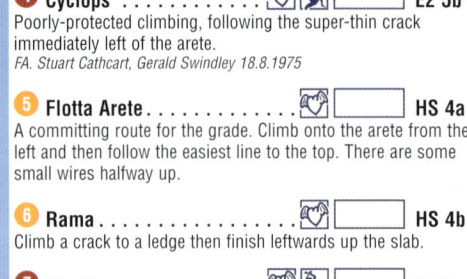

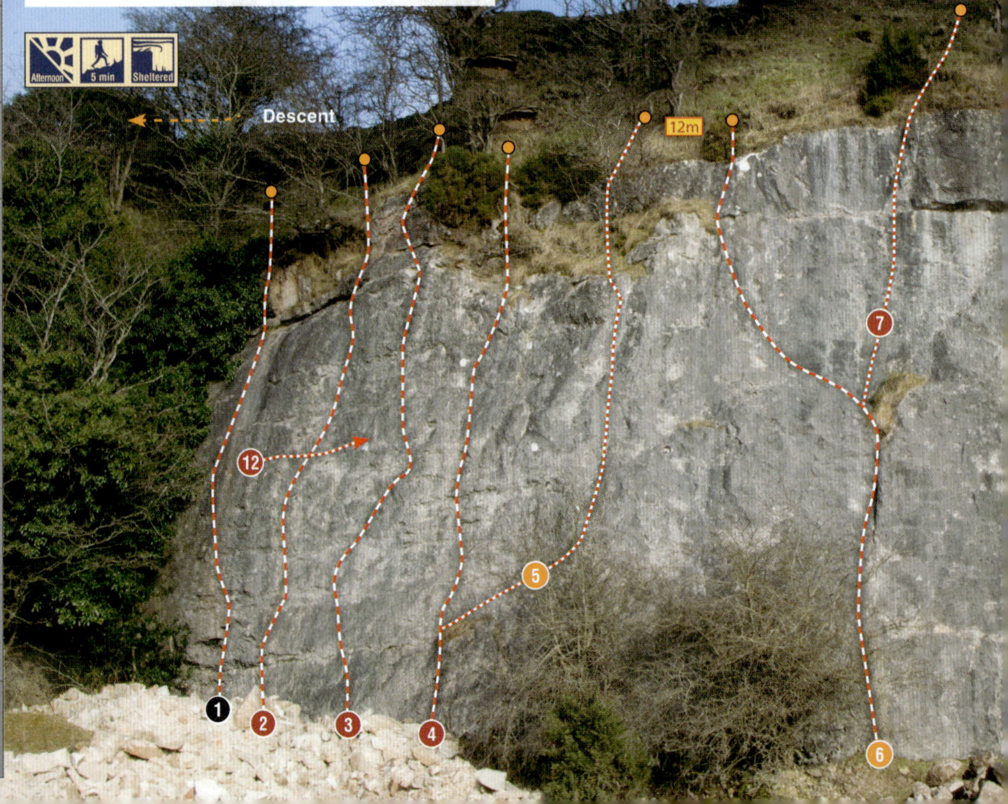

The White Wall — Maeshafn Quarry

10 White Spring .... HS 4a
The rightward-trending system of flake-cracks can be a bit dirty and overgrown.

11 Odysseus .... HVS 5a
A worthwhile route. Climb up into the groove beneath a small overlap which is passed on its left to a short grassy wall to finish.
FA. Stuart Cathcart, Gerald Swindley 15.8.1975

12 White Wall Traverse E3 5b
The left-to-right traverse. Start up *Hot Tin Roof*, traverse past the peg on *Running with the Wolf*, to finish up *Odysseus*.
FA. Stuart Cathcart, Tom Curtis 11 8.1976

There is a further small isolated wall situated in the trees 50m to the right (looking in) of the White Wall.

13 Maeve E2 5c
Start left of a tree then solo rightwards, on rounded holds, above the tree and onwards to the top. The tree needs cutting back.
FA. Stuart Cathcart, Tom Curtis 1979

14 Wilkinson Sword Edge ..... VS 4c
The right arete has some wonderful holds higher up but has some big brambles that can encroach from time to time.
FA. Stuart Cathcart 25.9.1977

Maeshafn Quarry — Main Wall

Main Wall

The main attraction at Maeshafn is this appealing wall of vertical thin cracks and the clean wall of excellent rock to its right. The climbs are very sustained and rely on small wires for protection. The left-hand side is a popular place that features a reasonable set of off-vertical routes with some technical climbing and the odd run-out section.
Descent - Walk off to the left.

There is a hidden buttress, 60m to the left of the Main Wall.

❶ **The Green Wall** E4 5c
The centre of the green wall has no protection.

❷ **Sita** E2 5c
A pitch up the crack and arete.
FA. Stuart Cathcart 23.9.1979

The slabby main wall gives good open climbing.

❸ **Joker** .... HVD
Pull steeply through the lower wall and then follow a leftwards line across the blank slab to the top. Bold.

❹ **Yellow** E1 5b
Climb trending left then right to beneath the bulging arete - nut on left. Move up onto a ledge on the arete before moving right. Finish more easily.
FA. Ryan McConnell 22.11.2008

❺ **Thrutch** .... HS 4b
A hard start and bold finish gives this route a bit of character.

Main Wall Maeshafn Quarry

6 Bumble Arete E1 5b
An extended boulder problem up the vague arete to a ledge, then finish through the small overlap above.
FA. Lee Proctor 1996

7 Jocca E1 5b
Bridge elegantly up the slim leftward-trending groove-line to reach a thin crack, which is followed to the top.
FA. Stuart Cathcart 5.1974

8 Brewing up with Les Williams
.... E4 5c
Varied and sustained climbing above a bold start. Move up to a peg then pull steeply past this to small holds and good gear. Move slightly right and finish up a short thin crack.
FA. Dave Johnson 15.3.1988

9 Moomba E4 6a
An alternative finish to *Inspector Gadget* that avoids its long reach by moving left at the undercut to join *Brewing up with Les Williams*.
FA. Stuart Cathcart, Gerald Swindley 23.9.1977

10 Inspector Gadget E4 6a
This one-move wonder is centred on an undercut at half-height. Climb easily to the undercut then make a long stretch for some small crimps. Pull up to better holds and an easy finish.

11 Apex E1 5b
Climb into the short steep corner beneath the tree then move left onto the arete and follow this, over an overlap, to the top.
FA. Stuart Cathcart 8.10.1975

12 Layback on Me .... VS 4b
The attractive layback flake is good but it ends too soon at a ledge. Finish easily up the slabby wall above.

13 Rambler .... S 4a
A smart well-protected pitch up the short corner and V-groove.

14 Puppy Power .... VS 4b
The best of the easier routes on the steep slab. Climb a thin leftward-trending crack to reach a shallow corner that is climbed to the top.
FA. Simon Williams, N.Stanford, C.Roberts 16.1.1988

15 Yobo .... HS 4b
A worthwhile pitch up the rib and cracks just left of the vegetation to a rightward finish. The mantelshelf finish is the hardest move. *Photo on page 58*.

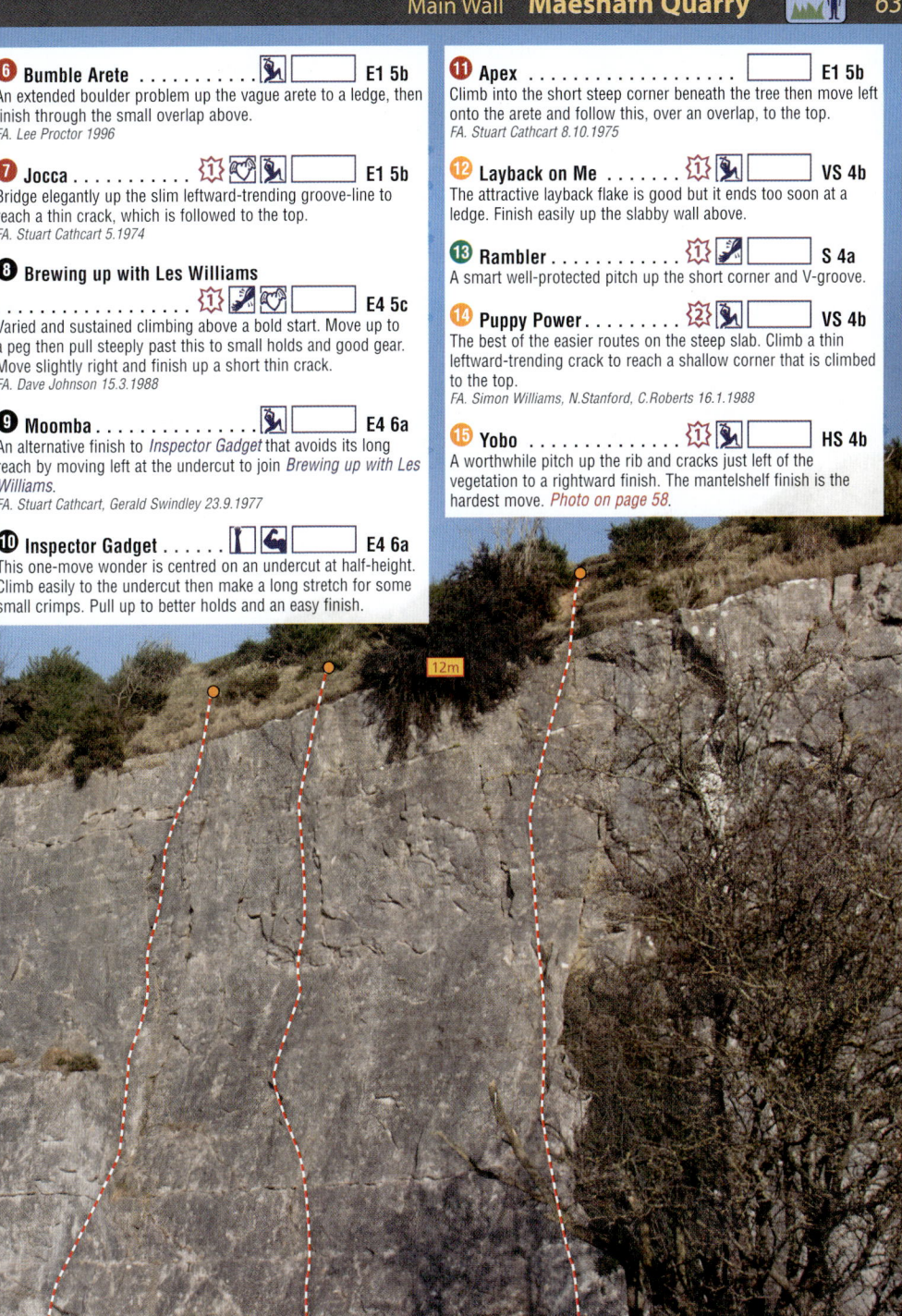

Maeshafn Quarry — Main Wall

16 Flying Block — E1 5b
The testing crack-line, right of the vegetated groove, requires big arms and a positive attitude to surmount the overhang.
FA. Stuart Cathcart, Gerald Swindley 15.8.1976

17 Royal Plume — E2 6a
The thin crack is continually challenging especially at the mid-height overlap. Finish direct through the narrowest section of the upper overlap.
FA. Stuart Cathcart, Tom Curtis 17.5.1979

18 The Minstrel — Top 50 — E1 5b
A finger-sized crack splitting the highest section of the main wall epitomises limestone crack climbing at its best - well protected, technical, awkward and slightly polished, but thoroughly entertaining! At the upper overhang, move right and then pull up using small holds to reach the top. *Photo on page 67.*
FA. Stuart Cathcart, Tom Curtis 11.8.1976

19 Alex's Crack — E5 6b
An eliminate line but with good climbing. There is a difficult and reachy move at half-height using a small finger-pocket. The route is normally climbed with a low side-runner in *Mathematical Workout* and is E6 without this.
FA. Dave Johnson 6.7.1988

20 Mathematical Workout — E3 6a
The perfect route for its size with technical and interesting climbing from the moment you leave the ground. Follow the thin crack to good holds and wires beneath the overlap, then make a long move rightwards to reach a flat hold. Pull up and stand on this and then follow the thin crack in the wall above.
FA. Stuart Cathcart, Tom Curtis 11.8.1976

21 Calculus — E4 5c
A good pitch up the arete with an awkward move through the overlap. The upper wall is climbed left of the arete and although easier, is a touch run-out.
FA. Andy Pollitt, Pete Bailey 11.5.1981

22 The Secret — E2 5c
A nice line following the corner. The start is awkward and polished but soon leads to a good rest and a peg. Pull past the peg and continue steeply to the top.
FA. Stuart Cathcart, Tom Curtis 15.4.1976

23 The Corner — E1 5b
A confusingly-named route that traverses right from the peg on *The Secret* to reach a good foot-ledge in the middle of the wall. Move up to another good ledge then finish easily up a slim corner. There is an alternative boulder-problem start 3m right of the corner - **6a**.
FA. Stuart Cathcart, Tom Curtis 15.4.1976

Main Wall — Maeshafn Quarry

24 Cousin M E2 6b
A highball boulder problem with a desperate sequence up the wall to reach the foot-ledge at the end of *The Corner* traverse. Finish up that route.
FA. Chris Durkin 1.7.1992

25 Think a Moment E6 6b
A technical exercise in crimping, with no real protection, taking a vague line up the wall. Climb *Laxix* to the small overlap, then move left and climb the smooth grey wall to the top.
FA. Chris Durkin 6.1992

26 Laxix E5 6a
Excellent climbing that has been slightly spoilt by recent rockfalls. Follow the rightward trending crack-line up the wall.
FA. Stuart Cathcart, Gerald Swindley 8.9.1975

27 Knotty Problem E1 5b
A good route that has become slightly harder due to recent rockfalls. Mantelshelf onto a flat-topped flake and continue up the wall, following the thin crack between two orange rock scars, to an awkward finish.
FA. Stuart Cathcart, Gerald Swindley 26.6.1975

28 So She Did E3 5c
A bold eliminate. Follow *Knotty Problem* to the lower rock scar then traverse right using stuck-on holds. When these disappear, blast straight up the wall, with a difficult move near the top.

29 Baraouche E2 5b
A short-lived but enjoyable pitch following the rightward-trending crack to a ledge and then the thin crack above to the top.
FA. Stuart Cathcart, Gerald Swindley 10.8.1975

30 Pengrail E1 5b
Climb the short crack and corner with a testing move half way.
FA. Stuart Cathcart, Tom Curtis 21.4.1976

There is a traverse of the walls - not shown on the topo.

31 Main Wall Girdle E3 5c
Originally done in four pitches, this exercise in horizontal movement starts up *Jocca* (page 63) then traverses right to belay on the ledge of *Layback on Me*. Continue easily to belay on *Yobo* before traversing across *The Minstrel* wall to a final belay in *The Corner*. The last bit is the crux which traverses across *Laxix* to finish up *Baraouche*.
FA. Stuart Cathcart, Gerald Swindley 25.11.1975

Maeshafn Quarry — The Amphitheatre

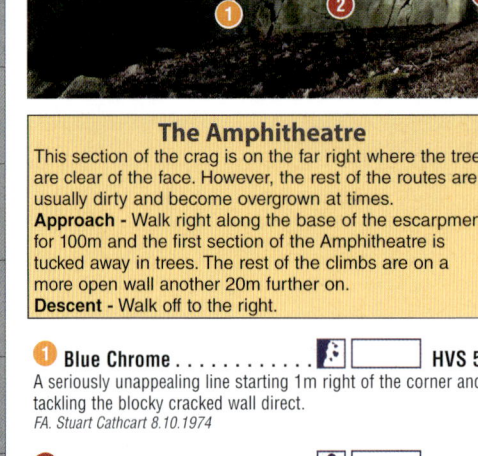

The Amphitheatre

This section of the crag is on the far right where the trees are clear of the face. However, the rest of the routes are usually dirty and become overgrown at times.
Approach - Walk right along the base of the escarpment for 100m and the first section of the Amphitheatre is tucked away in trees. The rest of the climbs are on a more open wall another 20m further on.
Descent - Walk off to the right.

① Blue Chrome .... HVS 5a
A seriously unappealing line starting 1m right of the corner and tackling the blocky cracked wall direct.
FA. Stuart Cathcart 8.10.1974

② Das Bolt E1 5b
The alternative slightly less worrying start to *Blue Chrome* goes up the thin crack in the bulging green wall.
FA. Dave Johnson 14.11.1985

③ The Rasp E3 5c
Start at the lowest point of the wall and climb steeply to a good hold. Pull awkwardly into the crack above and follow this through the overlap to a vegetated and prickly finale.
FA. Stuart Cathcart, Dave Johnson 29.9.1975

④ Itsu E3 5b
Steep, loose and unpleasant. Start up *Vulcer* then move left to climb the deep loose V-groove to a spiky exit.
FA. Stuart Cathcart, Gerald Swindley 5.1974

⑤ Vulcer .... HVS 5a
Although it looks like a good line, the crack running the length of the wall is loose and not recommended.
FA. Stuart Cathcart, Tom Curtis 15.4.1976

Mark Glaister starting up the initial crack of the Maeshafn classic *The Minstrel* (E1 5b) - *page 64* - a fantastic well-protected test of technique. Photo: Sophie Baring

Maeshafn Quarry — The Amphitheatre

6 Hiding in There E4 6a
Start 1m right of the cave and climb directly up the greasy wall and past the overhang using a drill hole.
FA. Steven Eccleson 30.8.2000

7 Ram Jam E2 5c
Climb easily up *Elephant Crack* to the overhang then move left beneath this to a roof-crack. This proves to be short and hard.
FA. Stuart Cathcart, Dave Johnson 30.9.1975

8 Elephant Crack .... S 4a
Climb the vegetated groove leading to, and finishing up, the body-width chimney.

9 Dandy Lion .... HS 4b
Follow the right-trending flake-crack to finish up the V-shaped groove with a hawthorn tree above.
FA. Gary Dickinson, P.Lockett 22.4.90

10 Sling .... HS 4a
The flake-crack in the short wall is popular and well protected.

11 Little Finger Jam .... HVS 5b
A frustratingly difficult start through the low overhang gains easier climbing above.

12 The Bulger .... HVS 5b
A nice technical pitch following the thin crack in the bulging wall left of the groove.
FA. Stuart Cathcart, Gerald Swindley 1975

13 Shattered Crack .... HS 4a
A popular route up the steep broken crack and groove until it is possible to escape left onto the grass terrace. *Photo opposite*.

14 The Arete .... VS 5a
The wall right of the groove is tricky low down.
FA. Stuart Cathcart, Tom Curtis 11.2.76

15 Wanderer .... HS 4b
A wandering line starting just right of *The Arete* at a short corner. Climb the corner to a ledge system, then traverse along this to join *Shattered Crack*.
FA. Stuart Cathcart, Tom Curtis 11.2.76

Sophie Baring on *Shattered Crack* (HS 4a) - page 68 - at The Amphitheatre, Maeshafn Quarry.

Pot Hole Quarry

	No star	★	★★	★★★
Mod to S	2	1	-	-
HS to HVS	9	12	1	1
E1 to E3	3	6	3	1
E4 and up	-	-	-	-

Debbie Roberts engaged in the intricacies of the technical thin crackline of *The Dog* (HVS 5b) - *page 74* - on the main face of Pot Hole Quarry. Pot Hole Quarry is a great little crag for an evening climb and only a short distance from a good pub.

Pot Hole Quarry

('Bryn yr Ardd' Quarry - Garden Hill Quarry)
Pot Hole Quarry is a small venue in an idyllic rural setting; it is a rather retiring little place though it has long been popular with locals. The crag has a good number of trad pitches in the lower and mid grades that make it worth calling in for an evening session, or for grabbing a couple of quick routes for those on the way to or from Snowdonia. The main attraction of the quarry is a long, low wall of solid quarried rock bounded on its left by a prominent corner and laced with finger-cracks. Generally the rock is good quality and the myriad of cracks offer small wire protection on most of the lines. There are many trees on top of the crag that provide convenient belay anchors. The crag can be easily combined with a visit to the more extensive Maeshafn Quarry which is only a five minute drive away.

Access
Pot Hole Quarry is on private land and managed by the BMC. No camping or fires are permitted. Dogs must be kept on a lead.

Approach Also see map on page 40
Take the A494 ring road around Mold, following signs for Ruthin. Once on the south side of Mold, the wide road climbs through the village of Gwernymynydd. After 2.5 miles, the village of Llanferres is reached. Park in the large lay-by 200m beyond the village. An information board in the lay-by marks the start of the path to Pot Hole Quarry. Head out across the field on a track and cross the river at a bridge. The less well-defined path links up with a better path at a stile and stream. Follow the path by the stream that quickly leads to the quarry on the left. Five minutes from the parking.

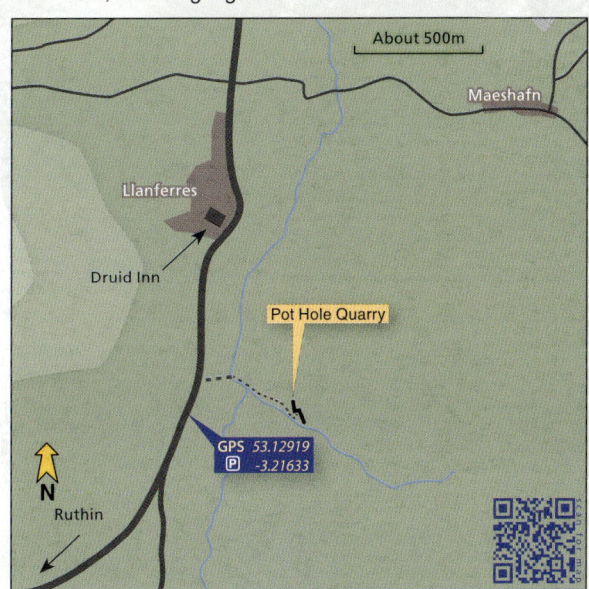

Conditions
Very sheltered and west-facing, Pot Hole Quarry is an afternoon suntrap and is often in condition, though the cracks do seep after persistent rainfall. The routes are well used with little loose rock, although polish can make things a little tricky in hot weather.

Pot Hole Quarry — Lower Wall and Main Wall

Lower Wall
A useful area should the Main Wall be busy, although the routes are of no great quality.
Approach - The Lower Wall is the short wall just below the base of the Main Wall.

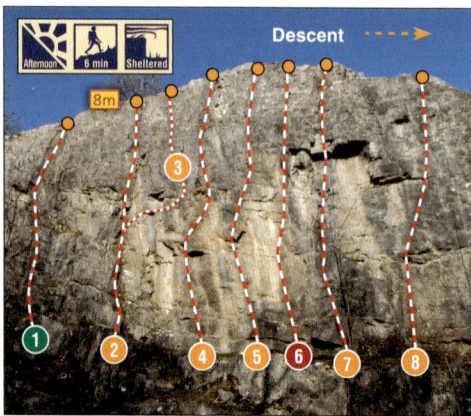

① Sunset .... ☐ **VD**
Starting from ledges just left of the corner, climb the juggy cracked wall.

Main Wall
The best climbing at Pot Hole is on the tall wall which stretches right and left from the prominent arete. The routes on the centre of this wall are superb, especially *The Dog* and *Ceba*. Further right the routes are a bit short, but they provide plenty of interesting lines at easier grades.

⑨ Owl Wall. .... ☐ **HS 4a**
Start left of the tree at a finger-crack and climb the wall past a tiny sapling to the top.
FA. Tom Curtis 17.6.1978

⑩ Mango .... ☐ **HS 4a**
A good line following the vague rounded scoop and cracks to reach a ledge by a small sapling. Pull up past this and climb the tricky wall above the ledge to reach the top.
FA. Tom Curtis 17.6.1978

⑪ Chutney .... ☐ **VS 5a**
Nice climbing up the wall right of *Mango* with an awkward finish up the thin V-crack near the top.
FA. J.Jones, P.Moore 19.7.2001

⑫ Droggo .... ☐ **VS 4b**
A well-protected climb following thin cracks in the wall left of the arete.

② Blindfold .... ☐ **HS 4a**
The corner has a few loose blocks low down.

③ Once Is Never Enough ...... ☐ **VS 4c**
From the corner, traverse right under an overlap to reach a juggy flake-crack that is followed to the top.
FA. A.Freeman, D.Romney 1.1990

④ Burning Bush. .... ☐ **VS 4c**
The wide crack with a thorny bush at half height.
FA. Stuart Cathcart, Tom Curtis 20.9.1978

⑤ Tosa .... ☐ **HVS 5a**
Short but entertaining climbing with a steep start. Ascend the yellow coloured wall to an easy but pleasant finish.
FA. Stuart Cathcart, Tom Curtis 20.9.1978

⑥ Badger Disco. .... ☐ **E2 5b**
The steep wall direct, finishing up a short crack between adjacent routes. Bold to start but never really desperate.
FA. Matthew West, Kate Surry 10.4.2011

⑦ Cima .... ☐ **HVS 5a**
The blocky crack right of *Tosa* through a small overlap.

⑧ Sideswipe. .... ☐ **HS 4b**
Start 3m right of *Cima*. From the right end of a ledge at 2m, climb rightwards up a bulging wall to finish up a tiny corner.
FA. Philip Biglands and team 27.7.2011

⑬ Epitaph. .... ☐ **HVS 5b**
Boldly climb the thin crack in the wall beneath the arete to reach a good crack in the narrow face of the arete. Follow this to a foot-ledge then move left to finish up the short wall.

⑭ Horn Dog .... ☐ **HVS 5a**
The arete direct is surprisingly independent.
FA. Dave Ayton 2005

Ed Booth on the tight eliminate line of *Ego* (E3 5c) - *page 75* - on the Main Wall at Pot Hole Quarry. Photo: Patricia Novelli

Pot Hole Quarry — Main Wall

15 Talking Legs E1 5b
Move up to an off-balance position on a ledge then tackle the short blocky crack above.
FA. Stuart Cathcart 28.9.1978

16 Talking Fingers .... HVS 5b
An entertaining route up the crack that feels steeper and longer than it really is.
FA. Stuart Cathcart 28.9.1978

17 Roger Rabbit E1 5c
This difficult eliminate squeezes up the cracked wall left of the right-angled corner.
FA. Roger Bennion, M.Frith 1990

18 Right Angle .... HS 4b
A classic struggle up the steep little corner.

19 Silly Lilly E1 5a
Nice climbing following the thin leftward-trending crack just right of the corner. Thin on gear high up.
FA. H.John, Jim Hewson 1984

20 Id E3 5c
A serious route up the fingery wall between the cracks.
FA. H.John, Jim Hewson 1984

21 Right Wall E2 5c
Good technical wall climbing that is quite bold in its lower half. The upper crack is well protected and sustained.
FA. Stuart Cathcart, Tom Curtis 28.9.1978

22 The Dog .... HVS 5b
A gem of a route and the line of the crag with well-protected and absorbing climbing following the finger-crack to the top of the wall. *Photo on page 70.*
FA. Stuart Cathcart, Tom Curtis 18.7.1975

23 Canine Meander E2 5b
A worthwhile eliminate, with just enough protection, taking the wall between *The Dog* and *Ceba*, finishing direct through the slim overlap on good holds.
FA. I.Doig, J.King 12.10.1984

24 Ceba E1 5b
An excellent technical route up the crack system with a tricky move to reach the right-hand edge of the high overlap.
Photo on page 40.
FA. Stuart Cathcart, Tom Curtis 21.3.1978

Main Wall — Pot Hole Quarry

25 Ego E3 5c
The blank wall between *Ceba* and *Vetta* is quite serious.
Photo on page 73.
FA. H.John, Jim Hewson 1984

26 Vetta E1 5a
A good route with a committing middle section. Climb easily to a ledge in a square niche, then move up to good holds before making a bold move left to reach the base of a crack-line and a welcome wire. Finish up the crack.
FA. Stuart Cathcart, Tom Curtis 18.7.1975

27 Vetta Variation E3 5c
A technical alternative finish to *Vetta* climbing directly up the wall from the square niche.
FA. Stuart Cathcart, Greg Griffiths 6.8.1978

28 Major .... HVS 5a
The crack is well protected and a good introduction to the harder routes on the wall.

29 Grizzly .... HVS 5a
A well-protected crack climb.
FA. Stuart Cathcart 10.7.1980

30 Un-Aided .... VS 4b
This crack runs the full length of the wall and is marked by a white splodge just above ground level.

31 Tre-Fynnon .... VS 4b
An eliminate up the wall between the cracks.
FA. Simon Williams, Alec Williams 29.12.1990

32 The Watzmann .... VS 4b
The left-hand of three finger cracks has a tricky finish.

33 Murren .... HS 4b
The middle crack of the three.

34 Cristallo .... VS 4b
The right-hand crack has a fingery exit.

35 Selva .... VS 4a
The wall and crack left of the arete.

36 Sesto .... HVD
The short arete is climbed on good flat holds.

37 Mestre .... S 4a
The short crack in the wall right of the arete.

There are a couple of traverses - not shown on the topos.

38 Diagonal Route E1 5b
25m. A mini-girdle. Start up *Un-Aided*, traverse across to climb the crux of *Vetta*, move up to the overlap on *Ceba*, then scuttle left across *The Dog* to finally finish up *Right Wall*.
FA. Stuart Cathcart, Malcolm Cameron 14.7.1979

39 Main Wall Girdle E2 5c
30m. Start up *Mango* and traverse around the arete, taking a belay in the corner of *Right Angle*, before continuing across to the top of *Vetta*.
FA. Stuart Cathcart, Gerald Swindley 9.8.1975

Minera Quarry

	No star	★	★★	★★★
up to 4+	-	2	-	-
5+ to 6a+	2	2	-	-
6b to 7a	-	2	1	-
7a+ and up	-	-	-	-

Minera Quarry is a vast abandoned limestone working with a couple of walls worth a look for those in the area. The climbs are fairly insignificant when set against the scale of the quarry as a whole and those on the Lower Quarry Wall are much trickier than first appearances would suggest.

Approach Also see map on page 40

From the A483 at Wrexham take the B5430 signed to Coedpoeth. Just beyond the village, turn left signed Minera. After 0.4 miles turn right at a fork in the road and drive a further 0.5 miles to a left turn onto a narrow lane - Maes-y-Ffynnon Road. Drive down the lane to parking at the entrance to the quarry. The walls are reached from here.

Conditions
The Minera Quarry is sunny, fairly sheltered and quick drying.

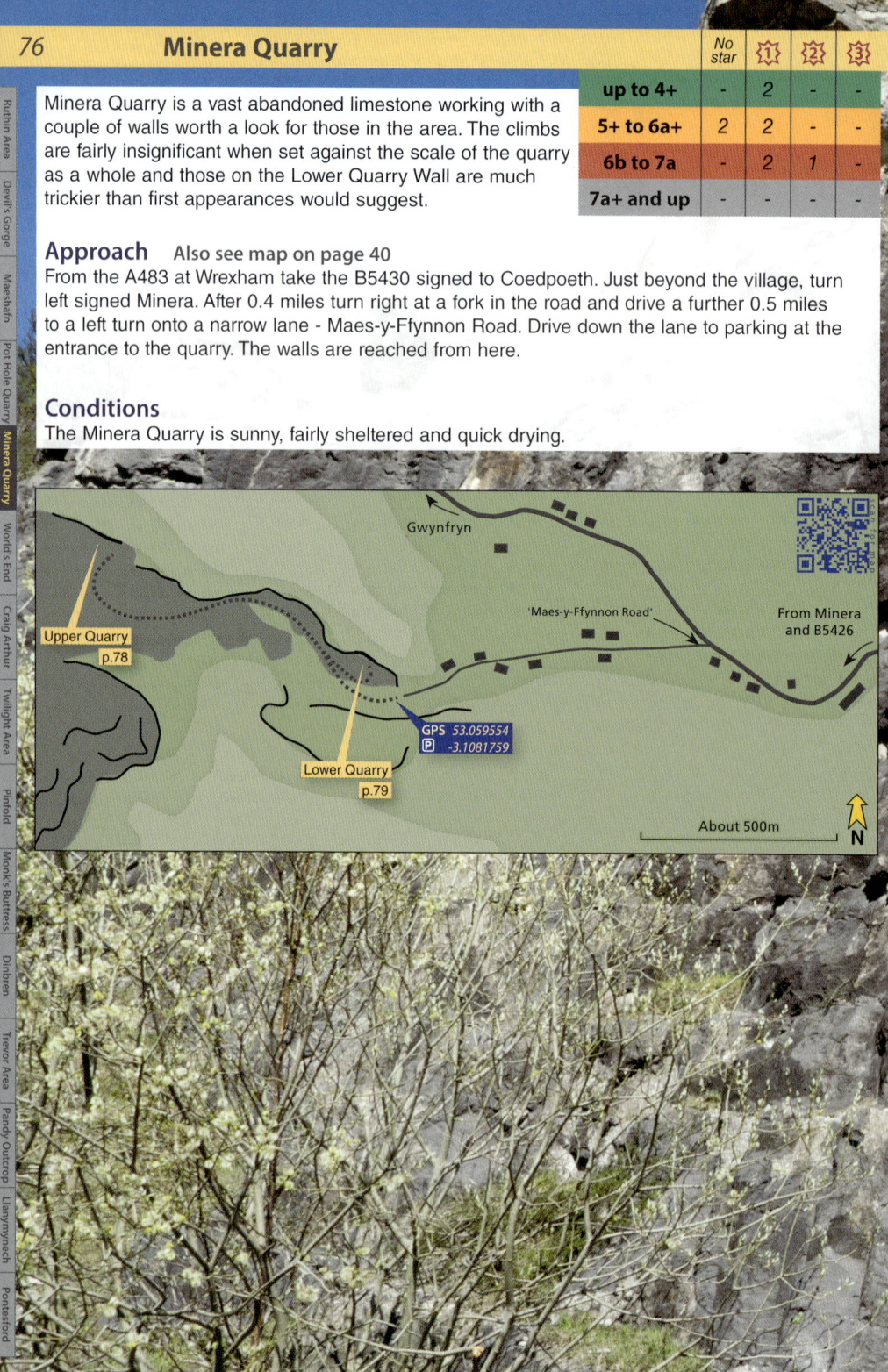

Minera Quarry

Paul Cox sizing up the top section of *The Quartz Slab* (6a) - *page 79* - at Minera Quarry. This wall has a small selection of deceptively tricky pitches on quartz-encrusted limestone which is a touch snappy.

Minera Quarry — Upper Quarry

Upper Quarry

An isolated wall with some good rock and one decent route at present.

Approach - Walk up through the quarry for 1km to a large grassy plateau from where the face can be seen up on the right.

1 The Calch .... 6b+
Superb technical climbing on flowstone with a tricky finale.
FA. Lee Proctor 11.6.2006

The thin wall to the right of The Calch is an open project.

Lower Quarry

A low wall of innocuous looking routes. The climbs themselves are actually quite difficult and whilst not strenuous provide plenty of technical interest. The rock has a quartz covering in places and is still a little friable. The first ascent details are not known.
Approach - Walk up the track for 200m, cross a fence and then walk back on another track to the face.

2 The Blocky Wall 6a
A touch unnerving on fragile-feeling blocks.

3 The Open Grey Groove . . 4a
Nice moves on good grey rock starting at the top of the earth bank.

4 Hard Start . . . . 6a+
A hard start! Keep on line away from poor rock out right. Finish up the easier wall to a lower-off below the ledge.

Lots of sun | 5 min | Sheltered

5 Narrow Arete . . . 6a+
Take the narrow arete to technical moves up and left to finish up the wall as for *Hard Start*.

6 Quartz Wall 6b
The wall of quartz is very pleasant. Finish direct via a hard pull to a good hold. Lower-off on large ledge.

7 Thin Grey Wall 6c
The thin grey wall has plenty of good moves.

8 The Quartz Slab 6a
Weave up to the slab via some less than straightforward moves to a single bolt lower-off. A good pitch at the top of the grade.
Photo on page 77.

9 Easy Grooves 4c
A brief but worthwhile easier pitch taking a series of short grooves and corners with one tricky step-up.

Just to the right is a low lone bolt.

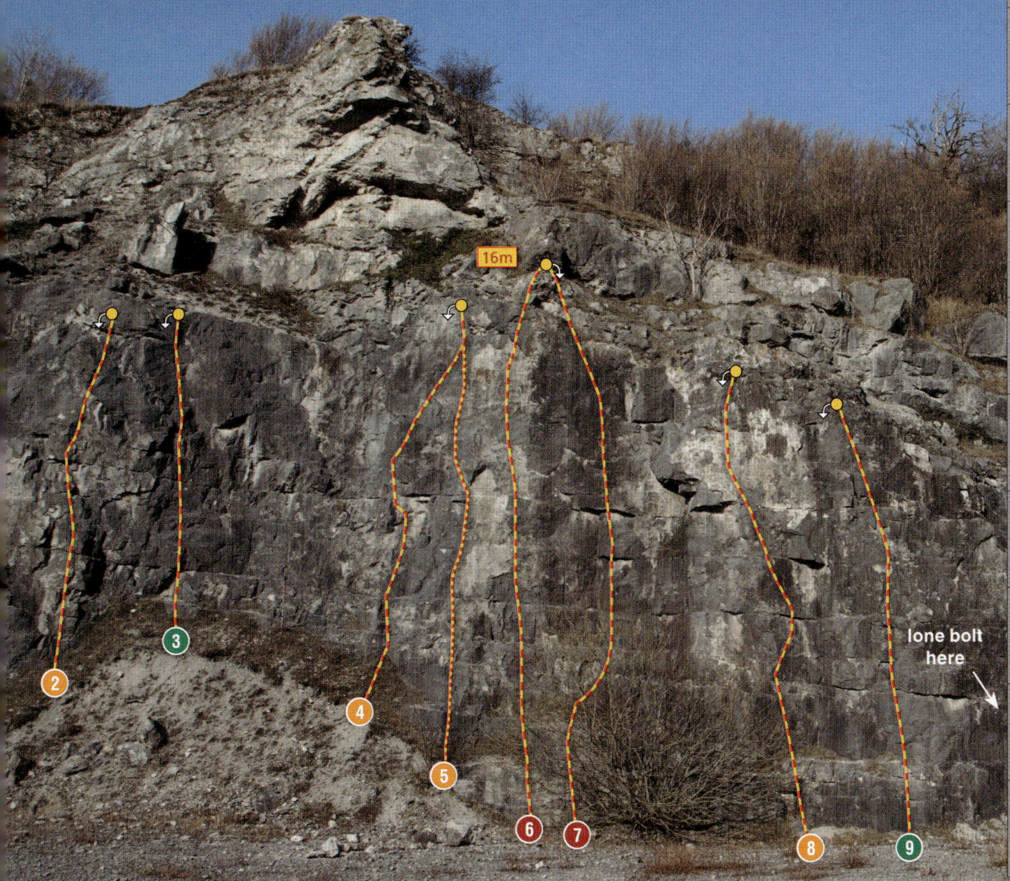

Ruthin Area
Devil's Gorge
Maeshafn
Pot Hole Quarry
Minera Quarry
World's End
Craig Arthur
Twilight Area
Pinfold
Monk's Buttress
Dinbren
Trevor Area
Pandy Outcrop
Llanymynech
Pontesford

Paul Ingham on *Back in Black* (7b+) - *page 165* - one of the many high-quality sport routes to be found at Dinbren. Photo: Patricia Novelli

Eglwyseg Valley

World's End, Craig Arthur, Twilight Area, Pinfold, Monk's Buttress, Dinbren

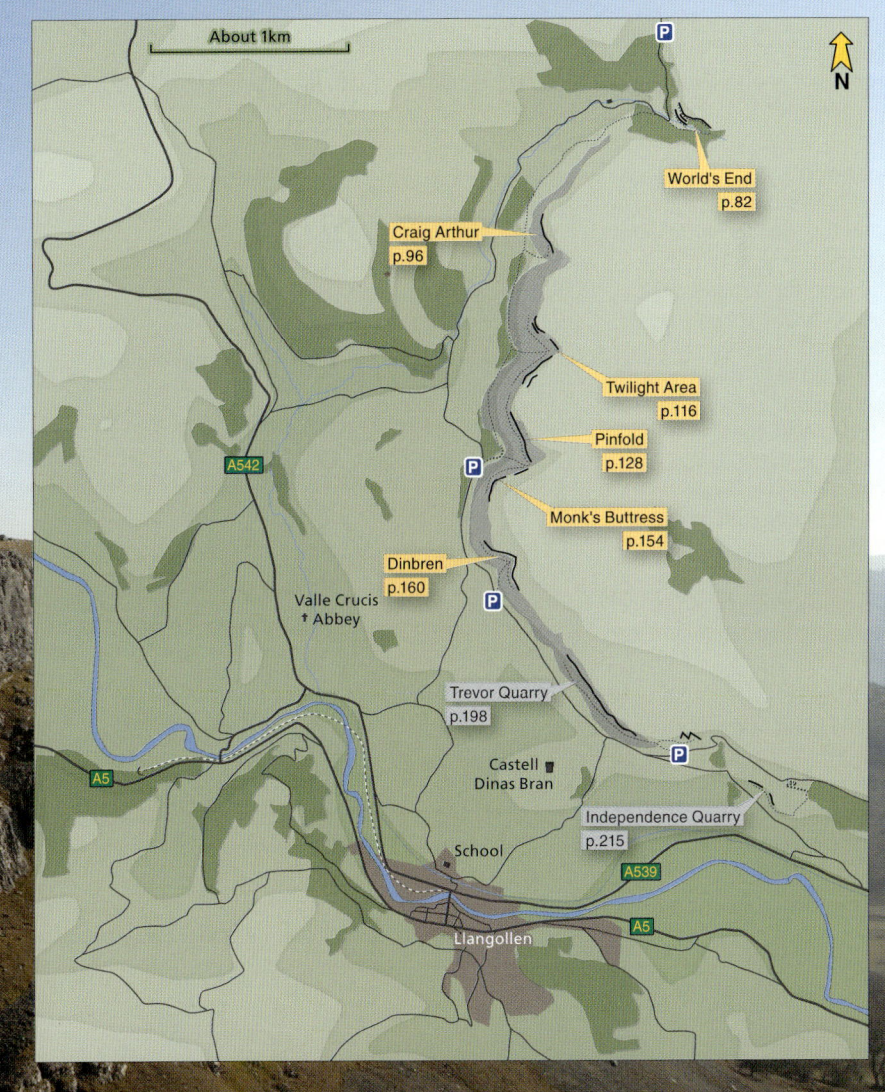

World's End

	No star	☆	☆☆	☆☆☆
Mod to S	24	4	3	-
HS to HVS	20	16	4	-
E1 to E3	23	14	4	3
E4 and up	5	10	5	1

World's End sits at the head of the Eglwyseg valley and is made up of a series of tiered cliffs that lean out from a forested hillside. World's End has always been synonymous with rock climbing on Clwyd limestone and, its ease of access and good spread of grades mean that many visitors get their first taste of Clwyd trad here. Many of the better routes are on good compact limestone that rises to around 12m and most of the climbs are vertical or slightly overhanging making them feel longer than their height might suggest. Several of the harder lines have protection from pegs, threads and bolts but treat all fixed protection with caution especially since the crag is covered by a drilling ban preventing replacement of old bolts.

Access

World's End is on private land. There is a total drilling ban. No camping or fires are allowed at any time.

Approach   Also see map on page 81

From Llangollen, follow the road to the junction at 1.8 miles and continue up the narrow valley road for 3 miles, until a ford on a sharp bend is crossed. 400m further on, just as the road exits the woods onto the moor, park on the roadside. Walk back to the ford and cross the fence on the left via a stile. Walk up the valley for 200m until the end of Coltsfoot Crack Area comes into view on the left. For the approaches to the various sectors, see the buttress notes.

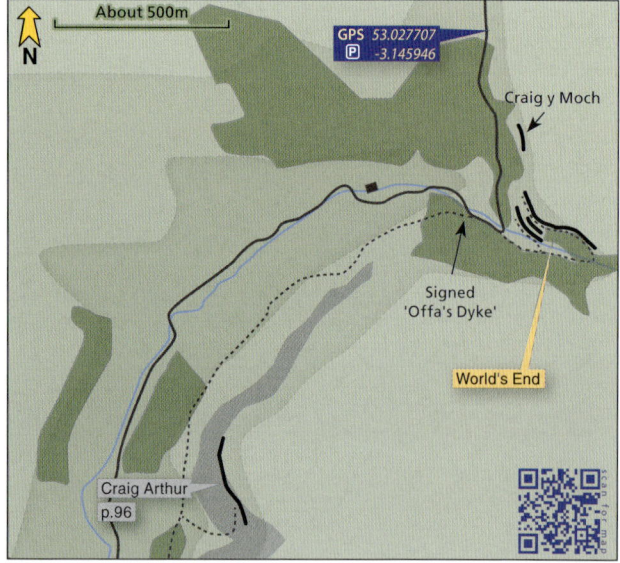

Conditions

World's End is a good place to head for if it is too windy on the other more exposed crags in the valley, although it offers no shelter from the rain. The rock dries quickly and persistent seepage is rarely a problem.

Craig y Moch Bouldering

This small spot is a great place to rattle off a few extended boulder problems in the evening sunshine. From the path above Taerg Wall, continue for 200m until a wall of good quality rock appears down on the left.

World's End

Ed Booth on one of the harder offerings at the perfectly positioned World's End cliffs - *Brigadier Gerard* (E5 6a) - *page 86*. Photo: Ryan McConnell

World's End — Taerg Wall Area

Taerg Wall Area

This fine exposed crag is the upper section of the tiers of vertical walls that hang over the road. The rock is generally excellent and the protection on the best lines is reasonable. The climbs are in a very exposed position and are likely to be windier than other areas on the cliff.

Approach - Follow the narrowing path under the crag to its far end. The ledge system that runs beneath this area is fairly narrow and care is needed. The climbs, although not long, are perched above a big drop-off and a belay at the base of the crag is advised.

1 Cathcart's Got a Brand New Brodrie E1 5b
Good rock and protection make for a worthwhile route. Start to the left of a fir tree and a small overlap. Pull up and move right to the base of a thin crack and follow this to the top.
FA. Phil Waters, Stuart Cathcart 5.7.1984

2 Finer Feelings .... HVS 5b
A little gem. The start is tricky but the rock, protection and climbing are superb.
FA. Stuart Cathcart, John Dee 13.5.1979

3 Warp Commander E1 5b
Pull onto the wall using good holds, then move up and right to a large layaway. Climb up to the overlap and reach above (peg) to good holds. Continue direct up the wall, past a second peg.
FA. P.Windsor 7.1984

4 The Trick .... HVS 5a
Follow the crack to the ash tree then tackle the problematic wall and crack above.
FA. Geoff Ashton, Rick Newcombe 30.8.1964

5 Vertical Games E3 6a
Climb up to the flake-crack in the smooth wall. Make a perplexing long move rightwards for a distant edge. Pull up, move back left, and sprint for the top.
FA. Paul Stott, Stuart Cathcart 7.7.1981

6 Chance E2 5b
A worrying route starting up flakes to the horizontal break. Pull up to a very hollow square flake and make a committing move off this, using shallow pockets, to reach a thin crack and the top.
FA. Paul Harrison, Steve Boydon 8.3.1984

7 Ash Bole .... S 4a
The unappealing vegetated crack.
FA. Geoff Ashton, Rick Newcombe 30.8.1964

8 Quill .... VS 4c
An entertaining test in jamming. Hand jam to a good ledge and finish up the short flared crack above. High in the grade.
FA. Stuart Cathcart, Nick Slaney 5.1975

9 Sting .... HS 4a
A good sustained minor classic. Climb the large flake to a ledge beneath the wide crack then follow this with conviction.
FA. John Hesketh, H.J.Tinkler 1962

10 Jennifer Crack ..... HS 4a
A powerful line following the wide crack splitting the buttress.
FA. John Hesketh, H.J.Tinkler 1962

11 World's Edge E4 6a
A well-positioned pitch. Start just right of the arete, and move up left to good holds - wires. Make a short but wild sequence of moves over the bulge to a peg. Finish more easily.
FA. Paul Harrison, Steve Boydon 8.3.1984

12 Someone Like You E5 6b
A difficult reachy and committing climb. Climb to a peg and continue precariously to beneath an overlap. Surmount the overlap before making a huge reach to some poor holds. A final pull gains jugs and the top.
FA. Gary Gibson, Hazel Gibson 2.7.1992

13 Soul on Ice E4 5c
An eliminate that follows a series of hollow flakes up the arete, with a hard move by a thin thread.
FA. John Moulding, John Codling 31.12.1983

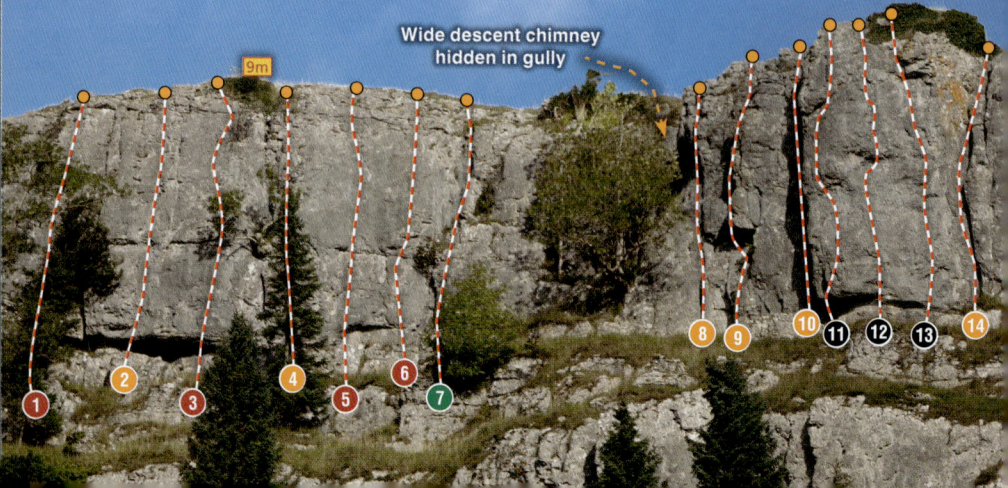

Wide descent chimney hidden in gully

Taerg Wall Area **World's End** 85

14 Les Elephants .... VS 4c
The chimney crack.
FA. John Hesketh, H.J.Tinkler 1962

15 Telegram Sam E4 6a
A delicate exercise up the left side of the wall, passing a very old bolt. Move left to finish up a slight crack.
FA. John Codling 11.1983

16 Taerg Wall E2 5c
A superbly-positioned climb taking the line of least resistance up the wall. Start up a short crack to reach a line of good but slightly rickety holds, move left, then rock up with conviction to stand on a good ledge. Step right to a thin crack and follow this to a peg. Make a long pull past this to reach the top.
FA. Stuart Cathcart, Malcolm Cameron 4.6.1981

17 Wasters Mall E4 6b
A rewarding climb with just enough protection. Start beneath a juggy flake and use it to climb straight up to good undercuts in the overlap. Move left and up to a peg then, using a pocket in the wall to the right, make a hard pull to reach a flake crack and good wires. Finish more easily up and leftwards.
FA. John Codling, John Moulding 31.12.1983

18 Heart of Darkness E3 5c
An airy route up the exposed arete that can be reasonably protected with small wires.
FA. Stuart Cathcart, Malcolm Cameron 24.7.1980

19 Half and Half .... S 4a
More like a cave route than a rock climb. Ascend the chimney into darkness and after 7m move onto the right wall and continue to the top.
FA. John Hesketh, H.J.Tinkler 1962

20 Sleeping Beauty E3 6a
Move up to an old inverted peg and make a hard move past this, over the bulge, to join the easy upper wall of *Xuxu*.
FA. Ian Dunn, Claudie Dunn 1985

21 Xuxu E2 5b
A nasty pitch. Pull through the large hollow bulge on big spaced jugs. The upper wall, just right of the yew tree, is easy.
FA. Stuart Cathcart, Malcolm Cameron 24.7.1980

22 Slither .... VS 4c
The thin crack in the wall left of *Ivy Crack* is awkward to start. Not vegetated despite appearances from below.
FA. Stuart Cathcart 3.10.1979

23 Ivy Crack .... S 4a
The arm-width crack eases after a couple of moves. The top is a lot cleaner than it looks from below.
FA. John Hesketh, H.J.Tinkler 1962

24 Wither .... Diff
The rather unappealing block-choked crack.
FA. John Hesketh, H.J.Tinkler 1962

25 Christmas Spirit E1 5b
Follow the finger-crack in the left edge of the wall to a thread. Continue up broken cracks and hollow flakes.
FA. Fred Crook, G.Crook 25.12.1983

26 Flash Harry E5 6b
Follow the finger-crack to a small overlap. Pull up to a peg, then make a very hard move above this, moving leftwards to finish.
FA. John Codling, John Moulding 31.12.1983

27 Flash Dance E4 6b
A technical, well-protected wall climb. Gain the thin crack in the right-hand edge of the wall and follow this past two pegs.
FA. John Codling 11.1983

28 Jumping Jack Flash E4 5c
A harrowing pitch. Start up *Flash Dance* and traverse precariously right to an old thread at the base of a massive hollow flake. Climb the flake to the top. Belayers stand well back!
FA. John Codling, Tony Bristlin 26.12.1983

World's End — Intensity Area

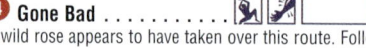

Intensity Area
The area is a good spot for those seeking out some decent mid grade trad lines and has one hard sport pitch.
Approach - The area starts as the path exits the trees and continues to the exposed arete.
Descent - Walk rightwards (looking out) and descend to the base of the tier via the wide chimney in the gully.
Conditions - Out of the shelter of the trees and therefore can be cold and breezy.

① Craznitch Crack . . . . HS 4a
The overhanging wide crack is easier than it looks.
FA. John Hesketh, H.J.Tinkler 1962

② Close to the Edge E1 5b
An exciting route. Follow *Intensity* to the first overhang, then traverse left beneath this (thread) to reach a V-shaped groove. Pull into the groove and continue to the top.
FA. Paul Stott, Mike Frith 26.5.1974

③ Intensity . . . . HVS 5b
An intimidating but classic testpiece requiring a forthright approach. Battle up the steep, wide crack using a variety of jams and face holds.
FA. John Hesketh, H.J.Tinkler 1962

④ Gone Bad E1 5b
A wild rose appears to have taken over this route. Follow the thin groove to the overhang and move right to reach a layback crack. Power up this, in a wild position, to the top.
FA. Stuart Cathcart, Nick Slaney 1971

⑤ Going Bad E2 5b
The crack and hanging pillar on the arete.
FA. Stuart Cathcart, John Dee 20.9.1978

⑥ Yew and Me . . . . . .  E3 5c
A hard and powerful start with no gear gains a good hold beneath the yew tree. Pull up onto a ledge and finish up the wall.
FA. Paul Stott 8.7.1981

⑦ Cigars of the Pharaohs . . 7b
The bulging wall has a hard and powerful start, followed by more hard technical moves above.
FA. D.Taylor 9.1990

⑧ Shooting Star . . . . . 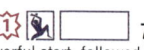 E4 6b
A striking line - one of the best routes at World's End. Climb the crack-line and bulge before finishing up the still taxing groove.
FA. Stuart Cathcart, Gerald Swindley 3.5.1979

⑨ The Final Solution . . 7c+
Technical climbing using tiny crimps and layaways on the lower wall is complemented by a powerful finish through the upper bulge on finger-locks. No lower-off.
FA. Nick Dixon 6.2002. The route supersedes Rudolph Hess that went to the third bolt and then traversed right to finish up Brigadier Gerard.
FA. (Rudolph Hess) Mike Collins 1988

⑩ Sisters of the Moon E5 6a
A poor eliminate that tries to climb the wall left of *Brigadier Gerard* but ultimately uses holds on that route. Protected by two bolt runners.
FA. Allen Price 1988

⑪ Brigadier Gerard . . . 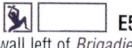 E5 6a
A good line blasting straight up the wall and over the bulge, following the crack-line. Some of the holds rattle but the gear is good. There is a peg in the lower crack. *Photo on page 83.*
FA. Steve Allen, John Codling 11.1983

Intensity Area **World's End** 87

⓬ Tripe and Landah E1 5b
A strenuous route climbing the thin crack past a peg.
FA. Paul Stott, Dave Greenald 18.8.1980

⓭ Fossil Finish . . . . VS 4c
A hard start gains a ledge with a thorn bush. Take the layback crack above and finish leftwards on loose rock.
FA. R.Tilston 6.1971

⓮ Ego Beaver E3 6b
A route with one very hard section.
FA. Fred Crook, Gary Cooper 12.1983

⓯ Titanium Man E3 6a
Good climbing. Climb easily to the top of a flake and continue up thin finger-cracks in the vague rib to a peg. Difficult moves past this lead to a second peg in a shallow groove and the top.
FA. Fred Crook, K.Crook, Gary Cooper 20.12.1983

⓰ Meth E1 5b
Steep to start. Make a crimpy pull over the bulge then continue up the groove via easier climbing.
FA. Ryan McConnell 3.2014

⓱ Crystal E1 5b
A nicely varied climb that starts up the rightward-trending layback flake to reach a finger-crack. Follow this, passing to the left of a ledge, and finishing up a short groove.
FA. Fred Crook, K.Crook, I.Barker 3.12.1983

⓲ Dr. Technical E4 6b
Climb nervously up the white groove to an old thread, then move up to the bulge and a welcome bolt. Span rightwards to better holds and an easier finish up shattered cracks.
FA. John Moulding, Steve Boydon 14.4.1984

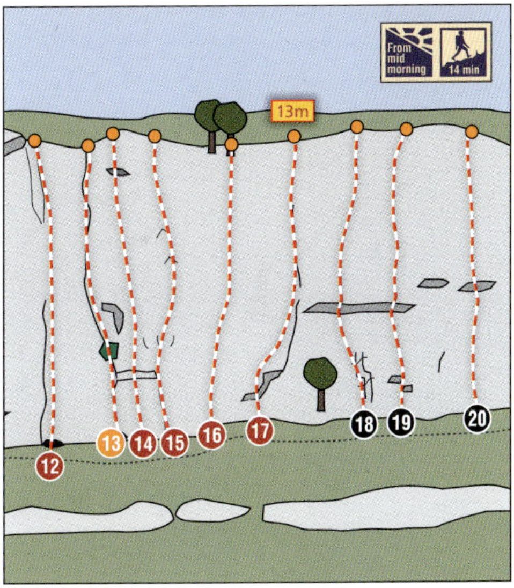

⓳ Nurse Nurse E5 6b
Climb boldly up to a bolt beneath the bulge and reach over this to big hollow jugs. Continue up easy ground, past a thread.
FA. John Codling 1983

⓴ Read My Lips E5 6c
The final route is also one of the hardest around with a very blind move at the crux. Climb up to a bolt beneath the bulge, continue over steep ground to a second bolt and pass this on the right with extreme difficulty, to reach a tree.
FA. Gary Gibson 3.8.1992

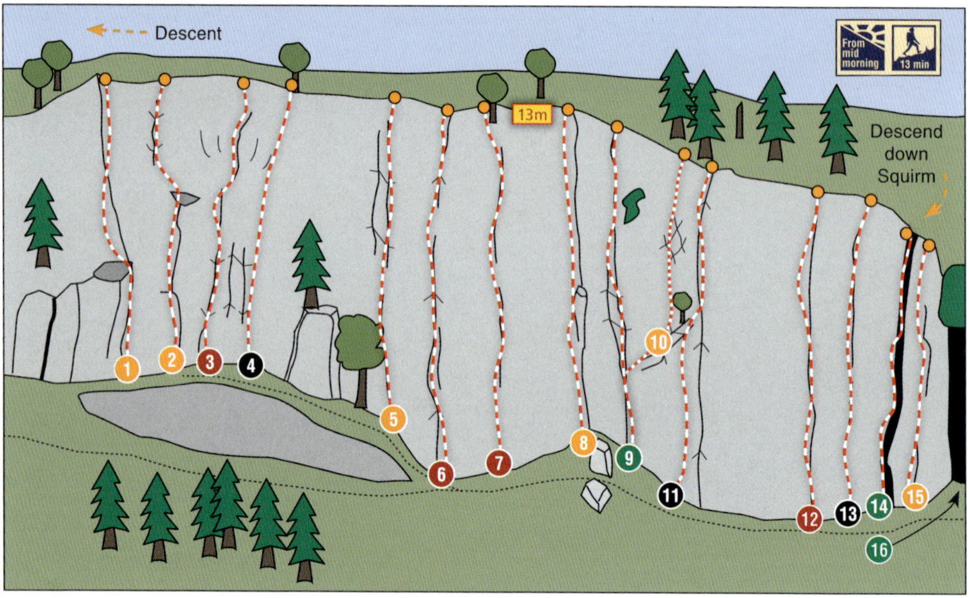

Open Book Area

Cracks, aretes and corners dominate in this area, which has some particularly good rock. *Suicide Crack* is a classic, well-protected, thin finger-crack. The fine corner of *Open Book* is the main feature in the middle of this area and a popular climb.

Approach - Follow the crag-base path until just before the final section of tree cover.

Descent - Either walk rightwards (looking out) and descend to the base of the tier via the wide chimney in the gully between the routes *Ash Bole* and *Quill* at the Taerg Wall Area; or down-climb *Squirm* (Diff).

Two routes have been recorded behind the yew tree - **Clartum Crack** *and* **Clartum Corner** *- both graded Severe and both now unclimbable due to vegetation.*

1 Margarine Arete . . . . 1 star **HVS 5a**
The rounded arete, with a brief detour left then back right, at half height.
FA. Steve Boydon, A.Orton 1985

2 Whim . . . . 2 stars **HVS 5a**
A good route following a line of flakes and cracks.
FA. Rick Newcombe, Geoff Ashton 30.8.1964

3 Windhover . . . . 2 stars **E2 5c**
A fine climb that feels run out at the start if the true line is adhered to. Climb cautiously up the white groove and wall to reach the base of a steep finger-crack. Arrange protection then blast confidently up the crack to a good jug and the top.
FA. Stuart Cathcart, Gerald Swindley 17.8.1979

4 Silver Shadow . . . . 2 stars **E4 5c**
The groove to the peg and headwall.
FA. Ryan McConnell 15.07.2013

5 Ivy Groove . . . . 1 star **VS 4b**
Well protected. Climb up cracks to reach a small corner.
FA. Mike Frith, Paul Stott 1975

6 Butter Arete . . . . 2 stars **E3 5b**
A bold route taking an excellent line on great rock. Climb leftwards to the arete. Arrange protection at half-height (reportedly placement has gone) then confidently follow the arete to the top.
FA. Stuart Cathcart, Malcolm Cameron 4.6.1981

7 Suicide Crack . . . . . 3 stars **E3 6a**
An immaculate thin crack with good gear. At the upper end of the grade.
FA. Stuart Cathcart, Nick Slaney 16.6.1975

8 J.T.P . . . . **HVS 5a**
An eliminate that just manages to avoid the easier ground to the right. Follow the jamming and layback crack, passing over some hollow-sounding blocks.
FA. Gary Dickinson, J.Drinkwater, P.Lockett 31.1.1993

9 Open Book . . . . 2 stars **S 4a**
The central line of the recessed bay has some fine climbing.

10 Slapalong . . . . 1 star **VS 4c**
Start up *Open Book*, go easily up right along a ramp to finish up the wall on the left side of the arete.
FA. Peter Biglands, Philip Biglands 23.9.1993

11 Hell's Arete **E4 6a**
A good line spoilt by some snappy rock low down. Start at the toe of the vague arete, underneath a crack. Pull up to undercuts, pinches and reasonable wires, then move up rightwards to hidden holds. Continue to jugs at the mid-height ledge then finish easily up the wall above a small sapling.
FA. Stuart Cathcart, Tom Curtis 14.6.1978

Ruthin Area | Devil's Gorge | Maeshafn | Pot Hole Quarry | Minera Quarry | World's End | Craig Arthur | Twilight Area | Pinfold | Monk's Buttress | Dinbren | Trevor Area | Pandy Outcrop | Llanymynech | Pontesford

Inelegance Area — World's End

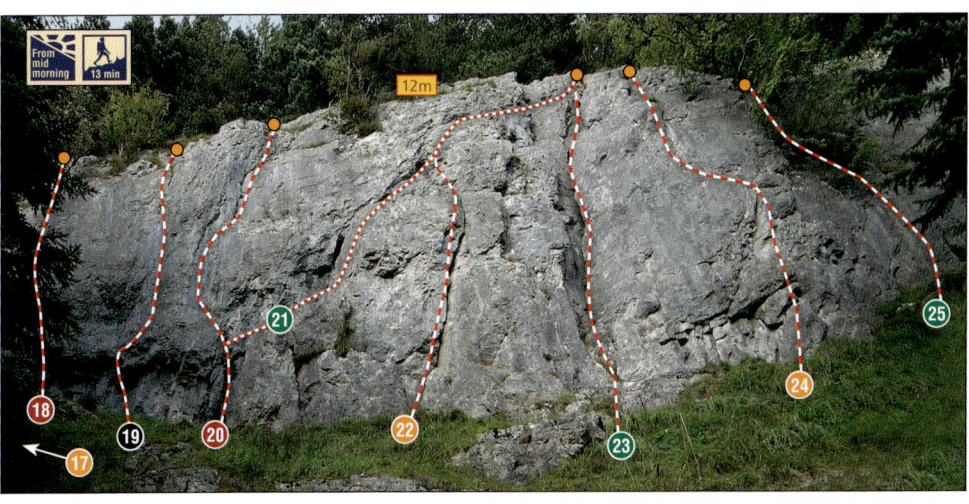

⑫ Fall Out E1 5b
A short but excellent and pumpy crack pitch with good gear.

⑬ Into the Fire E5 6a
A worthwhile climb that is far better than appearances suggest. Sustained with good but tough-to-place protection.
FA. Allen Price 4.1986

⑭ A'Cheval .... VD
A wide gully best used as a descent.
FA. John Hesketh, H.J.Tinkler 1962

⑮ Copper Pinnacle .... HS 4a
The crack between the gullies is poor.
FA. Geoff Ashton, Rick Newcombe 4.1.1964

⑯ Squirm .... Diff
The vegetated gully is a poor descent.
FA. John Hesketh, H.J.Tinkler 1962

⑰ Rough Cut .... VS 4c
Climb broken cracks and move right to a ledge with a precariously balanced flake. Move back left and climb the tricky wall.

⑱ Crystal Ship E3 5c
Good moves but serious. Deceptively technical climbing gains the diagonal overlap, then move left and pull over on good hidden holds.
FA. A.Windsor 1985

⑲ Dope on a Rope. E6 6a
Serious climbing up the centre of the grey wall. There is some gear but it is blind and hard to place as the crucial placement is blocked by your hand. Pull awkwardly into the scoop then move up on undercuts to small crimps. Move precariously right to a good side-pull and wire, then move up to small holds by a peg. Finish easily and safely to the top.
FA. John Codling, A.Dope 7.4.1984

Inelegance Area
Deep chimney cracks and juggy flakes contrast well with some bold but technically superb steep face climbs. The easier climbs are also very worthwhile.
Approach - Follow the crag-base path until a gap in the trees reveals an open section of wall with some eye-catching wide cracks splitting it.
Descent - Either walk rightwards (looking out) and descend to the base of the tier via the wide chimney in the gully between the routes *Ash Bole* and *Quill* at the Taerg Wall Area; or down-climb *Squirm* (Diff).

⑳ Dead Fingers Talk .. E3 6a
Excellent technical moves with a committing start. Move up to the top of the first crack of *Inelegance*, then step left with difficulty before moving up to the thin right-facing finger-crack. Follow this to the top.
FA. John Moulding, Simon Cardy 30.10.1983

㉑ Inelegance .... VD
A strong line with excellent climbing along the left-to-right diagonal line of pinnacles and flakes. Watch out for rope drag.
FA. John Hesketh, H.J.Tinkler 1962

㉒ Inspiration .... HS 4b
A very good climb taking the hand-sized crack direct to the upper pinnacle on *Inelegance*.

㉓ Incompetence ..... HVD
An excellent pitch of its type. The wide crack/chimney is sustained and protectable with slings and wires. Finish up the pinnacle on the right.

㉔ Insecure .... HVS 5a
Move easily up to a block-ledge at the start of the zig-zag crack. Well-protected moves up the initial crack lead to a committing traverse left on hollow but good holds. Pull into the continuation crack (good wires) then finish slightly leftwards up easier ground.

㉕ Ashgrove .... VD
Squirm up the chimney passing an ash tree at half height.

World's End — Black Ash Area

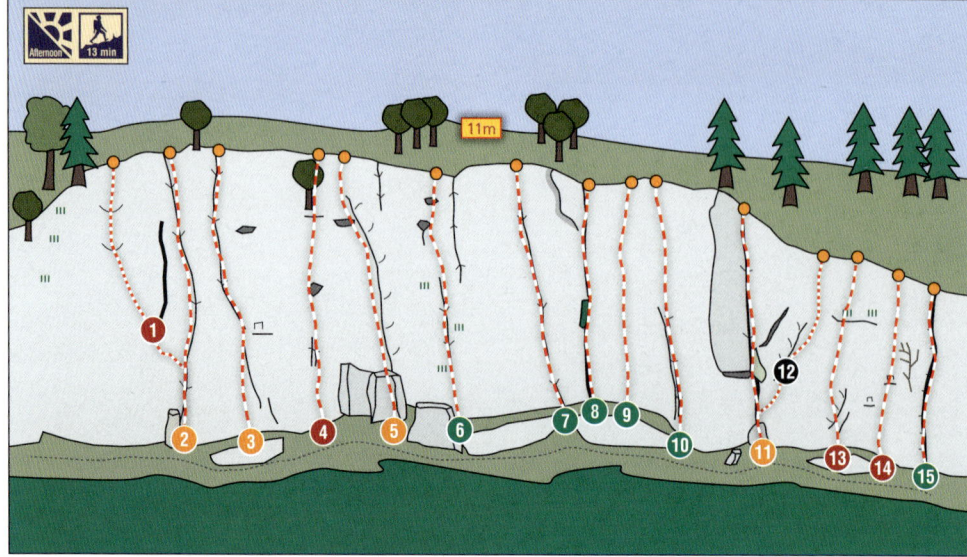

Black Ash Area

There is little of any quality here but a few reasonable routes can be found in the lower to mid-grades.
Approach - This area runs on directly from the Coltsfoot Crack Area.

① Crackstone Rib E1 5a
A bold route. Move left out of *Ashgrove Prelims* to climb the wall and scoop.
FA. Stuart Cathcart, Tom Curtis 21.8.1977

② Ashgrove Prelims .... VS 4c
The orange groove and layback crack. It is polished and can be dirty, but the climbing is enjoyable.

③ Black Ash .... HVS 5b
Climb the wall to a good ledge. Move left and follow thin cracks and flakes, finishing slightly rightwards.
FA. Andrew Casemore, Al Thompson 16.9.1990

④ Black Path E2 5b
Good rock and some thought-provoking moves but little in the way of meaningful protection.
FA. Stuart Cathcart, Gerald Swindley 1975

⑤ Flakeless Groove .... HS 4b
From the top of the left-hand pinnacle, climb the wall and finger-crack, moving leftwards to the top.

⑥ Gardener's Question Time .... S 4a
Start right of the right-hand pinnacle and follow the vegetated groove that is better than it looks.

⑦ Scarface Groove .... Diff
The groove has been cleaned up and is now regularly climbed.

⑧ White Crack .... VD
The leftward-slanting and broken crack system.

⑨ Rich's Robbery .... S 4a
Direct up the blank looking wall.
FA. R.Andrews, J.Howel 14.4.1990

⑩ White Groove .... S 4a
Climb the left-trending crack that is difficult to start.

⑪ Twisting Corner .... HS 4a
The fine wide crack takes some big gear. The grass at one-third height does not really detract from the route.

⑫ Bootlace Thread E5 6a
A fine sequence of moves but pretty much a solo. Climb *Twisting Corner* for 2m then move right onto the line using a good handhold on the bulge. A very fluffable move finishes the pitch. A thread is available low down and not normally in place.
FA. Stuart Cathcart, Gerald Swindley 26.4.1979

⑬ Cornucopia E1 5b
A good route with a hard layback start.
FA. L.Beaumont, D.Williams 5.5.1986

⑭ Shabby Slab E1 5a
Good climbing on immaculate rock with a bold start but easier climbing above.
FA. L.Beaumont, D.Williams 5.5.1986

⑮ As Yew Like It .... S 4a
Good, well-protected crack climbing.

Coltsfoot Crack Area **World's End**

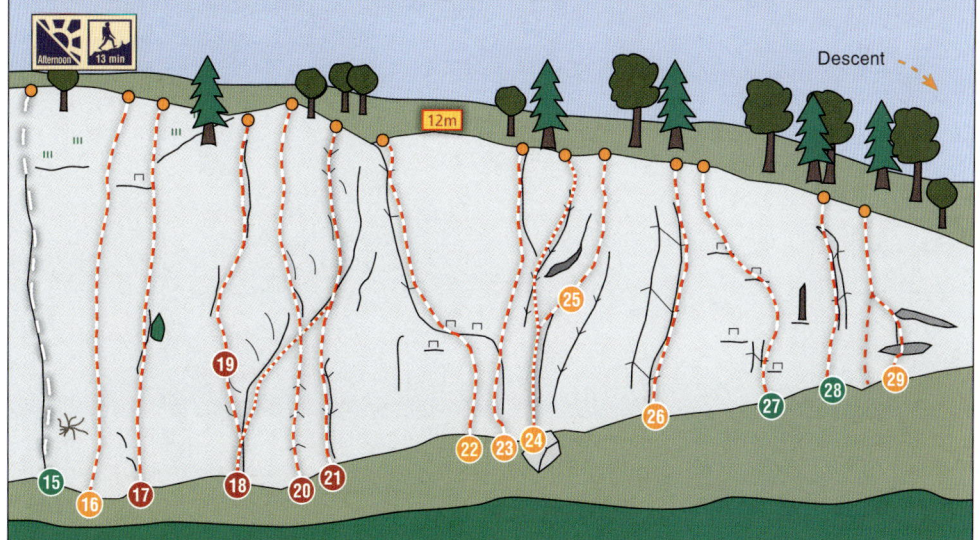

Coltsfoot Crack Area
This is the first section of the Upper Tier reached on the approach. Easy, polished lines on the right and tough technical lines on the left. Often busy.
Approach - This is the first area reached on the approach up the valley path to the Upper Tier.

16 Hornbeam Wall . . . . **VS 4b**
Climb up past the horizontal tree to broken ground above.

17 Hornwall **E1 5b**
A good little pitch with some enjoyable thin wall climbing in its lower half.
FA. Stuart Cathcart, Gerald Swindley 20.5.1977

18 Horny **E2 5c**
Smear up the polished wall to reach the flake-crack. Follow this rightwards to join and finish up *Hornbeam*.
FA. Stuart Cathcart, Gerald Swindley 20.5.1977

19 Hornblower **E2 5c**
A worthwhile pitch tackling the well-protected thin crack after a tough and slightly bold start.

20 Harvey Wall Banger . **E2 5c**
A bold start gains good flake holds and wires. Pull up to reach a good but hollow-sounding hold by a peg. Finish straight up the wall above.
FA. John Codling 7.4.1984

21 Hornbeam **E3 6a**
Powerful moves up the initial crack lead to a hidden peg. Pull into the flake-crack above and follow this rightwards to the top. A good pitch.

22 Coltsfoot Corner . . . . **HS 4b**
Climb the wall right of the corner, on good hidden holds, to a ledge. Step left into the corner that leads steeply to the top.

23 Left Edge . . . . **HS 4a**
Start up the polished flake, which is directly above a boulder at the base of the crag. Take the left-facing flakes above to finish.

24 Straight Edge . . . . **HS 4b**
Climb the wall between the two cracks.

25 Right Edge . . . . **VS 4b**
Good gear and moves up the flake line.

To the right is a faint rib with an old bolt hole. This was the route
The Gulag Archipelago, E3 6a.

26 Coltsfoot Crack . . . . **HVS 5a**
An enjoyable little pitch up the layback flakes, with good protection.

27 Shelfway . . . . **S 3c**
Climb rightwards to reach the tree and then move back left through ledges to the top. Reaching the tree is tricky and the upper section feels a bit bold.

28 End Flake . . . . **HVD**
Powerful moves up the flake-crack right of the tree. Big gear.

29 Recession Blues . . . **VS 4c**
An intense short pitch. Pull through the low overhang at a thin crack to reach a ledge. Step left and climb the bold wall to the top. It can be started direct at **5b**.

World's End Middle Tier

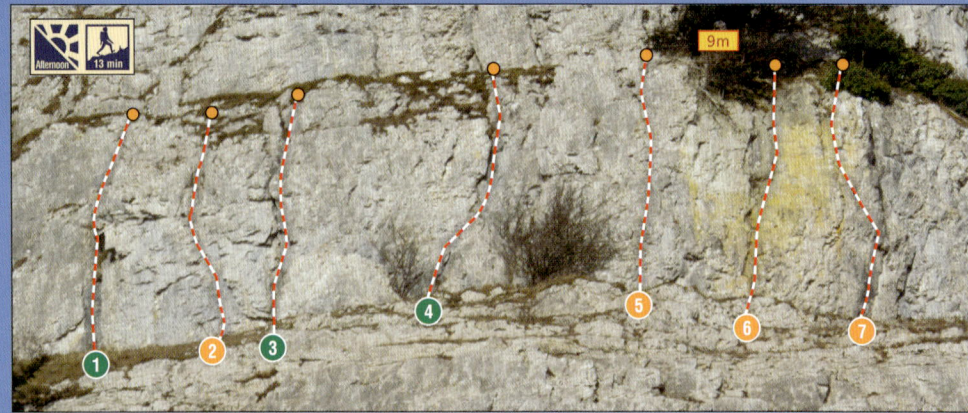

Middle Tier

A short section of crag with little climbing of any great merit. The belays at the top of the crag are awkward to arrange and some are a long way up the slope.

Approach - Best approached from above unless climbing on the Lower Tier. Drop down through the trees beneath the route *Whim* in the Open Book Area (page 88) on the Upper Tier, and follow a faint path along the base of the crag to the climbing.

1 Rumble . . . . **Diff**
The left-most major feature of the wall is a vegetated boot-wide crack with three good-sized chocks wedged along its length.
FA. H.J.Tinkler, John Hesketh 1962

2 Layback with Me . . . . **HS 4a**
The well-defined crack is easily protected and reasonably good though very short lived.

3 Handjam . . . . **S 4a**
The crack needs big gear and perhaps hands!
FA. John Hesketh, H.J.Tinkler 1962

4 Cake Walk . . . . **VD**
The crack just right of the flake at ground level is best tackled with some big gear.
FA. H.J.Tinkler, John Hesketh 1962

5 Desist . . . . **VS 4b**
The blank grey wall, with some very thin cracks, is well protected and on fairly good rock.
FA. Rick Newcombe, Geoff Ashton 1964

6 Mr Flay . . . . **VS 4a**
The yellow lichen-stained groove/crack is loose.
FA. Paul Stott 1975

7 Marjoun . . . . **HVS 5a**
The lower crack is steep. Make a difficult move left to the easier (but looser) upper crack.

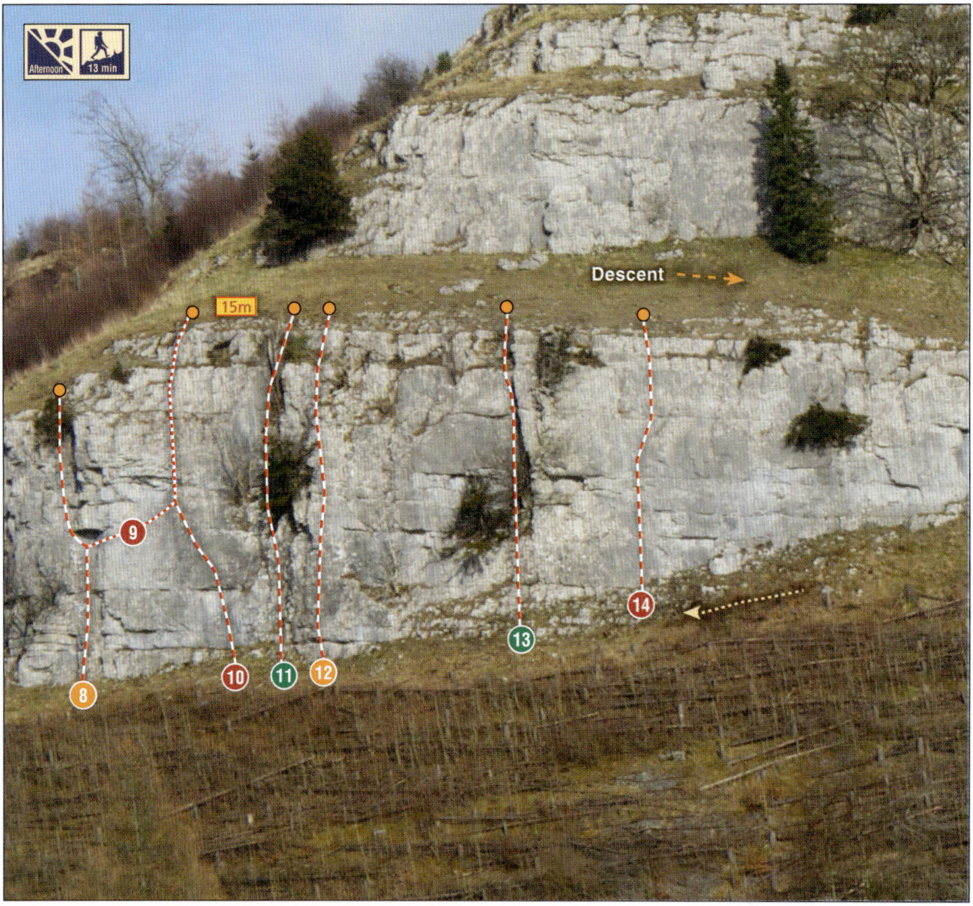

Lower Tier — World's End

Lower Tier
The crag has a couple of reasonable easier routes but the rock is not as good as first appearances may suggest. The belays at the top of the crag are awkward to arrange and some are a long way up the slope.
Approach - It is usually approached from below. Cross the fence by the ford and walk up the valley for 100m. Cross the small stream and walk steeply up the scree to the right-hand edge of the crag. It can be approached from above by dropping down a steep gully from the Middle Tier.

8 Diamond . . . . **VS 5a**
Climb the steep corner-line from the left side of the diamond-shaped roof.

9 Diamond Solitaire **E2 5b**
Climb up the vegetated corner to the diamond-shaped roof. Move right beneath the bulges to finish up past a tree.
FA. Stuart Cathcart, John Dee 20.9.1980

10 Prel **E3 6a**
Climb the blank wall leftwards into *Diamond Solitaire*.
FA. Stuart Cathcart, Phil Waters, D.Barber 1983

11 Grass . . . . **HVD**
Now totally overgrown.

12 Sunspots . . . . **HVS 5a**
The arete is serious with some poor rock at the top.
FA. Stuart Cathcart, Malcolm Cameron 17.5.1981

13 Pisa . . . . **S 4a**
Very overgrown.

14 Hypertension **E3 5b**
The blank wall past a slim horizontal break (peg). Loose.
FA. Stuart Cathcart, Tom Curtis 21.6.1980

15 Holly Tree Wall . . . . S 4a
The wall left of the small ground-level cave, moving right into the small corner-line of *Cato*. Very loose.
FA. H.J.Tinkler, John Hesketh 1962

16 Cato . . . . S 4a
From the right-hand side of the ground-level cave, move left into the small corner-line. Loose.
FA. Paul Stott 1975

17 Carter U.C.M. E2 5c
Hard moves up to and past a bolt, gain a loose but easier finish.
FA. R.Carter, Gary Dickinson 8.12.1991

18 The Cause . . . . HVS 5a
The short wall, via a thin crack, to the tree.
FA. Stuart Catthcart 16.8.1979

19 Plasuchaf Crack . . . . 1 S 4a
The steep and sustained flake-crack.
FA. John Hesketh, H.J.Tinkler 1962

20 Muscle Bound E2 5b
The thin crack in the wall.
FA. Stuart Cathcart, Malcolm Cameron 17.5.1981

21 Spetsnaz E2 5c
The blank wall past a bolt at mid height. Easier above.
FA. Doug Kerr, D.Woolger 11.10.1985

Ruthin Area | Devil's Gorge | Maeshafn | Pot Hole Quarry | Minera Quarry | World's End | Craig Arthur | Twilight Area | Pinfold | Monk's Buttress | Dinbren | Trevor Area | Pandy Outcrop | Llanymynech | Pontesford

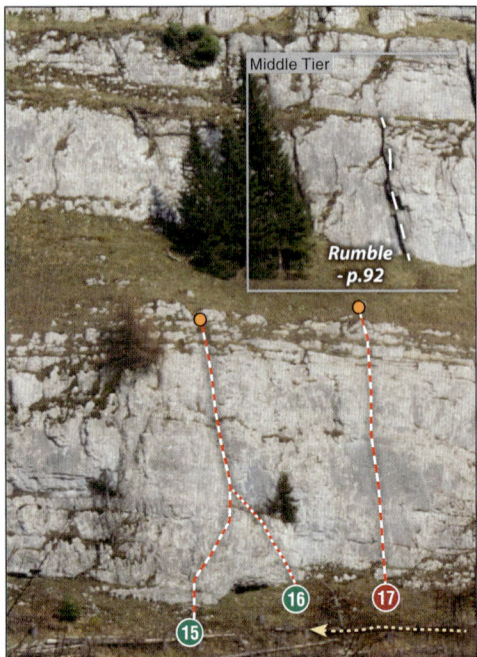

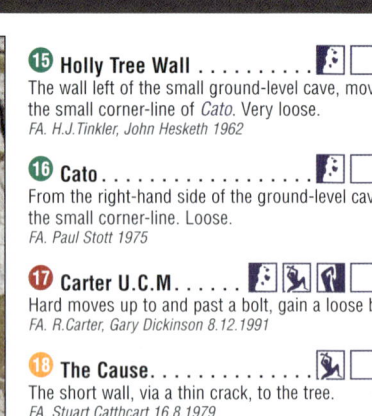

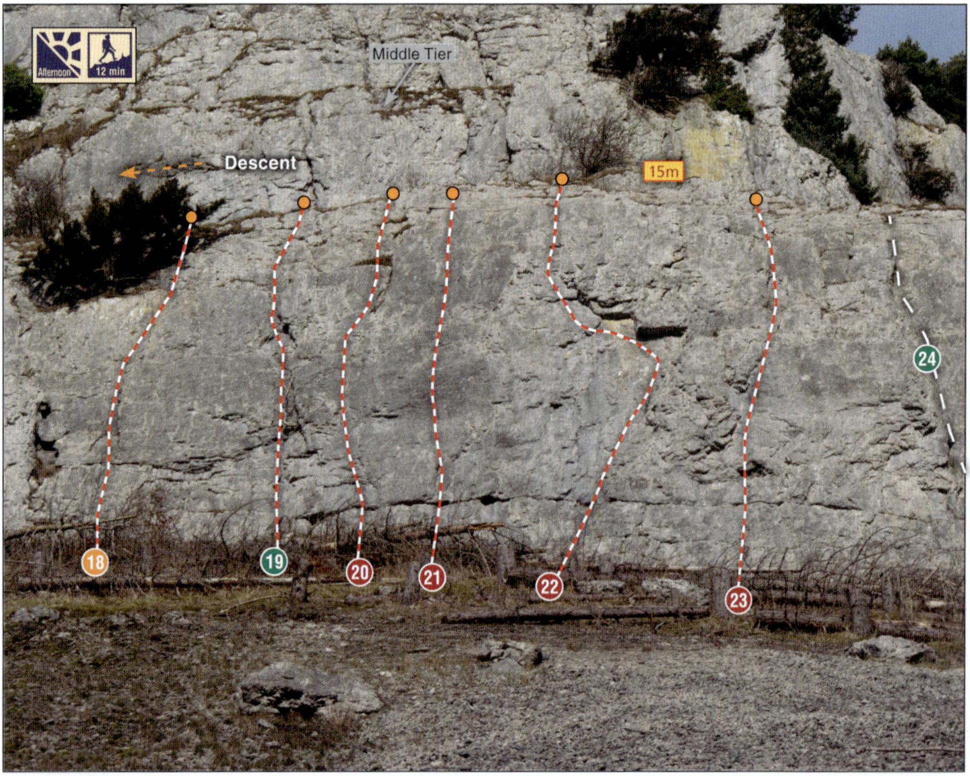

Lower Tier World's End

㉒ Icicle of Death E3 5c
Move up right to the roofs before traversing left to clear the largest of them. Finishing up a line of weakness just right.
FA. Stuart Cathcart, Malcolm Cameron 17.5.1981

㉓ Caveman Wall E2 5b
A poor line.
FA. Stuart Cathcart, John Dee 15.8.1980

㉔ Planerium .... S 4a
The fine-looking right-facing corner-flake. Take care at the top as loose rock is easily knocked down. AKA *Pleurnum*.
FA. H.J.Tinkler, John Hesketh 1962

㉕ Brinkman E2 5a
The crack leads to a loose finish.
FA. Stuart Cathcart, John Dee 15.8.1980

㉖ Kinky E2 5c
Climb the blank wall, past a bolt, to a loose finish.

㉗ La Di Da E2 5b
Climb the roof-capped corner and finish over the roof.
FA. Stuart Cathcart, John Dee 15.8.1980

㉘ Black Out .... VS 4c
The wide corner/groove to the right of a large blunt arete.
FA. John Hesketh, H.J.Tinkler 1962

㉙ Black Dog .... VS 4c
The wall past a small overhang.
FA. Stuart Cathcart 12.10.1980

㉚ Ganjah .... S 4a
The corner and continuation groove.

㉛ Brown Cracks .... S 3c
The dangerously loose corner.
FA. John Hesketh, H.J.Tinkler 1962

㉜ Picture Arete .... VS 4c
The arete passing the big curving crack.
FA. Stuart Cathcart, Malcolm Cameron 16.7.1981

㉝ Nose .... VD
Climb the cracks left of the gully.
FA. H.J.Tinkler, John Hesketh 1962

㉞ Ouja Chimney .... Diff
The inset gully has loose scree at its top.
FA. H.J.Tinkler, John Hesketh 1962

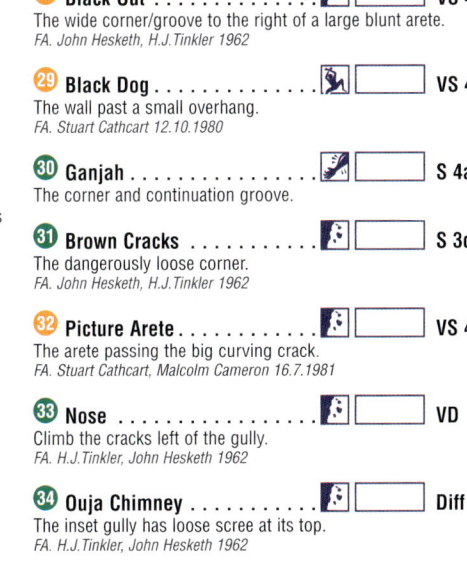

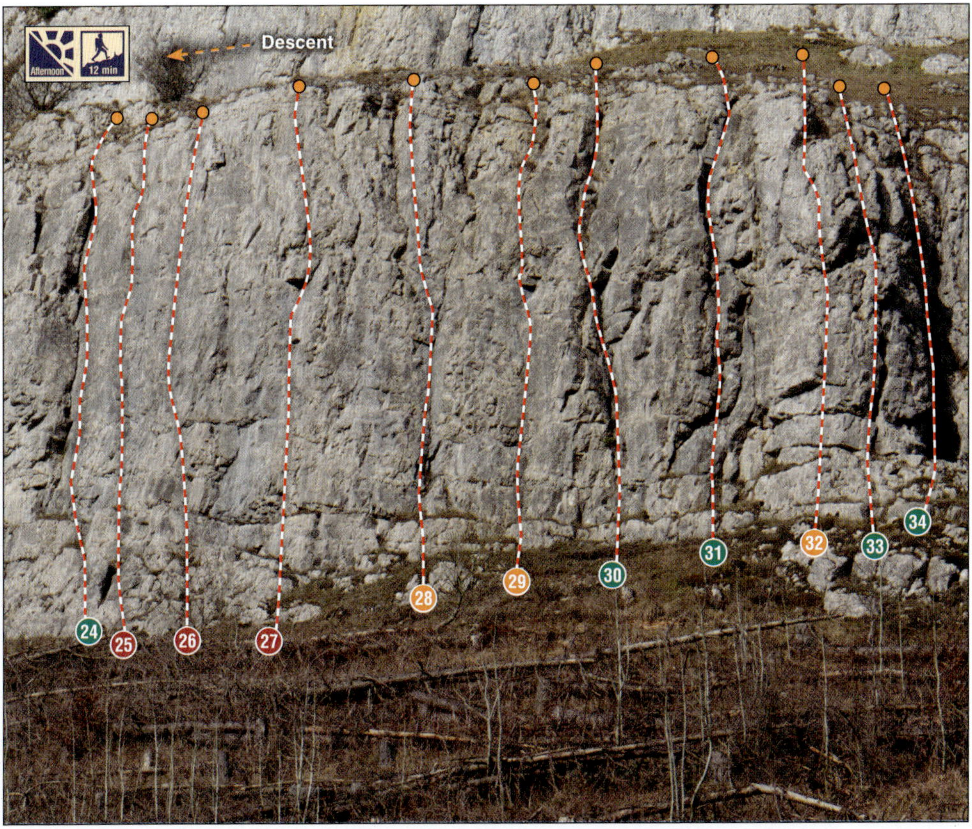

Craig Arthur

	No star	⭐	⭐⭐	⭐⭐⭐
Mod to S / 4+	-	-	-	-
HS-HVS / 5-6a+	6	2	-	-
E1-E3 / 6b-7a	21	20	6	3
E4 / 7a+ and up	2	13	14	13

The huge rampart of Craig Arthur looms impressively over the upper end of the Eglwyseg Valley. At around 40m it is by far the tallest of all the cliffs along the escarpment. The quality and length of the routes - both trad and sport - makes it a crag of national importance, with a number being multi-pitch offerings, adding a welcome dimension to the area that is otherwise dominated by shorter single-pitch climbs. The crag is mostly vertical but frequently crossed by horizontal bands of overhangs, especially in its upper reaches, making for some very exciting finishes. The rock is mainly composed of good-quality weathered white and grey sheets, seamed with some strong crack and flake lines. Some of the less frequented lines still have loose sections and can be a little vegetated. The crag's location is both spectacular and beautiful with expansive views above a base clear of vegetation. Its scree slope shelves away steeply making the exposure felt from the first moves on most routes. Many of the routes, both trad and sport, rely on fixed protection from pegs, threads and bolts although a full rack and double ropes are also required for the trad lines. A clip-stick may be useful as a number of the initial bolts on the sport climbs are fairly high.

Access
A restriction because of nesting peregrine falcons and ravens is in place on Rubberbandman and Sunnyside Areas between 15th February and 15th July (inclusive). This restriction is variable and may be applied to other sections of the crag. It may also be lifted early - see UKC or BMC RAD. The banned sections are delimited by markers at the crag base - see photo on page 28.

Conditions
High, exposed and west-facing, Craig Arthur can be very hot in the summer and bitterly cold in windy conditions, but on calm days it is superb. The tree under the Nemesis Wall provides shade and some shelter from rain but not the wind. The rock dries very quickly after rain but one or two small spots suffer seepage for longer periods.

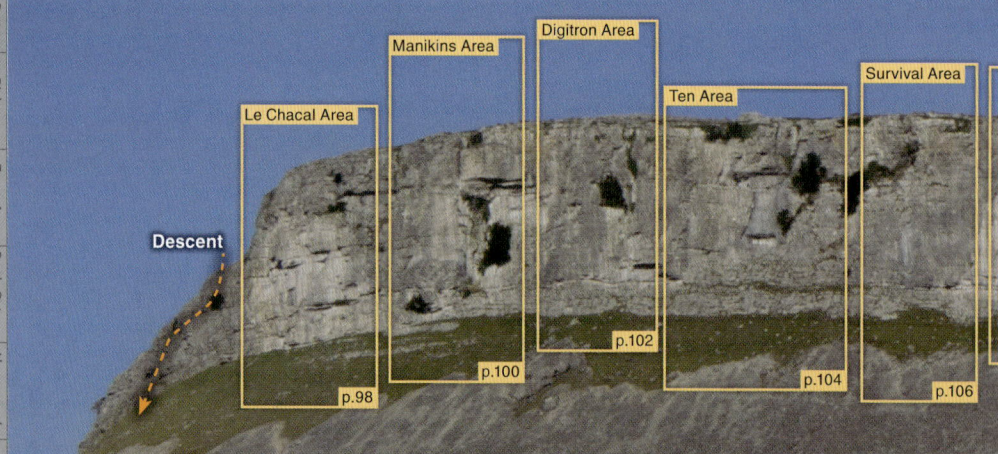

Craig Arthur

Approach See map on page 81
From Llangollen, follow the road to the junction at 1.8 miles and continue up the narrow valley road for 2.9 miles, passing under many of the Eglwyseg crags, until the road bends rightward and starts to climb. Continue up the road until a ford on a sharp bend is crossed, 400m further on just as the road exits the woods onto the moor park on the roadside. Walk back down the road to the ford and continue for 30m until the Offa's Dyke footpath on the left can be taken. Follow the path for 1.2km, until the stark profile of Craig Arthur is visible high on the left skyline. An old path leads diagonally up the steep scree slope to the base of the crag at the Le Chacal Area. For environmental reasons (the preservation of the scree slope), please walk a further 300m along the path and approach the base of the crag up a shallow grass gully.

Craig Arthur — Le Chacal Area

Le Chacal Area

The far left section of cliff is profiled starkly against the skyline as you approach. This section of cliff has a mix of sport and trad climbs that are both steep and exposed. In recent times a number of the older semi-sport lines have been fully bolted and equipped with lower-offs.

Approach - This is the far left section of the cliff.

Access - The 'no climbing restriction due to nesting birds' may include this buttress - see page 96.

An old route **Arthur's Pillar, VS 4b** followed some extremely loose ground and a potentially lethal detached flake.

❶ Kitten's Paws .... 6c+
A bizarre route touching the right-hand side of the detached flake and making hard moves from its top.
FA. Gary Gibson 4.6.2011

❷ Monkey's Claws E3 5c
A poor route taking in some nasty ground.
1) 5b, 24m. Move right to the large groove. Climb up to its top (peg) and pull over the overhang to a belay
2) 5c, 12m. Move right and up until below a bulging wall, then left on to the blank wall and a good hold. Finish up the crack.
FA. Stuart Cathcart, John Dee 8.10.1980

Le Chacal Area — Craig Arthur

③ Was it Stew........ 6c+
The well-bolted line up the wall to the left of the left-trending overhanging flake-line of *The Fall and Decline*. Technical climbing up the bolted white pillar leads to a junction with the last section of the left-trending flake. Continue up this to a large ledge and the lower-off.
FA. Gary Gibson 12.4.1993

④ The Fall and Decline E3 5c
The left-trending line through the overhangs is a spectacular route, featuring strenuous climbing and good protection.
1) 5c, 25m. Gain the flake-line and climb it to the overhangs. Traverse left (peg) and pull into a groove with difficulty. Move up and right to an arete (peg) and climb it and a wall to a stance.
2) 5a, 12m. The overhang above the stance to easier ground. Best avoided because of loose rock.
FA. Stuart Cathcart, Gerald Swindley 2.10.1977

⑤ Le Chacal........... E3 5c
A wild and exposed initial pitch through the overhangs.
1) 5c, 25m. Gain the flake-line and move right into a corner. Follow this to the overhang and traverse strenuously right to a peg. Make a difficult move to gain the lichen-covered wall above, and then go right to a ledge and belay.
2) 5a, 12m. Move up the crack on the right of the belay to a tree. Climb rightwards into an easier groove to finish.
FA. Stuart Cathcart, Dave Whitlow 14.6.1981

⑥ A Touch of Class ... E2 5b
An old classic up a series of slabs, corners and overhangs. Pitches 1 and 2 are easily linked together.
1) 5b, 28m. Climb easily to a ledge. Move right along the ledge to its end before making bold moves up the wall to a peg. Traverse thinly right (peg) to eventually make a step down onto a ramp. Take the ramp to the overhang and stance.
2) 5b, 14m. This pitch has some poor rock. Traverse right into a hanging corner and climb strenuously up it to a thread. Move out right and up to a tree. Above is another tree and a good stance.
3) 5a, 10m. Traverse left with difficulty before stepping down left on to a tiny exposed ledge. Finish up the juggy wall.
FA. Stuart Cathcart, Paul Stott 13.10.1980

⑦ Front of House..... 7a
A very good pitch that tackles the rib and overlaps to the belay of *La Chacal*. Move up to a rounded protuberance. Go up to a break and through the bulge before climbing the wall above to the traverse on *A Touch of Class*. Continue up through the bulges above to a ledge and lower-off.
FA. Gary Gibson 3.7.2011

⑧ Back Yard Holiday .. 6c+
Good sustained climbing. Follow *Front of House* to the junction with *A Touch of Class*. Move right and up to the bulge. Pull over the bulge and a finish up a shallow groove.
FA. Paul Stott, Dave Greenald 6.1988

⑨ Swelling Itching Brain .. 7b+
Climb to the break and then continue up the wall with great difficulty. Step right to the base of a ramp and continue more easily up this before climbing left through the bulge above to easier ground.
FA. Gary Gibson 20.7.1991

⑩ One Continuous Picnic .. 7b
A difficult and sustained line. Climb to the large break. Continue up a thin crack-line via a sustained series of hard moves to a roof. Move directly up to a good handhold and go left to a ledge and easier climbing.
FA. Gary Gibson, Phil Gibson 8.6.1991

⑪ Three Dimensions E2 5b
The impressive left-trending flake and corner system.
1) 5b, 26m. Climb the flakes to a peg. Move right and up to a crack in a corner. Move up to, and then left beneath an overhang, gaining the hanging corner of *A Touch of Class*.
2) 5b, 10m. Climb the corner on the left and move over the roof on good holds but suspect rock.
FA. Stuart Cathcart, Mike Hughes 29.6.1980

Sugar Sweet - p.100

Craig Arthur — Manikins of Horror Area

Manikins of Horror Area

The left side of this area provides a few superbly sustained and enjoyable pitches but the rock needs care in places. To the right is a tall white wall and some large overhangs that have a handful of harder lines. A yew tree at the base of the wall is just left of the start of *Manikins of Horror*. The area is to the left of a large tree 10m up the cliff under large overhangs.

Access - There no climbing restriction due to nesting birds may include this buttress - see page 96

❶ Sugar Sweet .... 6c+
A difficult lower bulge with fine upper section. The lower bulge is hollow.
FA. Gary Gibson, Hazel Gibson 4.6.2011

❷ Mon Miel 6c
A short route with a difficult bulge.
FA. Gary Gibson 30.7.2011

❸ A Bitter Pill .... 6b+
A pleasant pitch straight through a small mid-height bulge.
FA. Gary Gibson, Mark Elwell 3.7.2011

❹ A Cunning Plan .... 6b+
The direct line through the lower bulge and up the left-hand edge of the slabby face gives a reasonable pitch.
FA. Gary Gibson 1.9.2010

Manikins of Horror Area — Craig Arthur

5 The Marsh Flower — 7a
Climb the blank wall, moving right and then up and back left (very close to *Stratagem*). Continue with interest to a break and finish more easily via a crack just right.
FA. Gary Gibson 12.4.1993

6 Legacy — E1 5b
1) **5b**, 18m. Climb to a peg in a corner, on a slab. Move left and down to a ledge. Continue traversing over loose rock to a tree belay.
2) **5a**, 18m. Move to the right side of the bay and climb to the top via the easiest line on loose ground. A dangerous route.
FA. Stuart Cathcart, Gerald Swindley 28.8.1976

7 Stratagem — E2 5b
A reasonable climb although the rock is a little loose in places. Follow *Legacy* to the peg on the slab and continue to a bulge (peg). Climb up steeply leftwards to a break with difficulty and then move right and up (peg) to a tree. Finish up the crack.
FA. Stuart Cathcart, Gerald Swindley 28.8.1976

8 Manikins of Horror — Top 50 — E3 5c
One of the best pitches on the crag featuring sustained and technical climbing with generally excellent protection. Begin 4m right of the ground-level tree. Move up to a break and go left to a little corner with a peg above. From the peg move delicately left around the shallow rib to a slab beneath a slim crack. Follow the lovely crack past pegs to a horizontal break. Move left to a tree and climb the crack above to finish. *Photo on page 37.*
FA. Stuart Cathcart, Gerald Swindley 29.5.1976

9 Masquerade — 7b+
A fine direct line up the left-hand side of the buttress with a very technical move at half-height and sustained climbing above. The first bolt is high up - above where the line leaves *Manikins of Horror* - and needs some gear or a long clip-stick.
FA. Gary Gibson 1.9.2010

10 Swlabr Link — E3 6a
This excellent route has unfortunately suffered a rockfall at the end of the traverse and now has some dangerous loose blocks and unstable rock on it.
1) **6a**, 25m. Follow *Masquerade* to a thin horizontal break at mid height and traverse this right to easier ground (loose blocks). Move up to a good ledge by a tree.
2) **5b**, 14m. Move left and climb the excellent exposed crack as for pitch 2 of *Swlabr*.
FA. Stuart Cathcart, Nick Slaney 4.6.1981

11 Dance of the Puppets — 7b
A good sport route up the slender buttress. Climb directly up the grey nose then make a long stretch to gain the traverse line of *Swlabr Link*. Make some thin moves to a rounded break and then gain better holds in a scoop. Pull up and climb leftwards into a second scoop. A final hard move rightwards gains good flake-holds that lead to the lower-off.
FA. John Codling, John Moulding 5.5.1984

12 Hand in Glove — 7a
Straight up the right-hand side of the wall with a technical lower bulge and sustained climbing above, keeping just left of *Swlabr*. Move left and up to the belay.
FA. Gary Gibson 4.6.2011

13 Swlabr — HVS 5b
A great top crack but the lower section is unpleasant.
1) **4b**, 17m. Take the easiest line up the vegetated ground to a belay on a good ledge and tree. A poor pitch.
2) **5b**, 14m. Move left and climb the excellent, exposed crack.
FA. Bob Dearman, Martin Pedlar 1969

Craig Arthur — Digitron Area

Digitron Area

An attractive vertical wall of compact grey rock that has three great climbs on it. *Digitron* is one of the UK's better E2s and should not be missed.

Access - The 'no climbing restriction due to nesting birds' may include this buttress - see page 96.

❶ Rubs and Tugs 7c
A hard sport route through the left-hand side of the big roof.
1) **4b**, 17m. Move up and then left to a belay above the tree. Care needed with the rock but the climbing is easy.
2) **7c**, 16m. Follow the line of bolts leading across left through the roof to a lower-off.
FA. Marc Rooms 2003

❷ Eliminator E4 6b
An exceptionally positioned top pitch on some great rock.
1) **-** , 17m. Move up and then left to a belay above the tree. Care needed with the rock but the climbing is easy.
2) **6b**, 16m. The double roof stack above guards entry to the headwall. Climb to the roof and crank through it onto the headwall (two pegs). The rounded scoop of lovely rock is taken past a bulge to the top (thread and peg).
FA. John Moulding, F.Stevenson 5.9.1983

❸ Pi 8a
Craig Arthur's hardest route and one of its most impressive lines. Start at the first stance of *Eliminator*.
FA. Rob Mirfin 9.2005

❹ California Highway Patrol
. . . . 7c
A fine technical pitch on good rock after an unsavoury start. Climb up easy but very loose ground to the base of the bulge, thread and pegs. Pull through the bulge with difficulty and embark on a brilliant sequence up the wall with a final testing move to reach a pocket and then the lower-off.
FA. Pete Chadwick 2.7.2005. A route with a chequered history, originally equipped and chipped several years ago, hence the route name - 'CHiPs'.

❺ Tito E2 5b
This sustained route follows the left-hand side of the superb grey sheet of rock. Start as for the first pitch of *Eliminator*. Move up, as for *Eliminator*, then break right on a subtle line across slabby grey rock (peg) to a bulge. Climb up and then back right, with more difficulty, to an overhang and thread (possible stance). Pull up left through the overhang, via a crack, to reach a small tree. Easier ground leads to a large rounded scoop (loose). Follow this to finish.
FA. Stuart Cathcart, Tom Curtis 3.5.1980

❻ About Time 7b
A line that bisects *Tito* via some low technical moves and an easy central section before stepping right and climbing a shallow scoop in the headwall to a very taxing finale on small holds. Superb climbing but frustrating at the top. High first bolt.
FA. Gary Gibson 28.5.2009

❼ Pour Lulubelle E3 5c
A filler-in but a good one. Climb the difficult smooth wall - peg and bolt - to the main overlap. Above this take the superbly-positioned blunt rib via cracks and edges.
FA. Gary Gibson 30.7.2011

Descent

Dance of the Puppets - p.101

Digitron Area **Craig Arthur**

8 Digitron .... Top 50 E2 5c
An immaculate pitch and one of the best of its grade in the area with technically varied and absorbing climbing. The difficulty gently escalates culminating in a challenging finale. Climb easily to a peg then make a tricky move up and right to good holds by a small sapling. Continue up a slight groove following cracks to a second peg. Move left and step up to a good resting ledge beneath an overhang. Undercut rightwards beneath the overhang then pull around the slight arete to reach another good rest beside a small niche. Pull up and leftwards on small holds to reach bigger holds beneath a peg. Above the peg is a good jug and reaching it is hard. Once gained, pull up slightly leftwards - still difficult - to a small sapling, then finish easily to the right.
FA. Stuart Cathcart, Gerald Swindley 11.6.1973

9 Heaven or Hell .   E5 6b
Immaculate and extremely sustained climbing that is also fairly run out. Start below a yellow lichen-covered bulge at 8m. Make some committing moves up and then left along a slim ramp to a bolt, and make a long reach to a good hold at the base of a small groove. Move up onto the good hold and pull left to the arete. Climb the arete on its right-hand side, with some trepidation, to meet *Digitron* at a horizontal break. Step right (peg) and make hard moves up a flake to a bolt. Finish by moving leftwards into *Digitron*.
FA. Gary Gibson 1.6.1991

Craig Arthur — Ten Area

❶ Beta Beware .... 6c+
A short and intense affair through a series of difficult overlaps to an easier wall and tree belay. Loose.
FA. Gary Gibson 19.6.2011

❷ Omegod .... 6c+
Gain the prominent and worrying flake from below and exit it rightwards over a small overlap onto the wall above. The superb blunt rib above leads to the belay.
FA. Gary Gibson 3.6.2009

❸ Alpha Track Etch 7b
An impressive intricate line that has some hard moves. Start beneath the centre of the low offset roofs - the high first bolt usually needs to be stick-clipped. Pull up through the weakness to a slab. Undercut leftwards then make a very hard move to reach better holds. Continue up the wall to a break then move right along this before tackling the steep powerful capping bulge to easier ground and the lower-off.
FA. Martin Crocker 2.6.1990. FA. (Direct as described) Lee Proctor 2.7.2005. The route originally moved right along the undercut flake.

❹ Delta Force .... 6c+
The right arete of the face gives an interesting face climb with sustained but reasonable climbing to an intricate and fingery finale on the exposed final bulge. *Photo on page 1.*
FA. Gary Gibson 3.6.2009

❺ Badge E2 5c
A good airy upper half is preceded by a serious lower section. Start up broken ground and then move up to an overlap at the horizontal break. Pull through the overlap (poor peg), and push on carefully up the awkward wall to gain another peg. Easier moves gain the base of a scoop and much better rock and protection. Climb up the left wall of the scoop and exit with care.
FA. Stuart Cathcart, Tom Curtis 6.4.1975

❻ Keeping Secrets E5 6c
Start below a small bush in the break above broken ground. Climb through the bulge, just right of the bush, to a peg, and somehow reach a jug above. Go left to a flake and take this to a break. Easier climbing leads to another larger horizontal break. Move up the V-groove and exit left up the wall to finish at the shrub-lined crag edge.
FA. Gary Gibson 2.9.1991

Ten Area

The stacked roofs at the top of this area are taken by the excellent sport route *Ten*. The other lines on this section see little traffic. Most of the routes start up easy-angled broken ground. The large roof of *Ten* is high up on the crag around 100m left of the tree at the base of the Nemesis Wall.

Access - The 'no climbing restriction due to nesting birds' may include this buttress - see page 96.

Afternoon | 35 min | Windy

Ten Area Craig Arthur

7 Walls Have Ears .... 7b+
Climb a faint flake and bulge to a good ledge. The finish through the hanging scoop gives a hard sequence with a reachy clip.
FA. Gary Gibson 12.4.1993

8 Scary Fairy E3 6a
A meandering line with some good sections of hard and exposed climbing. Move up to the left-hand side of the oval niche of *Ten*. Difficult climbing leads to a steep flake-line, which is followed to easier ground. Traverse leftwards past a cave (possible belay) to the base of a V-groove. Move up the groove and exit left up the wall to finish at the shrub-lined crag edge.
FA. Stuart Cathcart, Paul Stott, Frank Bennett 20.7.1980

9 Ten .... 7b+
A stunning 'out there' sport route that starts in an oval niche. Scramble up to a ledge beneath the niche. Boulder out of the niche with difficulty to gain a brief reprise on the wall above. Move up to the roof and blast through this before any remaining power wanes. High in the grade.
FA. Gary Gibson 20.7.1991

10 Suite XV1 .... 7a+
A steady lower wall gains an excellent and problematic bulge.
FA. Gary Gibson 20.12.2014

11 Jungle Warfare .... HVS 5a
An appropriately-named expedition which follows rock and vegetation in about equal measures.
1) 5a, 20m. Climb up the centre of a slim buttress via a short flake and some vegetation to a large tree.
2) 5a, 15m. Climb up the tree and, from a jug, pull onto the rock. Traverse left past a block and ledge to finish up a yellow groove.
FA. Stuart Cathcart, Paul Stott 21.6.1980

12 When I was a Viking 6b
An easy lower wall leads to fine climbing above the ledge.
FA. Gary Gibson 29.1.2011

13 Ravenous 6b
Amble up the easy lower wall to access a fine upper section via flakes and cracks.
FA. Gary Gibson 19.6.2011

Craig Arthur — Survival Area

1. Charlain — E1 5b
The attractive grey slab.
1) **5b**, 20m. Start just right of a small tree/bush. Climb to a horizontal break (peg) and on rightwards to a hidden second peg. Continue trending right past some poor rock to another peg and a tree belay above.
2) **4b**, 12m. Climb the corner past a tree or abseil off.
FA. Stuart Cathcart, Greg Griffith 18.5.1980

2. Charlotte's Web — 6a+
Spaced bolts and a peg protect. Climb the blunt rib to the left of the shallow groove.
FA. Gary Gibson 30.7.2011

3. Now and Then — E2 5c
A good route up the left-hand side of the grey wall.
1) **5c**, 21m. Start below a small grey groove. Climb to, and up, the groove to its top (two pegs). Pull over a slim overlap and move up right, past a further peg, to easier ground and a tree belay.
2) **5a**, 12m. Climb up right to a tree. Traverse along a break to finish up a crack.
FA. Stuart Cathcart, Paul Stott 21.6.1980

4. Crocodile Shoes — 6b+
A surprising find up the smooth-looking wall right of *Now and Then*. Good moves but a tight line.
FA. Gary Gibson 3.6.2009

Survival Area — Craig Arthur

Survival Area
A fine wall of clean and featureless rock save for the subtle crack-line of *Survival of the Fastest*. There is a good deal of fixed gear on the routes here.

⛔ **Access** - There no climbing restriction due to nesting birds may include this buttress - see page 96

❺ **Dead Man's Creek** .. 6c
A good pitch. Pull up and left to access the line of tiny corners. Follow these and the face above to the lower-off.
FA. Gary Gibson 5.5.1984

❻ **Punch and Judy** . E5 6b
Fantastic technical climbing up the grey wall. Well protected with good wires and solid fixed protection. Pull powerfully around the lower bulge (bolt) to reach a thread. Move up and leftwards on tiny holds, passing a second bolt, and continue direct to a vague break and peg. Rock onto the break then tiptoe rightwards to a third bolt. Blind moves past this gain good holds and gear. Continue up easier ground to reach a shallow scoop and a final bolt, then move left above this with a long reach to the upper break (peg) and the lower-off.
FA. Gary Gibson 1.5.1984. FA. (Direct start and finish) Lee Proctor 12.9.2004, after the original start collapsed.

❼ **Full Mental Jacket** .. E5 6c
A variation on *Punch and Judy* that is more technical but less sustained. Start up the first few moves of *Survival of the Fastest*, then move left to reach an undercut hold. A technical sequence (peg) leads to a line of horizontal pockets in the vague break and a hidden bolt. Rock precariously upwards to join *Punch and Judy* at its third bolt. Finish up this to the lower-off.
FA. John Moulding, John Codling 3.7.1988

❽ **Survival of the Fastest** ..  E5 6a
An awesome pitch tackling the thin crack and flake-line bounding the left side of the Nemesis Wall. Extremely sustained and varied climbing throughout. One of the original protection pegs is no longer in place and the pitch is now more strenuous because it's difficult to arrange alternative nut protection. Pull up to the base of the line and follow the crack steeply to where it curves and fades. A thin traverse left past a bolt eventually gains easier ground. The right-slanting crack above is still tricky.
Photo on page 31.
FA. Stuart Cathcart 10.5.1978

❾ **Protect and Survive** . E6 6b
A good way up this section of the crag. The route makes a diagonal link from the initial section of *Survival of the Fastest* to the difficult upper bulges of *Survival of the Fattest*.
FA. John Moulding 8.2004

❿ **Survival of the Fattest** E5 6b
Climb up through low-level overlaps to a small corner. Continue up the wall and flakes above, on reasonable holds, to a bulge high on the wall. Difficult moves through this, and then left to break through the overlap above, gain a crack to finish.
FA. John Codling 1984

⓫ **Revival of the Latest** E 7a+
A short desperate wall pitch with a hard lower section and a fingery and technical upper section.
FA. Gary Gibson 25.6.2009

Shootin' Blanks - p.110

Nemesis Wall **Craig Arthur**

The 40m high Nemesis Wall is Craig Arthur's most impressive wall and hosts a number of high standard climbs both sport and trad in style. In this photograph Lucy Creamer is pulling over the final roof on the sustained and well named pitch *Relentless* (7b+) - *page 110*. Photo: Tim Glasby

Craig Arthur — Nemesis Wall

❶ Friday the Thirteenth — E5 6a
An adventurous mission up the huge face.
1) 6a, 22m. Start by the smaller tree at the base of the wall. Move up from either side of the tree to gain a small groove (peg low on left) before moving up left again to better holds. Above is a large, semi-detached jammed block at the right-hand end of a long narrow overhang. Take a rightwards line to the block and use it to access the wall above (peg). The belay is a little higher in the horizontal break.
2) 5c, 18m. Move right to the central groove and climb this to a capping roof. Pass the roof on the right and finish up the loose corner.
FA. Pat Littlejohn 13.4.1984
FA. (Direct start) John Moulding, John Codling 29.9.1987

❷ Oblivion — E6 6b
A direct assault on the wall passing through *Friday the Thirteenth* and starting and finishing as for *Manic Mechanic*.
FA. Gary Gibson 11.8.2009

❸ Manic Mechanic — E6 6b
A stunning, action-packed line involving a great deal of difficult climbing with a high crux. The streaked ramp is slow to dry and can be dirty. Start beneath the base of the ramp. Climb the wall past a bolt to the ramp. At the top of the ramp make blind moves up the steep wall, past two pegs, to reach the upper of two breaks. Move a little left then climb the fine pocketed wall rightwards, past a thread, to an intimidating perch beneath the roof. Traverse left (peg over lip - difficult to clip) and pull over the roof with difficulty, to a short wall and the top.
FA. John Moulding, John Codling (rests) 5.1984. FFA. Andy Pollitt 1984.

❹ Relentless — Top 50 — 7b+
A fine addition straight up the centre of the wall using a high hanging arete and with a super-exposed roof finale. Sustained despite two good rest spots. *Photo on page 108.*
FA. Gary Gibson 19.6.2011

❺ Smokin' Gun — E6 6c
Brilliant and technically sustained climbing up the centre of the Nemesis Wall. Good but spaced protection throughout.
1) 6c, 21m. Pull up and traverse left to a ledge beneath a groove. Climb into the groove (bolt) and continue to a second bolt. Using some poor undercuts, make a difficult reach for some tiny crimps, then rock up to reach a good flake and wires. Continue to a poor peg, then move rightwards into a niche and a rest (bolt on right). Move left around the arete (bolt) and climb the technical wall above to the break and belay (old pegs backed up with good cams).
2) 6a, 18m. Gain the overhung niche above, then move right past a shallow corner onto and across the wall (pegs). Keep traversing until it is possible to break through the bulge past two final pegs.
FA. John Moulding 21.5.1988

❻ Shootin' Blanks — E6 6c
The alternative direct finish to *Smokin' Gun* enables the centre of this superb wall to be climbed in one stunning pitch. Continue direct above the *Smokin' Gun* belay to reach the overhung niche. Pull around the overhang (bolt) then climb the technical wall, keeping to the right of the flakes in the finishing groove of *Friday the Thirteenth*.
FA. Lee Proctor 22.8.2004

❼ Tres Hombres — E6 6b
A big adventure that should not be underestimated. Start just left of the tree below a ramp at 8m.
1) 6b, 23m. Climb the deceptively difficult wall (peg at the start of the ramp), and move up to the top of the ramp (bolt). A series of hard moves past a peg and bulge (sometimes wet) are rewarded with a bolt. Move left around the arete (bolt) then climb the tricky wall above to the break and belay (old pegs backed up with good cams).
2) 5c, 18m. Traverse left to the steep finishing groove of *Friday the Thirteenth*.
FA. John Moulding, Nick Jowett, Steve Boyden 5.1984

❽ Mercury Rising — 7b+
A super direct plum up the wall with a hard technical groove to start, a reachy move away from *Tres Hombres* and a tough finale. A good no-hands rest is available at half height.
FA. Gary Gibson 28.12.2012

❾ Steppin' Razor — E5 6b
The first of two lines that begin at the large tree on the right-hand side of the face. The starts are concealed by the tree. Monkey up the tree and stretch left to clip a peg. Move onto the wall and up, past a bolt, to cross the long horizontal overhang on its left. Continue to an old peg and climb the groove above to another overhang (peg). Move right through the overhang to a slab (peg) and finish up the wall past a final peg.
FA. John Moulding, John Codling 24.4.1988

❿ Marie Antoinette — E5 6b
From a ledge at the base of the tree, move up and then out right onto the arete and a high bolt. The arete is a tight line and leads past a peg and another bolt to a break beneath a bulge. Good climbing up the finger-crack above attains the final roof which provides a strenuous tussle via a groove and peg.
FA. John Codling, John Moulding 22.5.1988

Survival of the Fastest - p.107

Nemesis Wall — Craig Arthur

Nemesis Wall
Craig Arthur's most impressive wall has a selection of hard, intimidating and adventurous routes that rely on a lot of fixed gear, some of which is old on the less well-travelled lines. The massive white wall capped by overhangs has a large tree below it on the path.

Access - The 'no climbing restriction due to nesting birds' may include this buttress - see page 96.

11 The Big Plop E3 6a
The hanging roof-capped corner high on the face.
1) 5b, 18m. Start right of a large tree. Climb to a tree and then leftwards past another to yet another tree and a ledge above. A steep wall (peg) gains a belay on a small ledge.
2) 6a, 18m. Enter and climb the corner, past pegs, with difficulty. At the roof, pull right to an arete and climb to the top more easily. Care needed with some of the rock.
FA. Stuart Cathcart, Tom Curtis (1pt) 14.5.1980
FFA. Paul Harrison, Steve Boyden 29.5.1985

12 Black and Blue 7b
Excellent climbing and positions. Follow the bald-looking wall to the right of the *The Big Plop* leftwards via some fine technical moves. The impressive snout above leads to a hanging groove.
FA. Gary Gibson 29.1.2011

Craig Arthur — Rubberbandman Area

① Craig Arthur Girdle .. E2 5c
Not on topo. A massive undertaking that visits many sections of the crag but also includes some poor rock and vegetation. Pitch 9 is the best.
1) 4b, 25m. Climb *Arthur's Pillar* to the top of the corner and then step right above an overhang to ledges. Move up and right to the belay at the top of *The Fall and Decline's* first pitch.
2) 4b, 25m. Traverse right and down to a horizontal break (peg). More traversing gains another peg at a niche. Leave the niche and continue to belay as for *A Touch of Class* pitch 2.
3) 4a, 25m. Move across the bay and climb down to another line (peg). Traverse this to a small tree on *Stratagem* and belay.
4) 5c, 15m. Climb down for 5m to pegs before traversing across the wall to a tree belay at the top of *Swlabr Link* pitch 1.
5) 5b, 26m. Climb a long way right and pick up two horizontal breaks (peg). Go up past two pegs to small trees and then head out to the arete on *Digitron*. Beyond the rock blanks out (peg). Move right into the large yew tree and down to a belay.
6) 5b, 18m. Traverse right via a thin break to a small corner and climb across the slab on *Alpha Track Etch* (two pegs) to belay just before the upper section of *Badge*.
7) 5a, 25m. Climb past a peg and beyond the V-groove of *Scary Fairy*. Step down and across the wall below the stacked roofs of *Ten* (bolt). Thrash past one yew tree to another and belay.
8) 5a, 26m. Traverse along broken ground and down to an ash tree. Continue along more grassy rock to a ledge. Move down and traverse past fixed gear, round an arete, to a tree and belay on the left-hand side of the Nemesis Wall.
9) 5a, 25m. Step down after 3m, past a peg, and traverse to below the dominating upper corner of the wall. Move right to a small niche and then down to the main break. Follow this to and around the arete and a belay at the top of *The Big Plop* pitch 1.
10) 5a, 25m. Traverse past a bush to a ledge (peg). Gain another lower peg and continue on good holds to a large terrace. Finish up a shattered wall and groove.
FFA. Stuart Cathcart, Tom Curtis, Malcolm Cameron in 1979
FA. Bob Dearman, Dave Riley, Tom Hurley (aid) 1969

② The Hoax .... HVS 5a
Climb to the first tree on *The Big Plop*. Move up right past another large tree via a crack. Step right with care above the tree, near the end of the crack, to a terrace. Climb up to an old yew tree and finish right.
FA. Tom Curtis, Stuart Cathcart 14.5.1980

③ Tranche de Vie .... 6a+
A direct line up the left-hand side of the face with a technical short wall above the bulge.
FA. Gary Gibson 1.9.2010

④ Voie de Bart E4 6b
Climb up to, and then right, along a ramp line to pegs in the bulge above. Hard moves through the bulge lead to a lower-off.
FA. Steve Boyden, John Moulding 31.5.1985

⑤ Rubberbandman 7b
Power moves through the overhang are the key.
FA. Gary Gibson 31.5.1991

⑥ Finger Press 6c
A short bouldery line finishing over a bulge.
FA. Gary Gibson 1.9.2010

⑦ Thumbs Down .... 6c+
A direct line via hard moves in shallow scoop. Start via flake.
FA. Gary Gibson, Steve Fowler 27.9.2009

⑧ Under My Thumb .... 6c+
A neat wall pitch involving intricate face climbing.
FA. Gary Gibson, Neville Barker 9.6.1991

⑨ Cold Finger E1 5a
1) 5a, 16m. Climb rightwards up the crozzly, off-vertical wall to a slim overlap. Traverse right to a terrace and tree belay.
2) 4b, 16m. Move left and climb a broken wall and groove.
FA. Stuart Cathcart, Greg Griffith 20.2.1978

Rubberbandman Area — Craig Arthur

⑩ Let's See Those Fingers 6c
Technical start and overlapping finale.
FA. Gary Gibson, Mark Elwell, 27.9.2009

⑪ Chopper Squad E2 5b
A serious route up the wall, through the left side of a bulge, to the tree on the terrace. Use the lower-off to the right.
FA. Neville Barker, Gary Gibson 27.5.1991

⑫ All Fingers and Thumbs . 6c
Easier lower wall and very tricky bulge.
FA. Gary Gibson, Alec Gibson 4.6.2011

⑬ Accidents Will Happen E1 5c
The right side of the bulge to the tree.
FA. Gary Gibson, Hugh Williams 25.7.1992

⑭ Octopus .... HVS 4c
Climb the wall past a low peg to the tree on the terrace. The second pitch is now overgrown.

⑮ Thumb Print 6a
A good little pitch straight up to the pillar.
FA. Gary Gibson 30.7.201

Rubberbandman Area
The cove between the much larger buttresses of the Nemesis Wall and the Sunnyside Buttress has a handful of useful sport pitches. The trad routes have either poor rock or poor gear, and some feature both. The area is just to the right of the large tree at the base of the Nemesis Wall.

Access - No climbing from 15th Feb to 15th July between markers because of nesting birds. This is a variable restriction - see page 96.

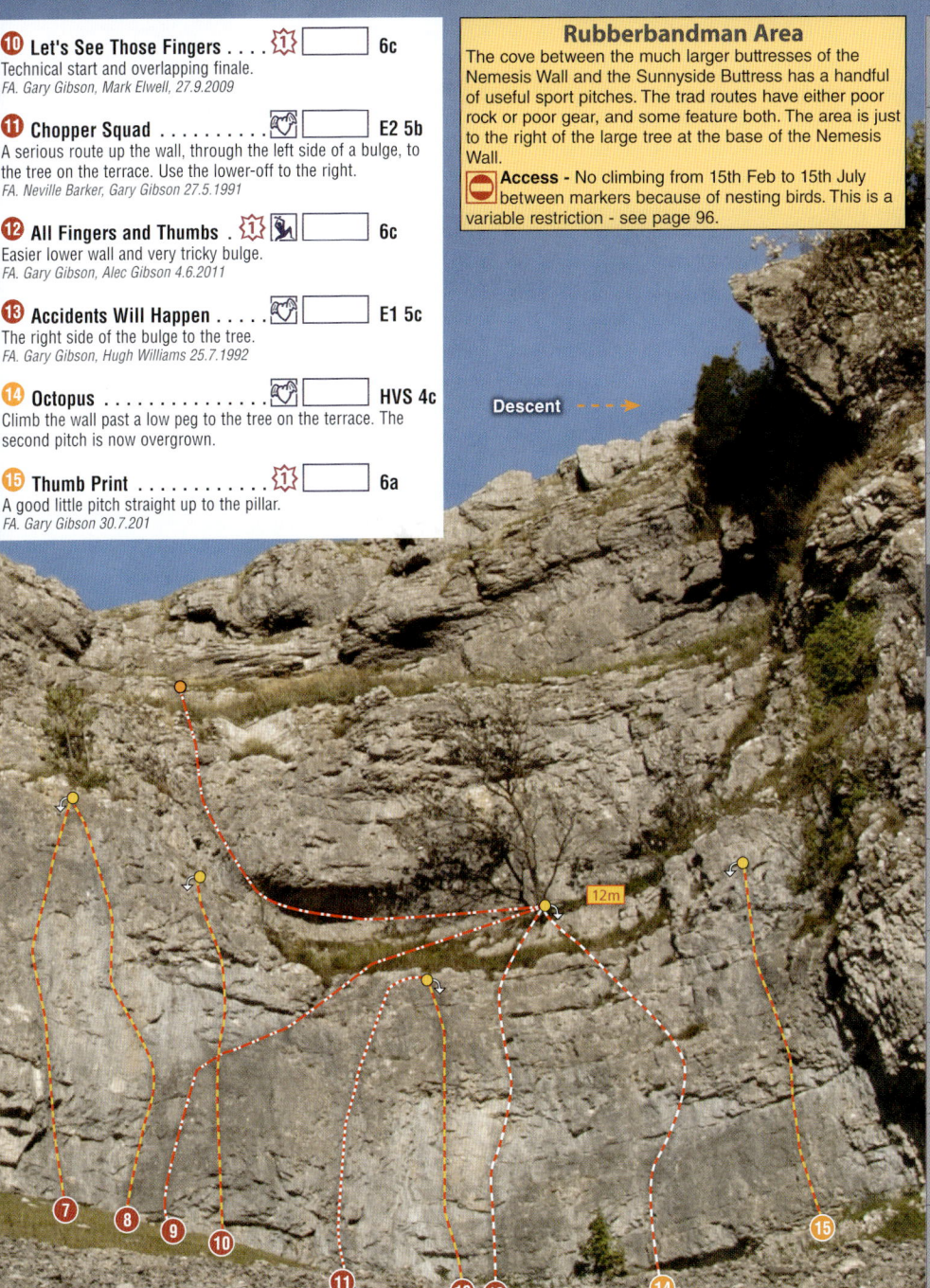

Craig Arthur — Sunnyside Area

Sunnyside Area

The final section of Craig Arthur, just before the descent gully, is a roof-capped wall of good rock. The wall has a selection of harder sport pitches and a couple of good trad lines. The area is the first reached on the approach - at the far right-hand end of the cliff.

Access - No climbing from 15th Feb to 15th July between markers because of nesting birds. This is a variable restriction - see page 96.

❶ Scrapyard Things E1 5a
1) 5a, 20m. Climb the dodgy-looking flake-crack on the left-hand side of a detached pillar to its top. Proceed up the wall above (peg) to a belay below an overhang on the right.
2) 5a, 12m. Move through the overhang on its left (pegs) to a large ledge. Finish up a chimney on the right.
FA. Bob Dearman, Martin Pedlar 1969. FFA. Stuart Cathcart 1979

❷ Uncrossed 7a
Climb direct up a rib, passing a ledge, to the bulge.
FA. Gary Gibson 20.12.2014

❸ Those Stumbling Words 7a
A direct line through two overlaps. A bouldery start (avoidable on the left) leads through poor rock in the mid-section to a good finale.
FA. Gary Gibson, Hazel Gibson 25.6.2009

❹ Double Crossbones E3 5c
1) 5c, 12m. A good little pitch up excellent rock, past a peg in a horizontal break, to a fluttery shallow scoop.
2) 5a, 12m. The overhang and corner to a belay on the left.
3) 5a, 15m. Move back to the corner and go right to the exposed arete below an overhang (peg). Move through the overhang on the right and traverse right to finish up a broken crack.
FA. Stuart Cathcart, Tom Curtis 18.5.1980

❺ Delaware Slide E4 6a
A good and demanding pitch. Climb up good rock past a thread and move right up a little ramp to an overhang (peg). Pass the overhang on the right and stretch for a good hold above. At the next overhang (old bolt which needs a wire over the bolt head) pull up to a peg in a small corner, avoiding some unstable undercuts, and move left and up with difficulty (old bolts above). Finish up the broken crack.
FA. John Moulding, John Codling 11.4.1984

❻ These Foolish Things . . . . 7a+
A brilliant technical route with hard moves at the top, although there are also some tricky sections lower down. There is a lower-off and a 60m rope just makes it down. *Photo on page 11.*
FA. Gary Gibson, Phil Gibson 1.6.1991

❼ Gates of the Golden Dawn . . . E5 6b
A fabulous line up the front of the buttress finishing in a wild position through the capping roofs. Better if started up *These Foolish Things* with a traverse to the belay at the top of pitch 1.
1) 5b, 20m. From the upper ledge. Step left to the bottom of a very lichenous corner. Climb this, to an overlap and then climb the groove-line on the right to a stance - many pegs.
2) 6b, 15m. Move up past a small ledge to the capping roofs - old bolt - and make tough moves through these to a final layback and the top. Threads and a peg.
FA. Stuart Cathcart, Greg Griffith (1pt) 15.5.1980.
FFA. John Moulding, John Codling 6.5.1987

❽ The Deadly Trap E3 5c
An old line that is now rarely attempted.
1) 5b, 20m. Pitch 1 of *Gates of the Golden Dawn*.
2) 5c, 21m. Move up towards the roof (old bolt) then traverse right (thread) and down-climb a short groove to a small ledge. Traverse right to finish up a groove and wide crack on the right-hand side of the roofs.
FA. Stuart Cathcart, Nick Slaney 22.8.1977

Sunnyside Area Craig Arthur

9 Sunnyside Up Mix 7b
A stunning pitch up the left-hand side of the buttress. The start is hard, the wall above is technical but the finish is as good as it gets - brilliant upside down jug-pulling across the capping roof in a wild position. There is belay at the start.
FA. Gary Gibson 31.7.1992

10 Black Poppies 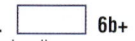 7b+
The hardest route on the buttress has some difficult fingery climbing on the lower wall and the finish is a real stopper unless you can confidently finger jam up overhanging flared cracks! Very memorable. There is a bolt belay at the start.
FA. Gary Gibson 27.5.1991

11 Chilean Moon 7b
A worthwhile route but not as good as its neighbours. Pulling through the lower bulge at the start is hard. Higher up there is some reasonable climbing but the finish feels a little eliminate in nature. Start at the *Black Poppies* belay.
FA. Gary Gibson 5.7.1992. The route was reclimbed after the loss of a large flake at the start by Lee Proctor 6.8.2002

12 Acapulco  7a+
Climb directly up the right-hand side of the buttress via the left-hand side of a huge ledge. It shares its start with *Chills of Apprehension*.
FA. Gary Gibson 25.7.1993

13 Chills of Apprehension E4 6a
A good natural line up the right side of the buttress. Climb up the rightward-trending line through the bulge (pegs and a thread). Above this difficult section, move left beneath some overhangs and climb up via a wall and groove that lead to the wide crack on the right-hand side of the overhangs.
FA. Steve Boyden, John Moulding 31.5.1985

14 Jam Spread 6b+
The short difficult bulge, shallow groove and wall.
FA. Gary Gibson 1.9.2010

15 Lemon Kerred E3 6b
A short semi-sport line to a lower-off on the tree.
FA. Gary Gibson, Doug Kerr 31.8.1991

16 Freshly Dug 6a
A pleasant face climb at far end of the wall.
FA. Gary Gibson, Hazel Gibson 25.6.2009

Twilight Area

	No star	☆	☆☆	☆☆☆
Mod to S / 4+	21	3	-	-
HS-HVS / 5-6a+	33	7	1	-
E1-E3 / 6b-7a	19	14	3	-
E4 / 7a+ and up	3	2	1	-

(Craig yr Ogof - Crag of the Cave)
When viewed from afar the Twilight crags look relatively insignificant, but closer inspection reveals a wealth of steep buttresses, walls and grooves that contain some quality routes. The Twilight Area is the least visited of all the Eglwyseg Valley cliffs and it's a good spot to get away from the crowds if the more popular areas are busy. The area is neatly split into two distinct sections: the shady Gully Walls and the exposed Twilight Tower Buttress. The Gully Walls are a good venue in hot weather, containing a selection of mid-grade sport routes and some worthwhile trad routes. Twilight Tower Buttress is the highest crag in the valley, with stupendous panoramic views and some good low-grade routes.

Approach   Also see map on page 81
From Llangollen, follow the road to the junction at 1.8 miles. Continue up the narrow valley road for 0.4 miles to a parking place on the right just before a gated track (also on the right) as the road drops down into the trees. More parking is available back down the road if the lay-by is full. From the parking, take the gated track and continuation path for 500m (this path passes below the Pinfold crags) to a wide valley on the right. Follow the wide valley above on scree to meet the cliff-line.

Conditions
Twilight Tower Buttress can be very windy but dries extremely quickly. The Gully Walls are less exposed and only receive sun in the evening. These walls tend to seep in winter but are dry by summer and offer shady climbing.

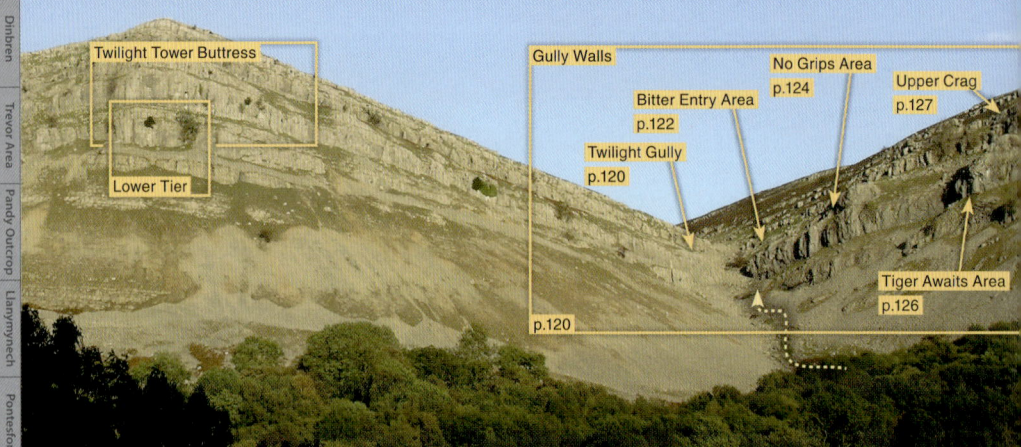

Twilight Tower Buttress — **Twilight Area** 117

Twilight Tower Buttress
A beautifully located spot with a number of worthwhile routes that are always quiet and worth the approach walk. The crag is very exposed and dries quickly but catches the wind so is not a good place to be in poor weather.

Approach - From above the scree at the top of the approach gully, head left on a narrow path to the start of the Upper Tier.

1 On Line . . . . S 4a
Power up the steep layback flake to reach easier climbing.
FA. Paul Stott 25.1.1981

2 Extension . . . . VS 4c
The rounded arete is slightly loose on its upper half.
FA. Paul Stott 6.1981

3 Funeral Corner . . . . HS 4a
A little gem situated high above the valley, at the tip of Twilight Tower Buttress. The perfect corner is a delight to climb - it is just a shame that it is so short.
FA. John Hesketh, H.J.Tinkler 1962

4 Inter Digital Pause . . . . HVS 5a
The arete right of *Funeral Corner* has a hard move high up past an old peg.
FA. Paul Stott, Stuart Cathcart 26.6.1981

5 Penetration Factor . . . . . VS 4c
An excellent and exposed route that follows the thin finger-crack and airy layback flake splitting the buttress.
FA. Paul Stott, Roger Bennion 11.5.1981

6 Sidestep . . . . HVS 4c
Climb the thin crack-line and take the right-hand fork where the crack splits to join a deep body-sized crack. Finish up the crack.
FA. Paul Stott 6.1981

7 Ruth's Ramble . . . . VD
Follow the broken crack system past two dead yew trees and up the slabby groove to the top.
FA. John Hesketh, H.J.Tinkler 1962

8 Loran . . . . S 4a
Good climbing following the flake-crack and groove to a blocky bulge beneath a dead yew tree. Pull up past the tree and climb the crack-line above on perfect grey limestone.
FA. Paul Stott 5.1981

Twilight Area — Twilight Tower Buttress

⑨ Hell Drivers .... 7a+
The thin bolted wall.
FA. Gary Gibson 4.1.2015

⑩ Sunday Driver .... VS 4c
A great route on immaculate rock following the wall and slab using a series of disjointed cracks.
FA. Stuart Cathcart, Paul Stott 26.6.1981

⑪ Wood Pigeon Crack .... HS 4a
A steep pitch that starts by a short V-groove right of a tree. Climb the groove to a small overlap then move right to finish up the crack and corner above the tree.
FA. John Hesketh, H.J.Tinkler 1962

⑫ Goin' to a Go Go .... 7b+
The direct line up the centre of the main buttress is excellent. A bouldery start accesses intricate face climbing. Finish rightwards through the upper overlap.
FA. Gary Gibson 28.7.1992

⑬ Go-a-Go-Go E2 5b
Fine climbing following the flake-crack in the wall. Start up *High Impedance* to the roof, then reach out left to access the flake-crack. The flakes feel creaky but the protection is sound.
FA. Stuart Cathcart, Paul Stott 26.6.1981

⑭ High Impedance E2 5c
Wild, well-protected climbing, that requires a bit of thought and a lot of brawn to surmount the wide roof.
FA. Paul Stott, Stuart Cathcart 26.6.1981

⑮ Attenuation .... VS 4c
An eliminate up the narrow buttress between the cracks with a technical finish up a short smooth groove.
FA. Paul Stott, Stuart Cathcart 6.1981

⑯ Moncrieff .... VD
The unappealing wide crack has several loose blocks.
FA. John Hesketh, H.J.Tinkler 1962

⑰ Ivy Tower Chimney .... VD
Climb past the low tree and up the left-hand chimney using ivy as much as rock to gain height.
FA. John Hesketh, H.J.Tinkler 1962

⑱ Cow Parsley .... VD
Start up *Ivy Tower Chimney* and then follow the right-hand chimney above the tree.
FA. John Hesketh, H.J.Tinkler 1962

⑲ Skullion .... VS 4b
Start at the foot of a large rectangular flaky niche. Climb to the top of the niche and continue up the cracked wall above.
FA. Stuart Cathcart 1980

⑳ The Clearout .... VS 4b
The steep, loose, blocky crack is best avoided.
FA. Paul Stott 6.1981

㉑ Helme's Highway .... S 4a
Follow the thin corner-crack and V-groove with an awkward move at half-height.
FA. John Hesketh, H.J.Tinkler 1962

㉒ Eclipse .... HVS 5a
A worthwhile route that goes up the steep slab using a series of shallow scoops.
FA. John Randles, Sean Roberts 11.8.1999

㉓ Onegin .... S 4a
The wide crack is becoming obscured by the tree.
FA. John Hesketh, H.J.Tinkler 1962

Twilight Tower Buttress and Lower Tier — Twilight Area

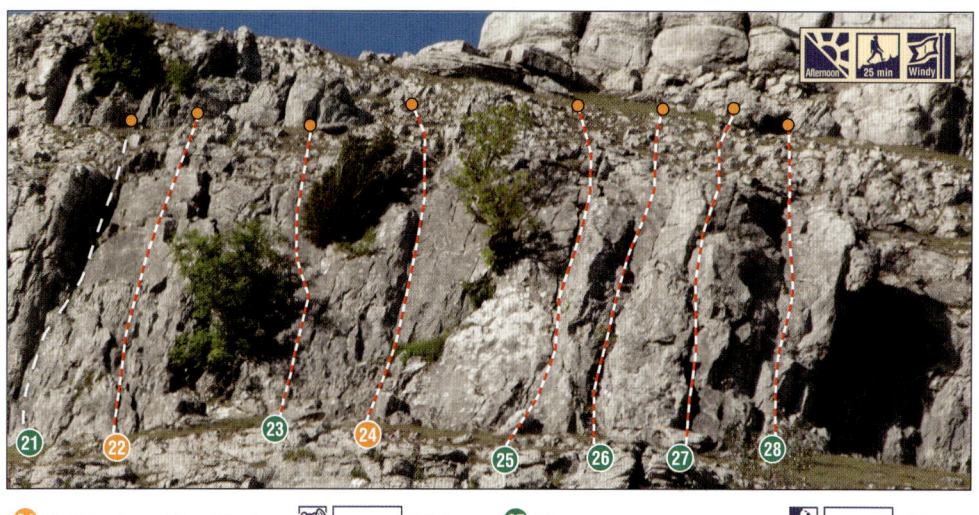

24 To Cut a Long Story Short ... VS 4c
Climb the short corner right of the yew tree. Bold.
FA. Paul Stott 4.1981

25 Pride .... VD
Good easy climbing up the crack-line right of the tree.
FA. John Hesketh, H.J.Tinkler 1962

26 Prejudice .... Diff
The deep crack.
FA. John Hesketh, H.J.Tinkler 1962

The next routes are on the tier below Twilight Tower Buttress.

29 Pinnacle Crack .... HVD
The steep leftward-leaning crack.
FA. Paul Stott 7.1981

30 Interface .... VS 4b
The short wall right of the wide gully separating the pinnacle.
FA. Paul Stott 6.1981

27 Flawse .... VD
A poor route up the crack-line in the vague arete.
FA. Paul Stott 4.1981

28 Sloth .... VD
A good route that tackles the hand-sized crack just left of a small cave.
FA. John Hesketh, H.J.Tinkler 1962

31 Riboflavin .... S 4a
Gain and climb the short rib left of a corner.
FA. Paul Stott 6.1981

32 Open to Offa's .... VD
Climb the chockstone-filled crack right of the yew tree.
FA. Paul Stott 6.1981

33 Terminal .... VS 4c
Thin cracks in the short wall right of the corner.
FA. Paul Stott 6.1981

Lower Tier
A nicely situated small crag but with little climbing of merit and the rock is poor in places. It can be reached from either end by descending steep ground carefully from the Upper Tier.

Twilight Area — Twilight Gully

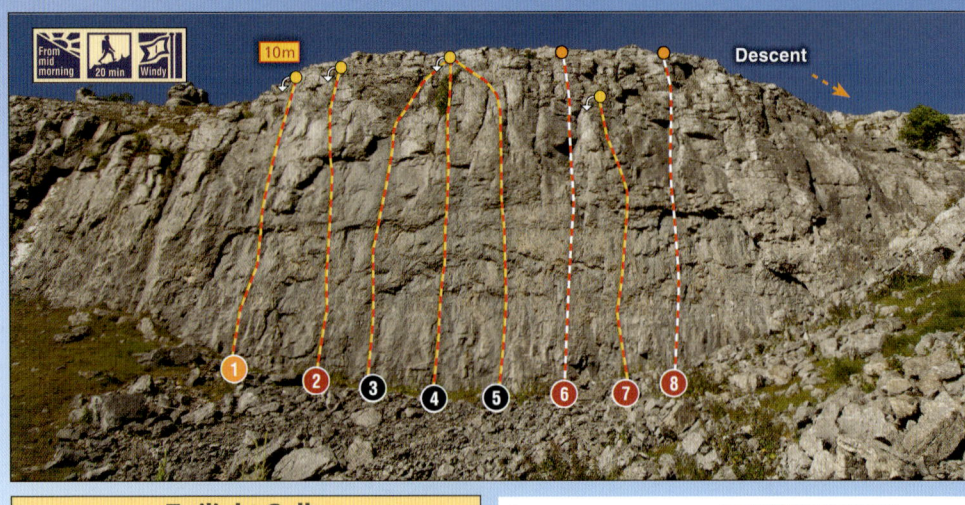

Twilight Gully

A short, compact and very sunny wall of solid rock that has a handful of intense and fingery pitches. Some of the routes have been equipped with economy in mind and a few small wires are needed on a couple of the harder lines.

Approach - The wall is easily seen on the left at the top of the approach path up the wide scree-filled valley.

1 Charlie's Podium 5a
A nice easier option on the far left of the wall. *Photo opposite.*

2 Spiderpig . . . . 6b+
Climb the wall crossing a right-slanting overlap.

3 Disappear . . . . 7a+
A short and fiercely technical face climb past two bolts.
FA. Gary Gibson, J.Shaw 9.7.1994

4 Manakin . . . . 7a+
The best route on the wall is a technical conundrum. Climb past two bolts to reach the rightwards-trending flake-crack (wires). Follow this easily to the lower-off.
FA. Allen Price 1988

5 Puppet Symphony . . . . . . 7b+
A super-desperate pitch requiring fingers of steel. The grade is unconfirmed since the route lost holds.
FA. Gary Gibson, Jim Shaw 9.7.1994

6 Bolt in the Snow E2 5b
Climb the bold lower wall, past an old bolt casing, to reach good holds and protection in the niche. Pull into this and finish easily.
FA. Allen Price 3.1986

7 The Muppet Show 6c
The technical face just right of *Bolt in the Snow*.
FA. Gary Gibson 30.6.2013

8 Jabberwocky E2 5b
A filler-in up the short wall and shallow groove left of the flake.

Claire Heaton finishing off *Charlie's Podium* (5a) - *opposite* - at the Twilight Area. Photo: Craig Bailey

Twilight Area — Bitter Entry Area

1 Shadow E3 6a
The leftward-trending shallow scoop and thin crack.
FA. Stuart Cathcart, John Dee 14.8.1980

2 Silhouette .... 6c+
Climb the really hard low bulge. *Photo opposite.*
FA. Gary Gibson 30.6.2013

3 Caricature .... 6c+
Neat climbing and another tough low bulge.
FA. Gary Gibson 30.6.2013

4 Slim Faster 6c
Climb past two staple bolts, then move right to the lower-off.
FA. Gary Gibson, Jim Shaw 9.7.1994

5 Crash Diet .... 6c+
A fun little pitch following a line through the widest part of the upper bulge, past thee staple bolts, to a lower-off.
FA. Gary Gibson, Jim Shaw 9.7.1994

6 Calorie Control 7a
A difficult start past 2 staple bolts reaches the right-hand side of the upper bulge (wires). Pull left around this to the lower-off.
FA. Gary Gibson, Jim Shaw 9.7.1994

7 Hungry Days E3 5c
A varied route. Start by a small ledge at chest height. Move up the light grey wall to reach the left edge of the overhang. Traverse left to join and finish up *Calorie Control* over the bulge.
FA. Stuart Cathcart, Malcolm Cameron 14.7.1981

8 Bitter Ender E1 5b
Start by a white painted square. Follow the flake-crack under and around the overlap, finishing up a thin crack/corner.
FA. Stuart Cathcart, John Dee 18.6.1981

9 Bitter Entry E2 5c
A powerful pitch. Follow *Bitter Ender* to the overlap and move left underneath this until a crack is reached in the bulge. A savage pull around this gains easy ground and the top.
FA. Stuart Cathcart, Malcolm Cameron 14.7.1981

10 Lemon Entry E3 5c
Climb the excellent thin crack with a difficult entry and exit!
FA. Gary Gibson 30.6.2013

11 Forced Entry E3 5c
Good technical climbing following the left-trending groove past two pegs (sometimes threaded). At the overlap, move right and finish up a thin crack.
FA. Doug Kerr 27.4.1986. FFA. Paul Harrison, Simon Cardy 4.1988

12 Tizer the Surpriser .... HVS 5a
Climb the first of three grooves, past a dubious block, to an awkward finish.
FA. Stuart Cathcart 4.3.1980

13 Central Groove .... HS 4b
The central groove is marked by a white painted square.

14 The Pancake .... HS 4b
The right-hand groove up broken ground.

15 Unbladed E2 5b
A line over bulges right of *The Pancake*.
FA. Gary Gibson 30.6.2013

16 Starting Block .... HVS 4c
Start by a white painted square at the foot of a short arete and right of an open groove. Climb up and leftwards into a second groove, and follow this to the top.
FA. Bob Dearman 1969

17 Race Riot .... HVS 5a
A reasonable pitch up the open groove.
FA. Stuart Cathcart, Malcolm Cameron 23.7.1981

18 Twilight Chimney .... HS 4b
A testing climb up the chimney at the left-hand side of the tower. There is a white painted square at the foot of the route.

19 Jittering Tower E1 5a
Climb the front face of the tower.
FA. Stuart Cathcart, John Dee 25.10.1980

Bitter Entry Area **Twilight Area** 123

Bitter Entry Area
The best bit of the Twilight Area. Compact, bulging rock with a mix of trad and sport pitches. It is shady until late in the afternoon and seeps after rain.
Approach - The crag is on the right at the top of the scree on the approach path.

Craig Bailey catching some evening sunshine on the tough little number *Silhouette* (6c+) - *opposite* - at the Twilight Area. Photo: Craig Bailey collection.

Twilight Area — No Grips Area

No Grips Area

A long low section of cliff with a larger buttress at the left-hand end and with the Upper Tier above.
Approach - It is reached by continuing a few meters along the narrow path from the Bitter Entry Area.

1 Frejus . . . . HVD
The wide fissure behind the right-hand side of the tower.

2 Agay . . . . S 4a
Climb flake-cracks in the wall behind the tower, to a finish right of a small tree.

3 Antibes . . . . VS 4b
Climb the wall to gain a layback crack. Finish up this.
FA. Stuart Cathcart 17.7.1981

4 Running Wild . . . . HVS 5a
From the start of *Antibes*, climb rightwards into a short V-groove. Finish up the left arete, keeping left of two trees.
FA. Stuart Cathcart 17.7.1981

5 Volenti . . . . S 4a
Follow the flake-crack to a small overhang then take the left-hand flake to the top. There is a white square painted on the rock at the foot of the route.
FA. Bob Dearman 1969

6 The Gift . . . . S 4a
Climb the thin crack to a tiny sapling then traverse left to below a yew tree. Scrabble up past this to the top.
FA. Bob Dearman 1969

7 Zilla . . . . VD
Start below a whitebeam tree and climb the left-hand of two cracks to reach a leftward-trending ramp leading to the top.

8 Frolic . . . . VS 4a
Climb the right-hand crack to reach the roots of the whitebeam tree and then finish direct up the wall above.

9 Roots . . . . VS 4c
Start behind a pointed flake and climb the slab to reach the roots of the whitebeam tree. Move right and finish through some small overlaps.
FA. Stuart Cathcart, Malcolm Cameron 12.5.1981

10 No Grips E2 5b
Step off the top of the pointed flake onto the arete then climb up and rightwards across the slab to finish just left of a small prow.
FA. Stuart Cathcart, Malcolm Cameron 25.10.1980

11 A New Bend in My Arm E1 5b
A counter line to *No Grips*.
FA. Nick Taylor 25.7.1998

There has been a rockfall and this has left the next two lines in an altered and unstable state.

12 Missing Link . . . . VS 4b
Altered by rockfall. Climb the short flake and corner system finishing just right of the small prow.
FA. Stuart Cathcart 15.8.1981

13 The Last Fling . . . . VS 4a
Altered by rockfall. The broken and cracked wall.
FA. Stuart Cathcart 15.8.1981

No Grips Area — Twilight Area — 125

14 Continental Chocs .... VS 4b
A short, steep crack climb above a painted square.
FA. Bob Dearman 1969

15 Pagoda .... HVS 5a
Bold and sightly loose climbing following the thin crack.
FA. Stuart Cathcart, Tom Curtis 13.10.1979

16 Rising Champ .... HVD
A poor route up broken ground left of the large ash tree.

17 Misty Dawn .... S 4a
Nice climbing following the wall and crack system right of the ash tree.
FA. Bob Dearman 1969

18 Tock Tick E4 6b
The left-hand line on a blank wall with peg in it.
FA. Gary Gibson 30.6.2013

19 Tick Tock E3 5c
The right-hand line.
FA. Gary Gibson 30.6.2013

20 Shakin' Stevens .... VS 4b
Truly awful climbing past a thorn bush.

21 Get a Grip of Yourself E2 5b
The face left of *Happy Valley*.
FA. Gary Gibson 30.6.2013

22 Happy Valley .... VS 4b
A nice route on flawless rock that follows the dark grey wall slightly rightwards. There is a white square painted at the bottom.
FA. Bob Dearman 1969

23 Rock Special ... E3 5c
A challenging route with a hard start that is both reachy and technical. Start by a slim overlap. Pull over the bulge with difficulty, then boldly traverse rightwards to reach a good hold. Mantelshelf onto this and finish easily up the slabby wall.
FA. Stuart Cathcart 1.7.1981

24 Howling E1 5b
Good climbing that feels a little fluttery. From the start of *Ten Percent Special*, climb the blank-looking wall leftwards on layaways to reach a short groove and the top.
FA. Stuart Cathcart 1.7.1981

25 Ten Percent Special . E2 5c
A compelling climb based on a pocketed scoop in the wall. Pull into the scoop then foot-traverse rightwards, beneath a slight bulge, to reach a series of shallow grooves. Climb up these to finish just left of a small whitebeam tree.
FA. Stuart Cathcart 1.7.1981

26 Masungi .... HS 4b
Climb direct to the small whitebeam tree using some good flake holds low down.
FA. Stuart Cathcart 1.7.1981

27 The Avenger .... VS 4b
A short wall climb following a thin crack in a brown streak.
FA. Stuart Cathcart 1.7.1981

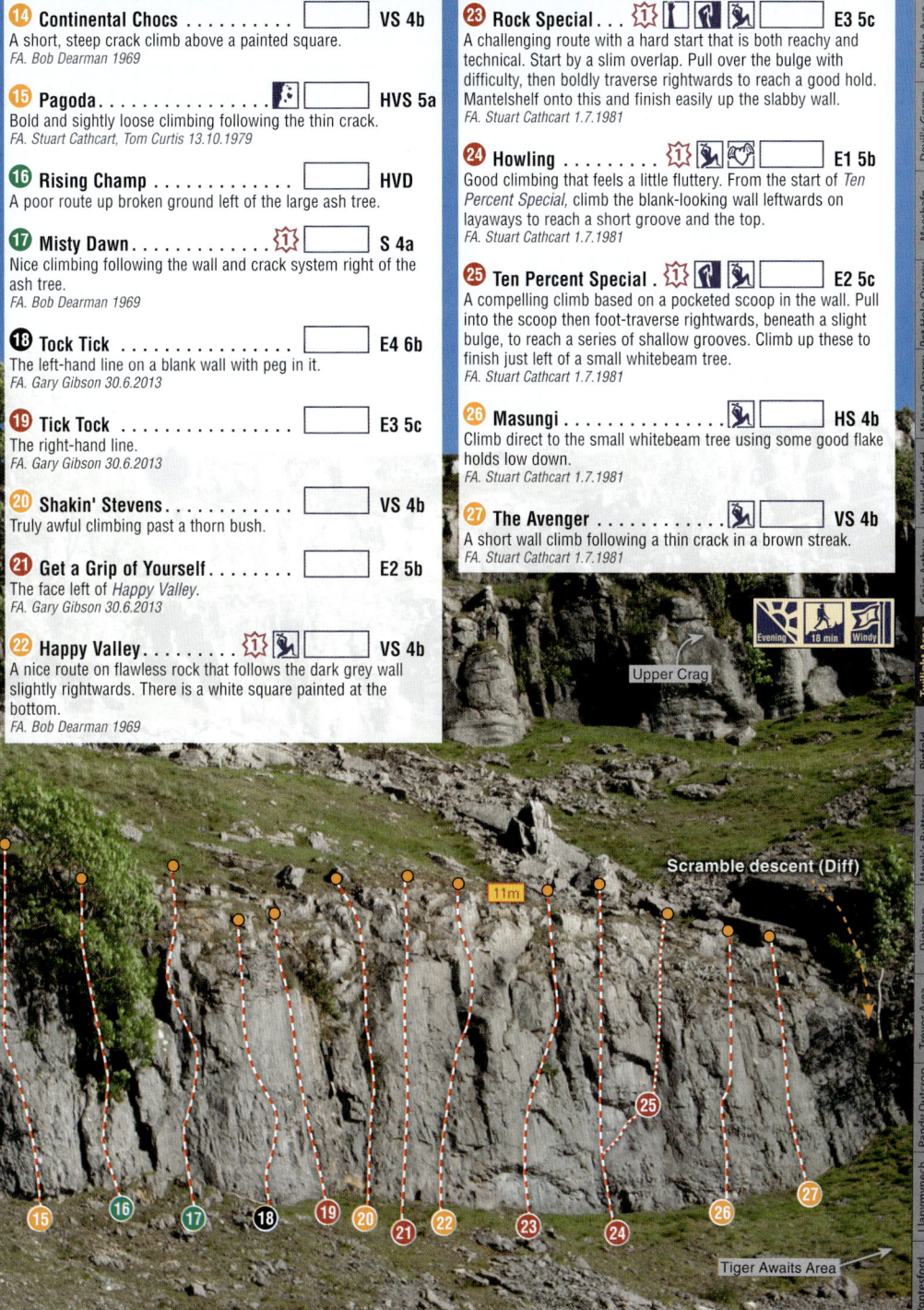

Twilight Area — Tiger Awaits Area

Tiger Awaits Area

The last section of substantial rock on the crag has a number of steep lines. To reach it, continue along the narrow path from the No Grips Area.

1 The Land of Fairies E1 5b
At the base of the wall, to the right of the grassy gully, is a small, knee-high, split flake. From the top of this, pull onto the wall and climb leftwards into a short, steep, hanging groove. A committing pitch.
FA. Stuart Cathcart, Andy Johnson 18.3.1980

2 Pitmungo . . . . S 4a
The loose-looking wall and crack system starting by a large flake.

3 Chateau . . . . VS 4a
Climb up broken grooves to reach a tree and move left past this to finish.

4 Unite . . . . S 4a
Follow the steep, reddish groove system.
FA. Bob Dearman 1969

5 H Block E1 5a
Start at the foot of a slim groove with a painted white square at its base. Climb the groove and continue over the rounded bulge at its top to finish up a short slab and corner.
FA. Stuart Cathcart, Malcolm Cameron 23.7.1981

Tiger Awaits Area and Upper Crag — Twilight Area

6 Bay of Pigs E1 5b
An entertaining route that starts at the same point as *H Block* but then follows the wall rightwards to reach a good crack below the roof. Continue to the roof then traverse left across the wall to finish up some cracks.
FA. Stuart Cathcart, Malcolm Cameron 23.7.1981

7 The Tiger Awaits E2 5b
A good climb that feels slightly artificial at the start. Climb the crack that contains a yew tree higher up, for 1m, then move left to a thin crack above the undercut base of the wall. Follow the crack, gaining the arete beneath the overhang, then move right and make an exciting pull around the overhang to the top.
FA. Stuart Cathcart, Malcolm Cameron 23.7.1981

8 The Heist .... VS 4c
Continue up the crack avoided by *The Tiger Awaits* and battle past the yew tree on its right-hand side. Follow the crack rightwards towards a second yew and avoid this by climbing the wall left of the tree direct.
FA. Stuart Cathcart, Andy Johnson 18.3.1980

9 Stay Alert Malcolm .... HVS 5a
This attractive wall climb follows the thin crack in the wall right of the yew tree. Climb up the crack, keeping to the right of some white splodges, to reach a slim overlap. Move right beneath the overlap and climb the wall above to the top.
FA. Stuart Cathcart, Malcolm Cameron 23.7.1981

10 Hyper Medius Meets Little Finger
.... E3 5c
A highball boulder problem testpiece. Climb the short smooth wall to reach a grassy flake-crack and the top.
FA. Stuart Cathcart 19.4.1980

11 Little Fingers .... VS 4c
A short-lived route up the slim groove.
FA. John Randles 25.4.1991

Further along the escarpment are two isolated routes.

12 Thumberline E3 6a
Climb a rib left of the rounded arete of *Fingerbobs*, passing a peg.
FA. Gary Gibson 30.6.2013

13 Fingerbobs E4 6a
Good technical climbing up the rounded arete that feels committing and is protected by a single bolt.
FA. Gary Gibson, Jim Shaw 9.7.1994

Upper Crag
Above the Tiger Awaits and No Grips Areas are a number of smaller buttresses that are composed of excellent and unusually-weathered limestone. A few easier routes have been put up and can be reached via the grass terrace that starts above the Bitter Entry Area.

14 Constantinople 6a
Pull over the low bulge and climb the slab.
FA. Gary Gibson 7.7.2013

15 Christiana 6b
Follow the arete right of the wide corner-crack. There is a big move near the beginning.
FA. Gary Gibson 7.7.2013

16 Copenhagen .... 6a+
Move up to and over the low bulge via some hard moves and finish up the slab above.
FA. Gary Gibson 7.7.2013

17 Bunter .... 6c+
The leaning arete is very bouldery.
FA. Gary Gibson 2013

18 Balling 6b
Short line passing a low bulge and layback edge.
FA. Gary Gibson 7.7.2013

19 Crumples 5b
The clean and crinkly slab.
FA. Gary Gibson 7.7.2013

20 Trending 6b
Take the arete on good holds.
FA. Gary Gibson 7.7.2013

21 Tweeting .... 6a+
Follow the arete to a lower-off at the tree.
FA. Gary Gibson 7.7.2013

Pinfold

	No star	⭐	⭐⭐	⭐⭐⭐
Mod to S / 4+	3	-	-	-
HS-HVS / 5-6a+	33	14	3	1
E1-E3 / 6b-7a	37	36	11	2
E4 / 7a+ and up	14	20	11	3

(Craig Tri Naid y Gath - Crag of the cat's three leaps)
Pinfold is a long series of crags that offers a variety of both trad and sport climbs. Nearly every grade is catered for making Pinfold a great venue for teams of mixed ability. The north end of the escarpment has a number of shorter technical pitches whilst the centerpiece is the huge open-book Atmospheres bay, clearly visible from the road, home to Pinfold's best hard sport climbs. Moving south, the crag takes on a more impressive character in the form of Two Tier Buttress, with its selection of tough two-pitch routes. Just before the stream bed at the head of the valley, there is an exquisite section of crag with some brilliant little trad pitches. On the far side of the stream, the bulging Monkshead Buttress has a selection of powerful and technical sport routes, well worth a visit in hot conditions if looking for some cool in the shade.

Access
An agreed climbing restriction due to nesting birds has been applied to certain sections of Pinfold in the past. This hasn't happened for many years but it is still a possibility. If there is a restriction it will be indicated by markers at the crag base.

Approach   Also see map on page 81
From Llangollen, follow the road to the junction at 1.8 miles. Continue up the narrow valley road for 0.4 miles to a parking place, just before a gated track on the right as the road drops down into the trees. More parking is available back down the road if the lay-by is full. From the parking, take the gated track for 100m and then follow the wide valley above to the base of the crag at the Solo in Soho Area. The small steep crag on the right of the approach path is Monkshead Buttress.

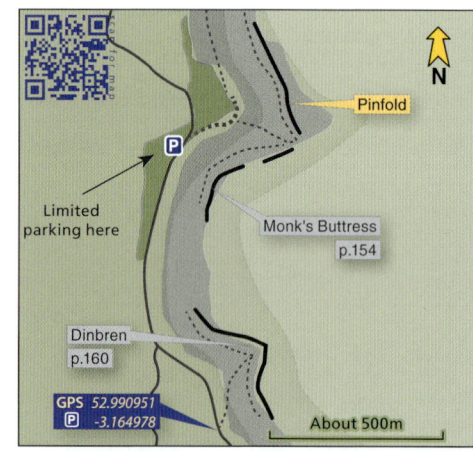

Conditions
The crags receive the sun in the afternoon apart from Monkshead Buttress which is a useful spot in hot weather. Seepage is only a major problem on Monkshead Buttress and in the *Atmospheres* corner in winter and spring. Elsewhere the crags dry quickly after rain. Windy days are best avoided. Little shelter from the rain is available except in the Atmospheres Bay which may offer some dry climbing in the rain.

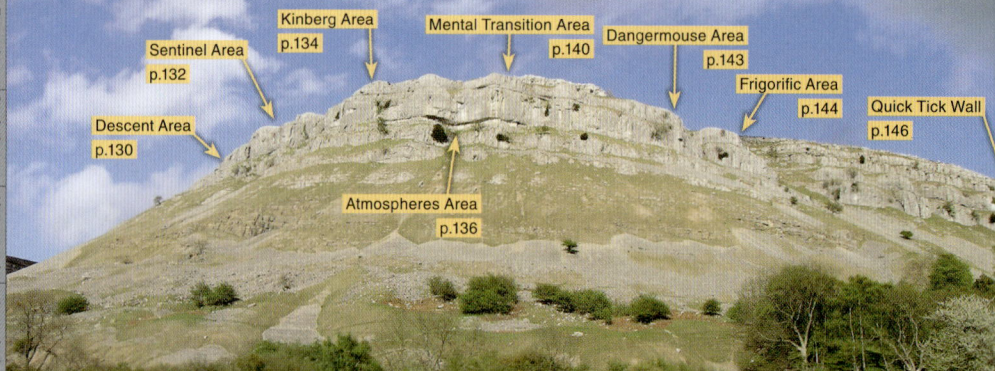

Chantelle Govier at the start of the dividing ways on *Y-Corner* (HVS 5a) - *page 150* - at the Solo in Soho Area, Pinfold. Pinfold has a huge range of route styles and grades with classic hard sport climbs rubbing shoulders with some excellent trad. Photo: Craig Bailey

Pinfold Descent Area

Descent Area
At the far end of the Pinfold edge, the crag gradually starts to break up into a series of smaller buttresses. There are a few good shorter pitches here but often they are more useful as quick ticks to pick off when descending from other routes. It is worth noting that the Twilight Gully Walls can be easily reached from here, in a few minutes, by continuing to walk along the base of the crag.

❶ Undercurrent E2 5c
The thin cracks 10m left of the descent route.
FA. Gary Gibson, Hazel Gibson 25.6.1994

❷ Smouldering Bouldering E3 6a
The smooth wall past a thread and peg.
FA. Gary Gibson 2.6.1985

❸ Ye Old Cod Piece E3 5c
The thin crack-line.
FA. Gary Gibson, Hazel Gibson 25.6.1994

❹ Sweet Satisfaction .... HS 4b
The groove and left-hand crack of the chimney. Loose at the top.
FA. Stuart Cathcart 20.6.1981

❺ Flighting .... HVS 5a
The crack right of the chimney and wall are best avoided.
FA. Stuart Cathcart 20.6.1981

❻ Sayfari .... VD
The corner past a grassy ledge.

❼ Fingernail .... HVS 5a
Climb the curving crack and slabby wall to the recess, continue up the steep crack to the right and finish airily up the arete. Care is needed with the rock at the top.
FA. Stuart Cathcart, Frank Bennett 26.7.1979

❽ One Carlos E5 6b
Trend left over the initial bulge to a bolt. Difficult moves, following the thin crack above (wires and peg) lead to the top.
FA. Gary Gibson 25.5.1992

❾ Franco .... HVS 5a
Layback up the crack and make an awkward move left to a grassy ledge. Finish up the wide crack.
FA. Stuart Cathcart, Frank Bennett 26.7.1979

Mark Glaister negotiating one of the typically powerful starts that are a common obstacle on many of the harder lines on the Kinberg Area at Pinfold. *Prickly Heat* (7a) - *page 135*. Photo: Phil Black

Pinfold — Sentinel Area

Sentinel Area

Some good little sport routes and a couple of fine trad lines stand out on this exposed section of the crag. It is reached by continuing along the base of the crag to an exposed arete and large head-height overhang in a bay just beyond.

1 Tweak E1 5b
Climb direct to the holly tree.

2 Et Tu Brutus .... 6b+
A smart little line with some puzzling moves to a lower-off.
FA. Gary Gibson 18.11.2012

3 Stoned Roman E1 5b
Reasonable climbing that follows the thin crack to the whitebeam tree, before moving left and up the slab.
FA. Stuart Cathcart, Frank Bennett 11.7.1980

4 Whilst Rome Burns 7a
Follow the compact wall to a lower-off.
FA. Gary Gibson 3.5.1992

5 A Stab in the Back 7b
Make desperate starting moves through overlaps to much easier climbing above.
FA. Gary Gibson 18.11.2012

6 U Got Me Bugged .... 7a+
Execute some powerful pulls to gain the recess above the lower bulge. Technical moves up the smooth wall above lead to the lower-off. A good pitch - if you can pull the start.
FA. Gary Gibson, Alec Williams 16.5.1992

7 Bug Off 7b
Once again a hard starting sequence precedes easier but still tricky climbing above.
FA. Gary Gibson 18.11.2012

8 Serengetti 7a
An alternative left-hand start to *Lurking in the Long Grass* - very hard to start.
FA. Gary Gibson, Alec Williams 16.5.1992

9 Lurking in the Long Grass
.... 7a+
A hard move gains the shallow scoop. Move up and leftwards to a line of flakes and follow these to the lower-off.
FA. Gary Gibson 29.7.1992

10 Rays and Hail .... 7b+
Climb the white wall to gain a thin crack beneath the overlap. Pull around this and tackle the wall above to a lower-off.
FA. Gary Gibson, Alec Williams 16.5.1992

11 Ray of Hope .... 6c+
Climb the thin and technical arete without much respite.
FA. Gary Gibson, Alec Williams 16.5.1992

12 Bennetto .... HS 4b
The broken corner.
FA. Stuart Cathcart, Frank Bennett 26.7.1979

13 Sentinel E2 5c
The best route in this area. Climb the appealing rightward-curving crack in the grey wall, with an awkward move low down. Pull through the bulge at the top of the slab to finish.
FA. Stuart Cathcart, John Dee 13.6.1981

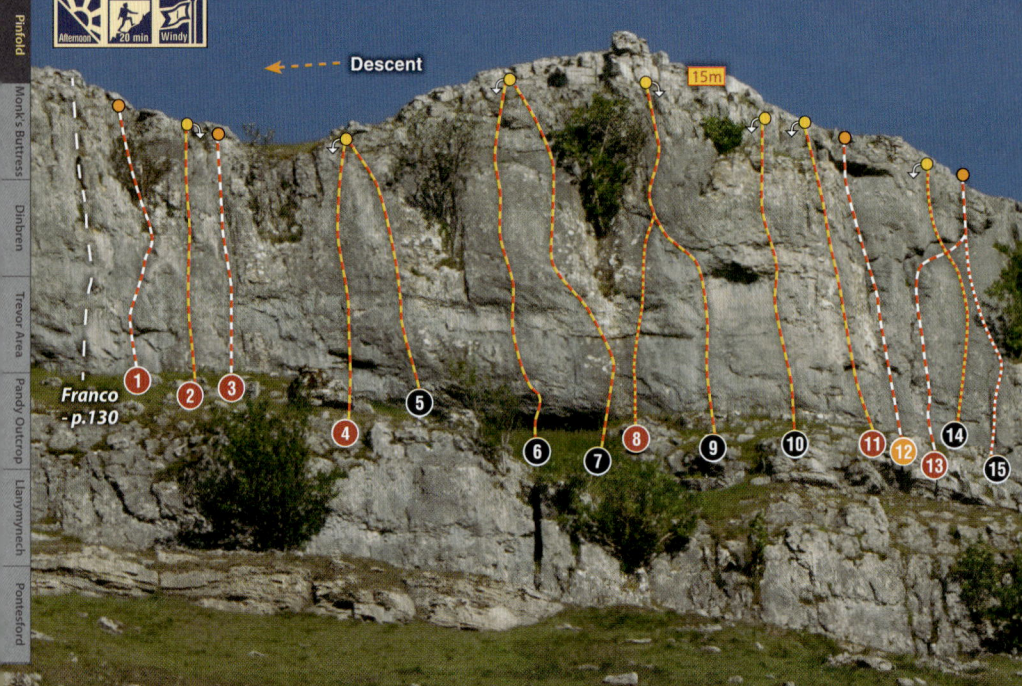

Sentinel Area — Pinfold

14 The Cycle Path — 7b
Thin and technical face climbing to join *Sentinel* with a fingery finale directly up the wall above the overlap. A large cam is needed at the break of *Sentinel*.
FA. Gary Gibson 31.5.2013

15 Freeway Madness — E4 5c
A bold route moving left from *Highway Hysteria* across the steep slab on pockets, to reach a good hold. The crack above is followed through the bulge to the top.
FA. Stuart Cathcart, Paul Stott 24.7.1981

16 Highway Hysteria — HVS 5a
Climb the flake, skirt under the ash tree and make a long move into the scoop on the right. Finish up the crack.
FA. Stuart Cathcart 12.6.1980

17 Soft Shoulder — 6a
Easy going face climbing follows a tricky start.
FA. Gary Gibson 31.5.2013

18 Buffoon — VS 4c
The vegetated cracks.
FA. Stuart Cathcart, Frank Bennett 23.6.1980

19 Hard Shoulder — 7b
A desperate start through the overlap to easier ground above.
FA. Gary Gibson 31.5.2013

The wide roof past a bolt to a nowhere finish may have been climbed but is probably still a project.

20 Polytextured Finish — 6c+
A good route. Climb the short compact grey wall with a difficult move. Finish up the shallow groove above.
FA. Gary Gibson 17.5.2013

21 Bold Poly — VS 4b
Enjoyable climbing up the corner with lots of big gear.

22 Sometimes Yes, Sometimes No — E3 6a
A good line that follows the thin curving crack up the steep shady wall with the lower bulge providing the difficulties (peg). There is a lower-off at the top of the wall.
FA. Gary Gibson 17.5.1992

23 A Dose of Barley Fever — 6c+
Climb the lower grey wall to near the left arete. Exposed climbing up this, leads to a thin crack that is followed to the lower-off.
FA. Gary Gibson 17.5.1992

24 Slippery Caramel — 7a+
The grey front face of the buttress features some technical and fingery moves above half height.
FA. Gary Gibson 17.5.1992

25 Nesting Crack — HVS 5a
The loose, vegetated crack is best left well alone.
FA. Stuart Cathcart 12.4.1981

26 Just a Treat — 6a+
The face to the right of *Nesting Crack*.
FA. Gary Gibson 8.6..2013

27 Monumental — HS 4b
Scramble past the yew tree, taking care with the rock, to reach a good ledge beneath the groove. Bridge up this to the top.
FA. Stuart Cathcart 13.7.1981

Pinfold — Kinberg Area

Kinberg Area

The corner defining the left-hand side of this fine wall of rock is taken by *Kinberg*, one of the Clwyd's easier classics. On the right-hand side of the wall a number of sport climbs provide plenty of technical climbing in a stunning position. The wall is best reached by following a narrow path around from the Atmospheres bay.

1 The Burger King E3 6a
Take the front of the jutting buttress left of *Kinberg* past two bolts.
FA. Gary Gibson 8.6.2013

2 Kinberg .... VS 4c
The best route of this grade in the valley and well worth the walk up. Bridge up the superbly-positioned groove with the feeling that the entire world is beneath your feet. There is a thread belay at the top.
FA. Paul Stott, Stuart Cathcart 26.9.1980

3 Atlantic Traveller .... VS 4c
A great climb that skirts across the wall from *Kinberg* to finish up cracks right of the *Unknown Feelings* overhang.
FA. Stuart Cathcart 5.6.1980

4 Osteophyte E5 6a
A superb, technical and bold route via face and shallow finishing groove system - two pegs.
FA. Gary Gibson 31.5.2013

5 Bone Orchard E3 5c
Good technical climbing on perfect rock. Follow the thin crack to the ledge and then move up to a peg in a small corner. Pull through the overlap and finish up the slab.
FA. Stuart Cathcart, Paul Stott 26.9.1980

6 Unknown Feelings E2 5b
A great route with a delicate start and an exciting finish through the widest part of the overlap. There is good gear just when you need it.
FA. Stuart Cathcart, Paul Stott 26.9.1980

7 A Spaceman in the Whitehouse E4 6a
An eliminate up the faint scoop and the pocketed rib above.
FA. Gary Gibson 5.4.1984

8 Space Ace E3 5c
A technical route on perfect rock that traverses left from *Mitsuki Groove* to a peg in a shallow scoop, which is followed to the top. There is a good direct start up pocketed rock, passing a bolt, which nudges the technical grade up to **6a**.
FA. Stuart Cathcart, John Dee 9.7.1981

9 Mitsuki Groove .... HVS 5a
Sustained climbing. Take care with the rock near the top.
FA. Stuart Cathcart, Frank Bennett 26.7.1979

Afternoon / 20 min / Windy

Abseil descent from above Kinberg possible
Descent
18m

Monumental - p.133

Kinberg Area **Pinfold** 135

10 Non Stop E1 5c
Climb the thin finger-cracks in the compact wall, passing a thread near the top.
FA. Gary Gibson 5.4.1984

11 Smokey Bear E2 5b
The flake-crack and left wall.
FA. Stuart Cathcart, Greg Griffiths 4.7.1981

12 Physical Transaction 7a
A powerful start (old bolt) gains undercuts and a second bolt. Pull awkwardly through the overlap to reach better holds and a convenient tree to lower off from.
FA. Gary Gibson 13.10.1991

13 Freely Slapping Upwards ... 7b
A hard and powerful start past a bolt gains a good hold at the base of a short corner (bolt). Move left past a peg to reach good holds and the tree.
FA. Gary Gibson 8.5.1994

14 Out of the Fire, Into the Furnace 7b
Desperate moves through lower overhang but pleasant above.
FA. Gary Gibson 8.6.2013

15 Prickly Heat 7a
The best on this section of wall. Power through the undercut start to reach a good side-pull. Climb the technical wall above, moving left and then back right. Taking a direct line and cutting out the left and right moves increases the grade to **7a+**.
Photo on page 131.
FA. Gary Gibson 13.10.1991

16 Pictures of Living ... E4 6a
From the top of a flake-crack (on *Dying Tonight*), move up to reach a threaded peg. Continue leftwards on undercuts to reach a yellow block ledge beneath a thin crack. Pull onto the ledge with difficulty and follow the crack (peg required, may be missing) to a lower-off on *Prickly Heat*.
FA. John Codling, John Moulding, Gary Gibson 8.4.1984

17 Mr Wobbler E3 6a
Follow *Pictures of Living* to the threaded peg, then make a committing pull into the hanging groove. Follow this, past a thread, moving right at the top to a lower-off.
FA. Gary Gibson 2.6.1985

18 Dying Tonight ..... 7a+
Climb the lower grey wall with your left hand in the flake-crack to reach a large undercut. Now tiptoe rightwards to reach more undercuts, then power up the difficult wall to reach big jugs in the easy groove. Follow this to a lower-off.
FA. Gary Gibson, Hugh Williams 27.2.1992

19 Slap and Tickle .... 7a+
A very hard start using tiny undercuts, gains a good hold beneath a short corner. Easier but technical climbing above reaches a large flat hold. Rock onto this and step left into the final groove of *Dying Tonight*.
FA. Gary Gibson, Hugh Williams 27.2.1992

20 Wibbly Wobbly World 6c
Pull through the initial thuggy bulge then follow a rightward-trending line to the top.
FA. Gary Gibson, Rob Hilditch 24.4.1994

Atmospheres Area **Pinfold** *137*

Arran Deakin starting out on the complex wall climb of *Generation of Swine* (7b+) - *page 139* - at Pinfold. The classic Pinfold crack-line of *Atmospheres* (7a) is the diagonal line cutting through the overhangs to the left.

Pinfold — Atmospheres Area

1 Funky Monkey Pie .. 7c+
A desperate start, requiring a huge reach across the horizontal roof, gains a positive jug at the lip. Pull into the niche above and then continue up the bulging wall, following a vague crack-line.
FA. Gary Gibson 25.6.1994

2 Killer Gorilla ...... 7a+
The impressive overhanging crack-line is a good test of layback and finger-locking technique. **7c+** if the start is climbed free.
FA. John Moulding 1985

3 Planet Claire 7b
A superb alternative finish to *Atmospheres* with a brilliant 'spacewalking' finale. Finger-traverse left from *Atmospheres* to reach tiny holds at the bottom of a shallow groove. Pull up this and over the roof above to reach good holds and the lower-off.
FA. Gary Gibson 24.5.1992

4 Atmospheres 7a
One of the best routes in the valley incorporating sustained climbing in a wild position up a superb natural line. Stand in a long sling on the first bolt to reach a good hold beneath the large undercut flakes. Pull onto the rock and move rightwards to gain a good flake hold. Follow the spectacular line strenuously all the way to the lower-off. **7c+** if the start is climbed free.
FAA. Stuart Cathcart, Gerald Swindley 6.1979
FFA. John Codling, Andy Grondowski 28.7.1984

Atmospheres Area
The imposing bay of steep limestone is easily picked out from the road and has some outstanding llines. Most of the routes require some aid moves to get past the blank roof at the base of the wall.

5 Private Idaho 7c
An excellent technical wall climb. Aid up to the second bolt and start with your left finger in a mono and your right hand on a side-pull. Move up to good undercuts and climb the technical wall above using small crimps, undercuts and side-pulls, before moving rightwards to reach good holds and a rest in the niche. Tricky bridging out of this gains the lower-off.
FA. Gary Gibson 5.8.1992

Atmospheres Area **Pinfold** 139

6 Generation of Swine. 7b+
A good sustained wall climb with a sting in the tail. Aid up to the second bolt and start with your left hand in a shallow pocket just underneath the bolt, and your right hand on a side-pull. Move up using tiny crimps to reach better holds in the shallow groove. Climb up to the bulge and use undercuts to reach a series of energy-sapping layaway holds leading to a good small hold. Pull up on a rounded hold and then rock up to some tiny crimps. Finish rightwards through the small bulge to a lower-off.
Photo on page 136.
FA. John Moulding, John Codling, Ian Dring, M.Mitchell 4.6.1989

7 Brain Box 7b+
Pull up to a good hold at the lip of the roof using an undercut. Climb the short awkward lower wall to reach a good ledge beneath the upper bulge. Move up and follow a line of undercuts rightwards to better holds. Finish by moving up and then left to the *Generation of Swine* lower-off.
FA. Gary Gibson 18.5.1992

8 Aphrodizziness 7a
A worthwhile eliminate with some good climbing after the aided start (uses a bolt for aid to get going). Take care with a hollow shield midway.
FA. Gary Gibson 18.5.1994

9 Oxygen E3 6a
A fine route with a well-positioned finish. Use a bolt for aid to reach a good hold by a peg. Continue up the lower wall until it is possible to move left to the base of a fine finger-crack. Follow this to the top.
FA. John Moulding, John Codling, J.Lockett 29.4.1984

Pinfold — Mental Transition Area

Mental Transition Area

The major feature of this area is the barrel-shaped wall of immaculate rock. It is situated just before the path narrows and drops down to round the arete into the Atmospheres Bay.

1 Eddie Waring Lives On . . 6c+
A surprising little climb with some interesting moves. Pull through the lower bulge (with the help of a glued-on hold) to reach the bottom of a left-facing flake. Rock up onto the slabby wall above and climb this, swinging rightwards to the lower-off.
FA. Gary Gibson, P.Lockett, Gary Dickinson 29.7.1992

2 Demolition Man E4 6b
From the block ledge, pull over the bulge and move right into a shallow groove. Climb this, passing a thread, to the top.
FA. John Moulding, John Codling 17.3.1984

3 Mental Transition . . Top 50 E4 6b
The faultless central line of the wall. A difficult start, protected by two pegs, accesses superb wall climbing up the pocketed groove above, with a tricky move past the third peg. There is a lower-off at the top. Brilliant. *Photo opposite.*
FA. Stuart Cathcart, Phil Waters (1pt) 21.5.1981
FFA. John Codling, John Moulding 8.4.1984

4 Through the Grapevine . . 7b
The excellent powerful direct start to *What's Goin' On* requires strong fingers.
FA. Gary Gibson 2.6.1985

5 What's Goin' On 7a
Move left out of *Spastic Spider* around the arete onto the wall. Thin climbing up this leads to a high and well-hidden lower-off on the left.
FA. Gary Gibson, Fred Crook 5.4.1984

6 Mercy Mercy Me . . . . 6b+
The blunt arete above the start of *Spastic Spider*.
FA. Gary Gibson 24.9.2015

7 The Sinking, Shrinking, Shrimp E2 5c
An alternative finish to *Spastic Spider*. Traverse leftwards to the *Mental Transition* lower-off.
FA. Gary Gibson, Nick Dixon 16.2.1984

8 Spastic Spider E2 5c
A stiff pull through the lower bulge (thread) gains easier ground. Traverse right to a groove and climb this.
FA. Stuart Cathcart, Tom Curtis 22.4.1980

9 Spastic Spider Direct E2 6a
Climb direct to join and finish up *Spastic Spider*.
FA. Gary Gibson 18.2.1984

10 Shy of Coconuts 7a
Follow the technical narrow crack.
FA. Gary Gibson 24.4.1994

11 Candy 7b
A technical wall climb on small crimps with an easier finish through the upper bulge.
FA. Gary Gibson, Neville Barker 7.11.1993

12 Lickin' Lollipops . . . 7b
Very similar to *Candy* and slightly easier.
FA. Gary Gibson 18.5.1994

Lots of sun · 18 min · Windy

Descent →

16m

Rich White moving up to the pocketed groove on the immaculate rock of *Mental Transition* (E4 6b) - *opposite* - at Pinfold.

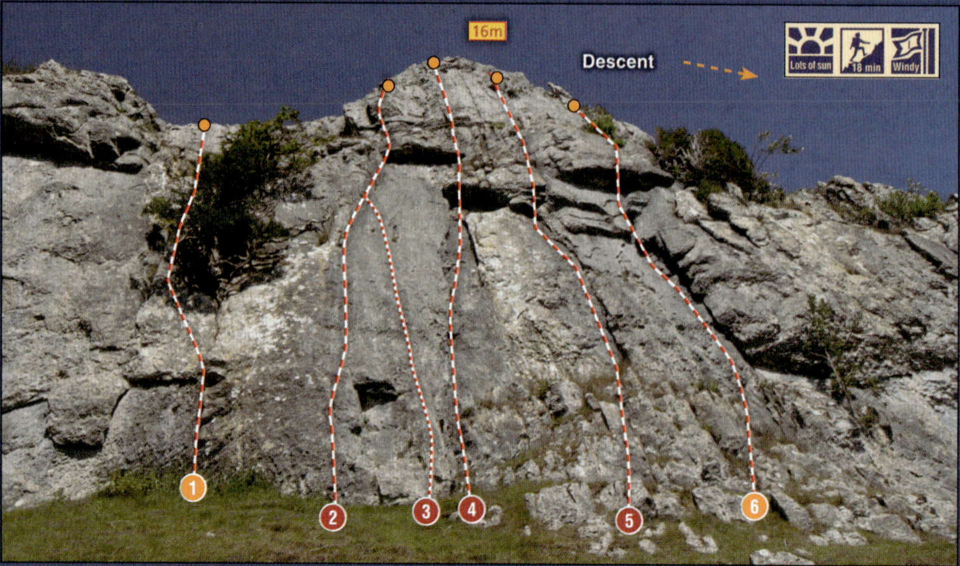

Pinfold — King of Fools Area

Descent

16m

King of Fools Area
The major feature of this area is the barrel-shaped wall of immaculate rock on the left. To its right is a tall roof-capped buttress of well-featured rock and a wall dominated by a large bulging overhang on its right.

1 Condessa .... HVS 5a
The hand-sized crack passing the large yew tree on its left.
FA. Stuart Cathcart 20.4.1980

2 Friction Factor E2 6a
Good climbing up the smooth grey wall, passing a peg.
FA. Fred Crook, Gary Gibson 5.4.1984

3 Fraction Fictor 7a
A super thin and technical exercise just right of *Friction Factor*.
FA. Gary Gibson 31.5.2013

4 Hard Fought E2 5b
The thin left-hand crack is a little vegetated but the climbing is worthwhile.
FA. Stuart Cathcart 20.4.1984

5 Last Fandango E1 5b
An enjoyable route following the thin finger-crack right of *Hard Fought*, with a steep finish up a layback flake.
FA. Stuart Cathcart 30.5.1980

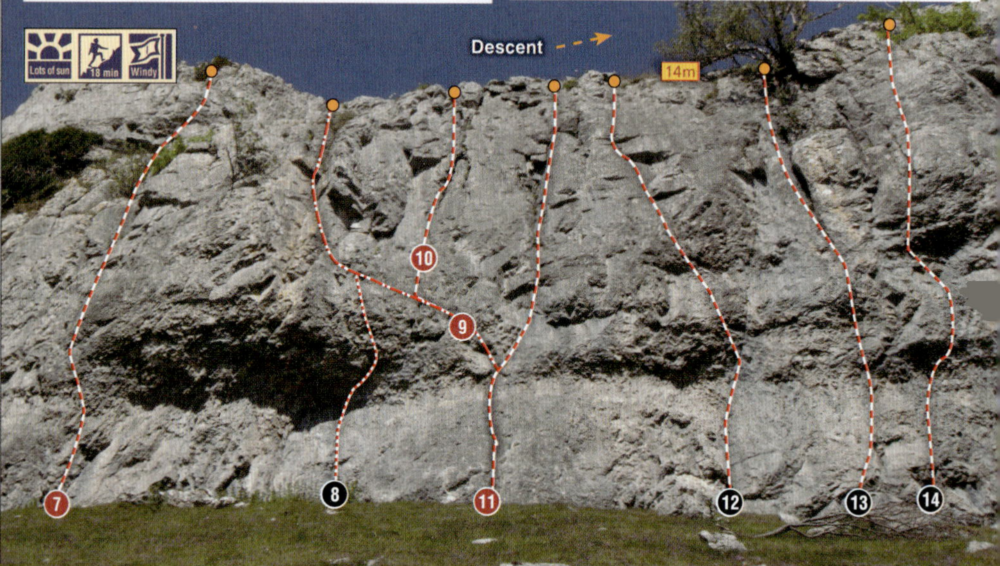

Descent

14m

King of Fools Area — Pinfold 143

6 Wafer Way .... VS 4c
A good route up the crack to a small roof which is climbed on the right, close to a large yew tree.
FA. Stuart Cathcart, Frank Bennett 17.5.1980

7 Shasavaan E1 5b
A poor route up the broken crack to a small tree.
FA. Stuart Cathcart 24.3.1980

8 Foolish Pride E4 6b
A powerful direct start to *King of Fools* past a bolt, on poor rock.
FA. Gary Gibson 8.5.1994

9 King of Fools E3 6a
Start up *Basket Case* and then traverse left above the bulge, before making an exciting pull around the sharp arete into the hanging yellow-flecked V-groove.
FA. Stuart Cathcart, John Dee 11.6.1979

10 Mainstay E3 6a
Start up *Basket Case* and pull up slightly leftwards to reach twin flake-cracks.
FA. Stuart Cathcart, John Dee 11.6.1979

11 Basket Case E3 6a
Climb direct up the V-groove in the grey wall. Care is needed with some loose blocks at the top of the groove.
FA. Stuart Cathcart, John Dee 18.6.1979.

12 Stress Test E4 6b
A powerful start up the bulging wall, past two pegs, reaches twin flakes above.
FA. John Codling 8.7.1985

13 The Soft Machine E5 6b
The steep thin crack is well protected by a peg and two threads. Lower off the whitebeam tree.
FA. John Moulding, John Codling, Paul Harrison 8.4.1984

14 Vicious Circles E5 6b
Boulder up to the first bolt and then make a difficult blind move rightwards to a second bolt. Pull up to a ledge and finish easily.
FA. Gary Gibson 10.10.1993

15 Ornamental Art Mark 2 .. E5 6b
A serious and poorly-protected start on loose rock. Above the bulging start it follows the groove and is both easier and safer.
FA. Gary Gibson 28.7.1992

16 Origami Today E4 6a
An eliminate direct to the crack in the rounded arete, after a slightly loose start protected by a bolt and thread.
FA. Gary Gibson 3.5.1992

17 Poison Letter E3 5c
A difficult start, that is hard to protect, gains good holds at the base of the shallow groove. Technical moves up this lead to a lower-off on the right.
FA. Stuart Cathcart, Malcolm Cameron 21.5.1979

18 Bagpus E5 6a
A strong test of nerves. Boldly bridge up the blue/grey groove to reach some wires at half height. Easier but still technical climbing above leads to the top and a lower-off on the left.
FA. Gary Gibson, Phil Locket 3.5.1992

19 Baron Greenback E6 6a
Boldly climb the smooth wall to reach a 'thank god' peg at half height, then finish direct. Lower-off on the left.
FA. Nick Dixon 16.2.1984

20 Storm Rider E3 5c
Follow thin cracks in the wall left of the large ash tree.
FA. Stuart Cathcart, Malcolm Cameron 18.5.1979

Pinfold — Dangermouse Area

Dangermouse Area
This good compact wall. On its right-hand side is a fine arete next to a larger roof that is home to a couple of interesting hard routes and one well-positioned easier pitch. The wall is situated just left of a large tree and broken section of crag.

1 Centre Line .... VS 4c
The groove right of the ash tree, passing a dubious block.
FA. Stuart Cathcart 15.6.1980

2 Trophy .... HS 4b
The square-cut groove.
FA. Stuart Cathcart 19.5.1979

3 Whispering Wall E2 5b
Good climbing up thin cracks and a vague scoop to a tree.
FA. Stuart Cathcart, Frank Bennett 17.5.1980

4 Dangermouse .. E5 6b
An absorbing route up the bold arete to a fixed wire at the left edge of the large roof. From the wire, pull strenuously into the vague groove above (thread and peg). Finish direct, moving right past a small overlap at the top.
FA. Stuart Cathcart, Dave Barker, Bryan Philips 1983

5 Baby Frogs with Dirty Little Lips E3 6a
Climb easily to a bolt underneath the right edge of the large roof. Pull around the roof to reach a flake-crack in the wall above and follow this passing a peg to the top.
FA. John Moulding, John Codling, Ian Dring, Mark Mitchell 4.6.1989

6 Just a Tad E1 5b
Climb directly up to and past the overlaps (peg) to gain the upper wall and a lower-off.
FA. Gary Gibson 8.6.2013

7 Obelisks Fly High .... HS 4a
An exciting climb for the grade. Follow the thin curving crack to a sloping ledge. Move left to a good foot-ledge on the yellow-flecked wall above the overhang. Follow the thin crack above moving left at the top to avoid some blocks.
FA. Stuart Cathcart 27.9.1980

8 Unmegaladon 6c
A short tricky exercise up the blunt arete.
FA. Gary Gibson 24.9.2015

9 Megalith .... HS 4a
Climb the thin vegetated groove to a small tree, taking care with the rock at the top.
FA. Stuart Cathcart 12.11.1979

Frigorific Area

A crack and flake-seamed buttress with a couple of worthwhile lines, but also some poor rock. The buttress is just left of the wide descent gully.

10 Transient .... HVS 5a
Climb up to a leftward-slanting ramp. Move right to an old thread and climb the short pocketed wall above.
FA. Stuart Cathcart, Mike Hughes 16.5.1981

11 Pugilist. .... HS 4a
Squirm up the wide chimney-crack taking care with the rock.

12 Scaremonger. .... HVS 4c
A hard start leads to a layback flake that is followed to a whitebeam tree near the top.
FA. Stuart Cathcart, Frank Bennett 12.7.1980

13 Lax .... M
Scramble up blocks and ledges to the top of the wall.

14 Auto-De-Fe .... S 4a
Climb to the tree and layback the flake above to the top.

15 Frigorific. E1 5b
The narrow groove is followed to a small overlap. Pass this on the right and follow good holds to the top.
FA. Stuart Cathcart, John Dee 18.4.1979

16 Centrefold .... HVS 5b
A technically-interesting climb up the centre of the buttress.
FA. Fred Crook, K.Crook 4.1984

17 Calefaction .... VS 4c
Start up the well-protected crack and groove to reach large undercuts at the base of the overlap. Step right and pull through the overlap on good holds then move left to easier ground.
FA. Stuart Cathcart, John Dee 18.4.1979

18 Exostosis .... HVS 5a
Start 1m left of the small cave and climb broken cracks to reach a layback flake at half-height. Follow this to the top.
FA. Stuart Cathcart 16.4.1979

19 Heloma Durum .... 6a+
Nice little wall of smooth rock.
FA. Gary Gibson 8.6.2013

20 Swell .... VS 4c
Climb the jamming crack above the small cave to a tree.

21 Blister .... HVS 4c
A poor route on poor rock. Start on top of a large block leaning against the wall. Climb rightwards to a scoop and finish direct.
FA. Stuart Cathcart 16.4.1979

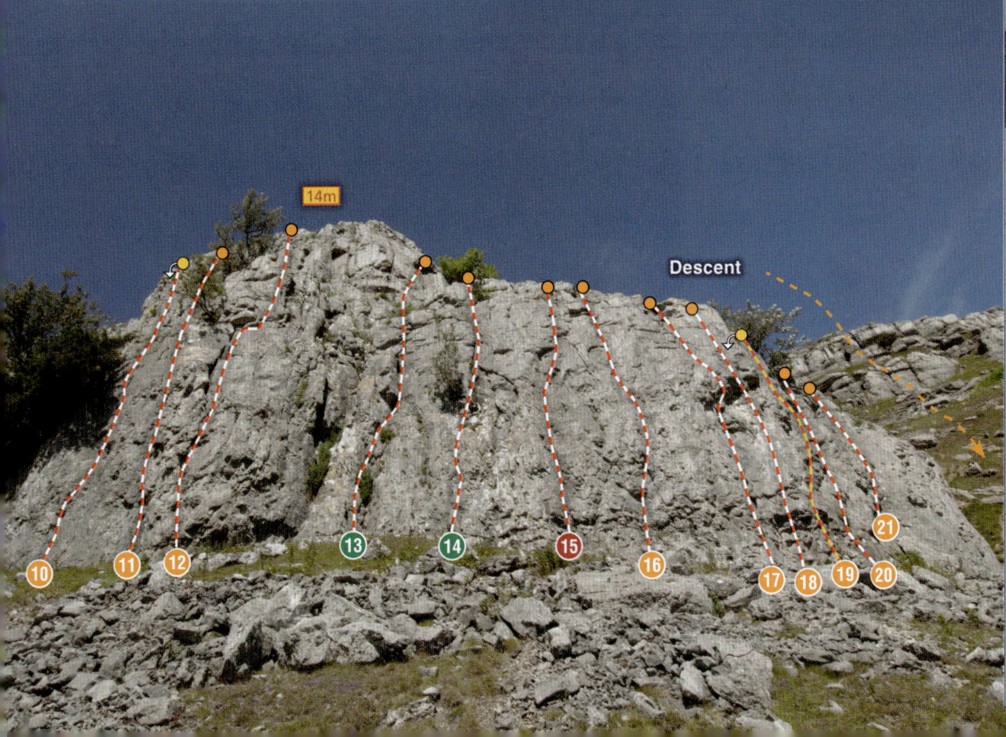

Pinfold — The Quick Tick Wall

The Quick Tick Wall

A long, low wall of excellent vertical rock above a steeply-sloping grass base. It has some short and tough pitches that should not be underestimated. Some of the belays are on the back wall of the upper crag. Descent from the bulk of the best routes is by abseil from a fixed bolt belay on the mid-way ledge.

1 Minnie Minor 6c
A short, technical wall with a bolt and a peg.
FA. Gary Gibson, Alec Williams 16.5.1992

2 Happy Slapper E4 6a
Climb the left-hand arete of the buttress.
FA. Ryan McConnell 4.7.2011

3 Sister Moon E3 5c
A short and worthwhile eliminate. Climb straight to a peg, move left and surmount the bulge. Move back right above to finish up a thin crack.
FA. John Randles, Sean Roberts 20.8.1997

4 Unknown Crack .... VS 4b
The wide crack in the short buttress.

5 Gilly Flower .... HVS 5b
The twin cracks passing a thread.
FA. K.Crook, Fred Crook 3.1984

6 Waffle and Crackers E2 5c
The crack to the left of *Toe Bitter*.
FA. Ryan McConnell 4.7.2011

7 Toe Bitter E2 5c
The bulging wall, passing a peg and some dubious flakes.
FA. Fred Crook, S.Smith 3.1984

8 Flied Lice E1 5b
The rounded corner leads to a short steep crack.
FA. John Codling 18.3.1984

9 Crypt Tick .... HVS 5a
The best easier route on the wall with good protection. Start up some juggy flakes then make a thin move up the smooth slab to big holds in the scoop above (thread).
FA. Barry Barrett, Andy Popp 18.3.1984

The Quick Tick Wall **Pinfold** 147

10 Pig Pen E3 6a
After a difficult start, climb direct to a small tree.
FA. Andy Popp, Nick Dixon, Barry Barrett 19.2.1984

11 Winterhill E3 5c
The best hard route on the wall has a difficult start to enter the rounded scoop and a technical finish up the thin rightwards-trending crack.
FA. Andy Popp, Nick Dixon, Barry Barrett 19.2.1984

12 Old Chipatti E3 6a
The razor-sharp flake in the centre of the wall is gained direct by a hard and bold start. Some of the undercuts at the start are a little wobbly.
FA. Nick Dixon, Andy Popp, Barry Barrett 19.2.1984

13 El Crapitan .... HVS 5a
Climb the short, steep layback flake to an easy finish.
FA. S.Lowe 18.3.1984

14 Pumpkin Seed E1 5b
A tricky start but the rest is easy.
FA. Fred Crook, K.Crook 18.3.1984

15 Lentil Man E1 5b
A good pitch with some blind wire placements.
FA. Fred Crook, K.Crook 18.3.1984

16 Fingerbobs .... HVS 5b
The technical lower wall is climbed, past an old thread, into a bubbly scoop.
FA. Andy Popp 19.2.1984

17 Celery Stick E1 5c
Start just left of the corner at a vague bubbly rib. Climb the rib to a shallow scoop, then move left to a flake-crack and follow this to the top.
FA. Nick Dixon 18.3.1984

18 Short Trip .... VS 5a
The short groove immediately left of the large yew tree leads to a compact wall and then a final battle through the upper branches of the yew tree to finish.
FA. Fred Crook, K.Crook 4.1984

Pinfold — Two Tier Area

Two Tier Area
This impressive buttress, the largest at Pinfold, is easily picked out on the walk up from the valley. It gives some good two-pitch routes split at mid height by a ledge. Care needed with loose rock on some of the routes.

1 Lay Me Back .... HS 4b
A short route up the layback crack in the right-facing corner and over the juggy overhang. Either continue up *Pinfold Right-hand*, or walk off leftwards with care.
FA. Stuart Cathcart 6.1980

2 Splitting Finger Crack... E2 5b
An easy first pitch gains the exposed second pitch which you will remember for quite some time.
1) 5a, 18m. Tackle the short, steep crack then move up easily to the crawl terrace. Traverse right along this, passing a narrow section, and belay just after this on small wires.
2) 5b, 12m. Move back left then make a challenging, balancy move up in a very exposed position, to reach a line of flaky holds in a shallow groove. This leads leftwards to the top.
FA. Stuart Cathcart, Tom Curtis 16.6.1979

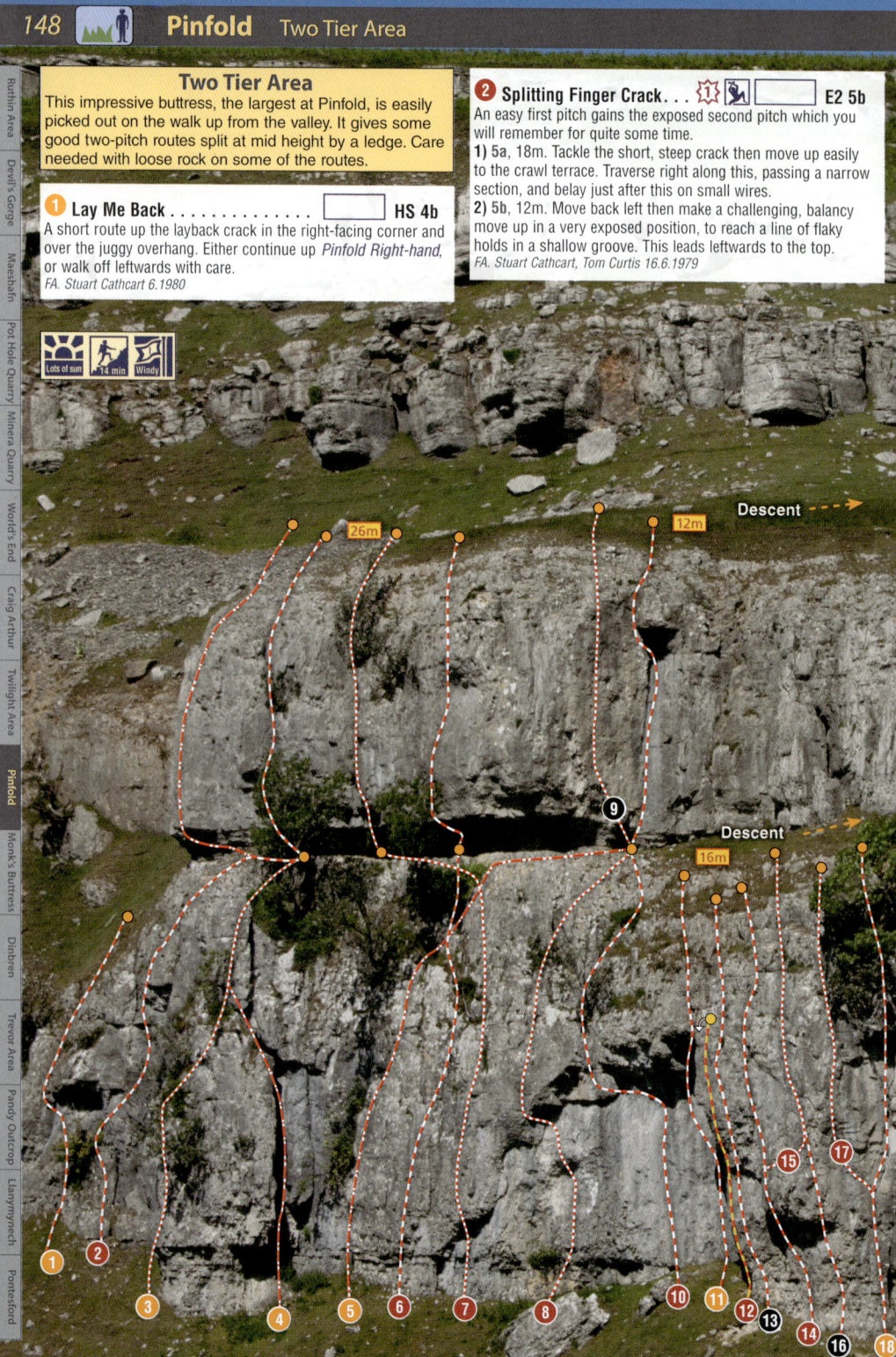

Two Tier Area — Pinfold

❸ Pinfold Left-hand .... VS 4b
An alternative left-hand start to *Pinfold Right-hand*.
1) 4b, 18m. Venture into the darkness of the large chimney crack and follow this to the *Pinfold Right-hand* belay.
2) 4b, 14m. Follow the second pitch of *Pinfold Right-hand*.
FA. H.J.Tinkler, John Hesketh 1962

❹ Pinfold Right-hand .... VS 4b
A good line which is unfortunately spoilt by some loose rock.
1) 4b, 18m. Either climb the deep chimney or, better, the layback crack to its right, to attain a standing position on top of the huge flake. Carefully move up, past a patch of ivy, to the crawl terrace. Shuffle left along this past an exposed narrow section, and under a low roof, to a poor belay on wires.
2) 4b, 14m. Stand up and climb the left-hand side of the rounded arete on slightly loose rock.

❺ Wooly Ramble .... VS 4c
An unappealing route spoilt by a large thorn bush. Climb the steep scoop beneath the bush then battle past it to reach a smooth grey wall. Climb this, passing over a small overhang, then scramble past the large tree above to the crawl terrace. Crawl right to escape. The route can be finished up the easier right-hand finish to the second pitch of *Progressions of Power* at a good **5a**.
FA. Stuart Cathcart 16.4.1981

❻ The Moving Finger E3 6a
The wall left of *Buster Bloodvessel* has some friable rock and is slightly vegetated. When clean it is a worthwhile route with a committing initial pitch and powerful second.
1) 5c, 16m. Start underneath a sharp right-facing flake at 2m. Bold moves from the top of the flake gain a good crack and wires. Move right, past a hidden thread, onto a sloping ledge. Continue up broken ground on the right, passing a second thread, to a tree belay just below the crawl terrace.
2) 6a, 12m. A hard pitch tackling the bulge and crack behind the tree belay after a difficult start on finger-locks.
FA. Adam Hudson, Gary Gibson 18.2.1984

❼ Buster Bloodvessel E3 6a
A good route with an intricate first pitch and butch second.
1) 6a. 16m. Start at the foot of the rightward-trending line of overhangs. Pull leftwards around the lower bulge to reach thin cracks and small wires. Continue up the technical shallow scoop to better holds and good gear. Move up past a dead yew tree and then left across broken ground to reach the crawl terrace. Scuttle leftwards along this for 5m and belay on high wires beneath a downward-pointing flake.
2) 5c. 12m. Pull onto the smooth wall, using the downward pointing flake, and layback up the wall with a stretchy move to reach a ledge and tree near the top.
FA. Stuart Cathcart 17.4.1980

❽ Red Flag Day E3 6a
A good technical pitch. Start at a white scoop next to a small thorn bush. Move left to a good flake hold and wires. Move up and right on large undercuts to beneath a square roof. Overcome this on its left-hand side and climb the wall above (thread) to easier ground. Move right to the belay of *Progressions of Power*.
FA. Gary Gibson, Adam Hudson 18.2.1984

❾ Thin White Line E5 6a
The compact white wall, marked by two threads, has a bold and committing start with an immediate sense of exposure. The climbing is superb, technical and pumpy.
FA. Gary Gibson, Adam Hudson 18.2.1984. Previously described as pitch 2 of Red Flag Day.

❿ Progressions of Power E3 5c
A nicely varied route with two good pitches: the first pitch is a little bold and warrants E3; the second involves well-protected technical bridging at E2 but probably has a harder move. The upper pitch can be done on its own by approaching along the mid-height terrace.
1) 5c, 18m. Climb the bold, slabby wall to the overhang. Traverse leftwards, using undercuts, to a slight rib beneath a crack (hidden peg on the left). Pull up into the crack and follow this to the terrace above. Belay at the bottom of the corner/groove. The crack can also be reached direct - **Scratting Hen Start**, at bold **E4 6a**.
2) 5c, 11m. Layback and bridge the immaculate groove to a small overhang and pull through this on its left-hand side to the top. The right-hand finish past the overhang is substantially easier at **HVS 5a** and worth doing on its own.
FA. Stuart Cathcart, Tom Curtis 22.8.1980

⓫ Gerald's Dilemma .... VS 4c
An excellent pitch requiring big gear. Follow the wide corner-crack to the roof and pull through this to finish up the right wall.
FA. Stuart Cathcart, Gerald Swindley 24.3.1974

⓬ Inglorious 6c
A good little route up the arete and crack in the right wall of *Gerald's Dilemma*.
FA. Gary Gibson 24.9.2015

⓭ Glorious Wobblegong E4 6b
Finger jam the thin crack to the bulge and power through this (bolt). Breeze up the wall above.
FA. Gary Gibson 26.5.1992

⓮ Overhanging Crack E1 5b
Excellent climbing up the wide crack.
FA. T.Williams, J.O'Niel 1969

⓯ Rock a Little E2 6a
Start up *Overhanging Crack* then move onto the right wall above the bulge. Climb the wall direct passing two pegs.
FA. Allen Price 4.1986

⓰ Pocket Rocket E4 6b
The direct start to *Rock a Little* is powerful and reachy.
FA. Gary Gibson 3.5.1992

⓱ G.M.B.H. E3 6a
Start up *E.C.V.* and move left onto the arete beneath a bolt. Difficult moves past this gain a crack and groove that is followed to the top.
FA. Gary Gibson, Gary Dickinson, Phil Lockett 3.5.1992

⓲ E.C.V. .... VS 4c
An excellent steep crack climb with an intimidating and wild finish through the upper overhangs. The name is painted on the rock at the start.

Pinfold — Solo in Soho Area

Solo In Soho Area
A great little wall with a host of neat pitches on mostly excellent rock. A good spot to clock up some mileage but take care not to knock scree off of the top of the crag onto those below. The crag is on the left at the top of the approach.

1 Eagle's Nest Crack .... HS 4b
One for the masochist. Scrabble up the wide crack, battle past the tree, then pull and squirm up the awkward chimney.
FA. John Hesketh, H.J. Tinkler 1962

2 Dead or Alive .... VS 4b
Climb the wall between the two trees to reach a large ledge, then follow the pocketed wall rightwards to the top.
FA. Stuart Cathcart 1.4.11980

3 Alive Not Dead .... VS 4c
Climb the groove beneath the large whitebeam tree to a ledge on the right. Continue up the wall above passing the stunted yew tree on the right.
FA. John Randles, Sean Roberts 8.5.1999

4 Neon Knights E2 5b
The slim and technical groove has an awkward start.
FA. Stuart Cathcart 7.4.1980

5 Phallic Tower .... HVS 5a
Climb the broken wall, moving right to a small pillar - the phallus. Carefully move left and up a short groove to the top.
FA. Stuart Cathcart 17.5.1980

6 Marnie .... HVS 4c
The superb hanging V-groove is gained from the left. The groove itself feels bold but there is just enough protection where needed and loads of holds.
FA. Stuart Cathcart, Gerald Swindley 3.9.1975

7 Life of Dubious Virtue ... E4 6b
A surprisingly independent pitch following the technical thin crack in the arete.
FA. Dylan Smith 28.7.1999

8 Y-Corner .... HVS 5a
The steep cracks are very good and harder than they look. Either branch is the same grade. *Photo on page 129.*

9 Too Many Women E2 5c
An eliminate up the wall left of *Vacances Verticales*.
FA. Alec Williams, Simon Williams 17.7.1992

10 Vacances Verticales E2 5c
An excellent wall climb with a hard move by the peg.
FA. Steve Boydon, Paul Harrison 13.3.1984

11 Darling Rose E3 6b
A fierce eliminate up a thin crack to a small overlap (bolt). Continue on tiny holds to reach good jugs and easier ground.
FA. Gary Gibson, Alec Williams 16.5.1992

Solo in Soho Area — Pinfold 151

⑫ Foot Loose and Fancy Free .. — **E1 5b**
A steep, strenuous pitch following the broken crack direct to the wide finishing groove of *Marander*.
FA. Stuart Cathcart 29.9.1980

⑬ Marander .... — **E1 5a**
A good climb. Start at a red 'W' and arrow painted on the rock. Pull up to a ledge then follow a leftwards trending line of ledges to reach a groove and the top.
FA. Stuart Cathcart, Gerald Swindley 26.3.1974

⑭ Russian Roulette .... — **E2 5b**
A route of differing halves. Climb the problematic wall direct to a whitebeam tree, or make a start from *Marander*. Pull into the wide groove above and follow this easily to the top.
FA. Stuart Cathcart 12.4.1980

⑮ Solo in Soho ...... — **E3 6a**
A stunning pitch which is the best E3 on the Pinfold escarpment. Delicately climb the shallow scoop (small wires and a good peg). Move up to an overlap, then reach leftwards into a thin crack and follow this to the top. It is possible to finish direct from the small overlap at the same grade.
FA. Stuart Cathcart (solo) 3.4.1980

⑯ Alchemy .... — **E3 6a**
The blunt arete feels less committing with a high side-runner in *Devil's Alternative*.
FA. Steve Boydon, Paul Harrison 15.3.1984

⑰ Devil's Alternative ..... — **HVS 5a**
Enjoyable climbing up the shallow scoop. Use double ropes to take advantage of all the gear placements.
FA. Stuart Cathcart 3.4.1980

⑱ Toccata............. — **VS 5a**
A fantastic pitch tackling the crack with testing moves to reach and pass a small protruding block.
FA. Stuart Cathcart, Gerald Swindley 24.3.1974

⑲ Play to Kill .... — **E2 5c**
An eliminate direct finish to *Banana Splits* over the bulge.
FA. Simon Williams, Alec Williams 17.7.1992

⑳ Banana Splits .... — **E3 6a**
A circuitous way up the wall with an airy finish. Climb *Toccata* to a small protruding block at 3m, then move right into a shallow scoop and briefly climb this before delicately foot traversing right to join the finish of *Shoot to Thrill*.
FA. Stuart Cathcart 1983

㉑ Shoot to Thrill .. — **E7 6b**
A bold route requiring precise footwork and strong fingers. Boulder into a shallow scoop and continue rightwards to a good side-pull. Move back left and make a committing move up to reach a good hold and a bolt. Pull straight up to some undercuts then move right into a short groove to finish.
FA. John Moulding 16.8.1987

㉒ Midnight Special .... — **HVS 5b**
The broken wall has a difficult start. The upper section is easy, but take care with the rock.
FA. Stuart Cathcart 3.4.1980

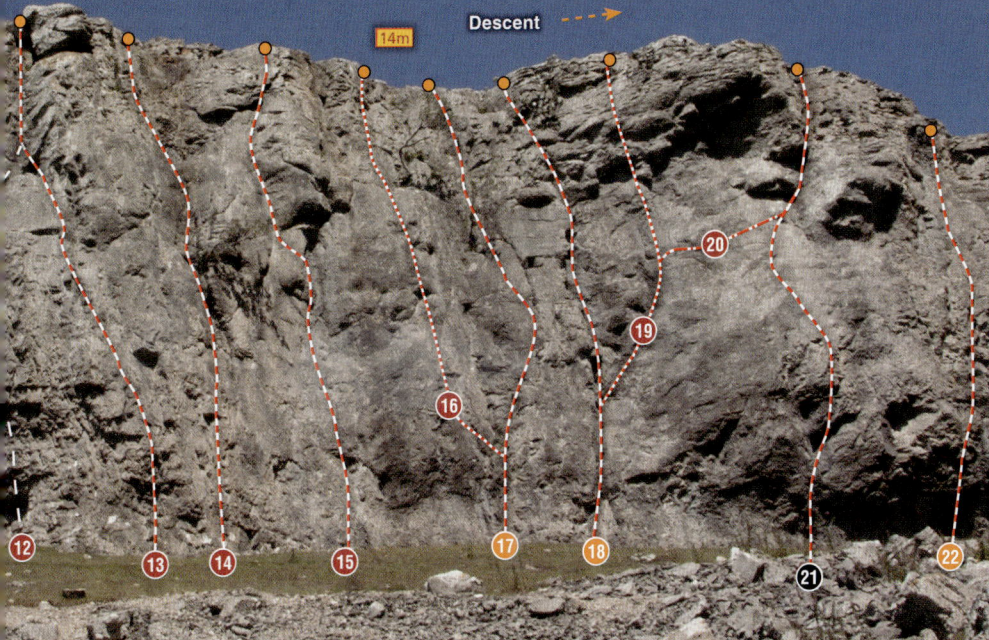

Pinfold — Monkshead Buttress

Monkshead Buttress

A squat but power-packed little buttress that has been re-equipped and gives mostly sport routes. The crag does not look much from the approach path but is well worth a look, as it is in the shade until late and dry in the summer. This area is immediately on the right at the top of the approach valley.

1 Hunky Monk 6c
The first line on the left takes the low bulge and wall above to a lower-off.
FA. Sarah Daniels 2005

2 The After Eights .... 7b+
Powerful moves through the left-hand side of the bulge lead to a thin finish.
FA. Gary Gibson 26.5.1992

3 People Give Me the Eyes 7c
The best route on this sector is a powerful and technical concoction that saves its hardest move for last. Move right at the top, past the tree, to the lower-off.
FA. Gary Gibson 18.5.1992

4 Yankee Doodle Dandy .... 7b+
Climb direct to the tree using undercuts and big biceps.
FA. Gary Gibson, Doug Kerr 8.9.1991

5 I Feel Like a Wog 7b
A short and powerful pitch that can feel a lot harder if you get the sequence wrong at the start.
FA. Gary Gibson 8.9.1991

6 Too Monk to Funk 7c
Hard pulling through the overlaps.
FA. Rob Mirfin 2005

Monkshead Buttress **Pinfold**

7 Yo yo yo yo E3 6a
Something a little easier. Boulder past a bolt to gain a flake and thread. Move past a peg to the top.
FA. Doug Kerr, Gary Gibson 8.9.1991

The next four routes are essentially sport routes but lack bolt protection on their easier upper sections.

8 Golly Gee .... 6b+
A good pitch with a difficult start. Climb the thin wall to reach good holds and a peg at 2/3 height before an easier finish. Lower-off above.
FA. Doug Kerr, Gary Gibson 1.9.1991

9 Golly Gosh .... 6b+
Slightly harder than *Golly Gee*. Climb easily to a good hold then move up to reach the base of a shallow groove. Pull up past a peg, then step left to the *Golly Gee* belay.
FA. Doug Kerr, Gary Gibson 1.9.1991

10 Indian Summer 6c
A difficult sequence up and leftwards around the arete, to finish at the *Golly Gee* lower-off.
FA. Gary Gibson, Doug Kerr 1.9.1991

11 Golly Wog 6c
Climb up using a series of small side-pulls, to reach a good hold around the bulge. A stiff pull past a peg gains easy ground and the lower-off.
FA. Gary Gibson, Doug Kerr 8.9.1991

12 Swiss Drum Roll E5 6b
The bulging featureless wall has no real protection. It has been bolted at **6c+** but bolts have gone missing.
FA. Gary Gibson 8.9.1991

Lee Proctor on *Life* (E1 5b) - *page 158* - one of a good number of trad lines at the little visited Monk's Buttress. The crack-line of another of the recommended pitches, *Jibber* (E1 5b), is to the right.

Monk's Buttress 155

	No star	☆	☆☆	☆☆☆
Mod to S	3	-	-	-
HS to HVS	13	2	-	-
E1 to E3	14	5	2	2
E4 and up	2	9	1	2

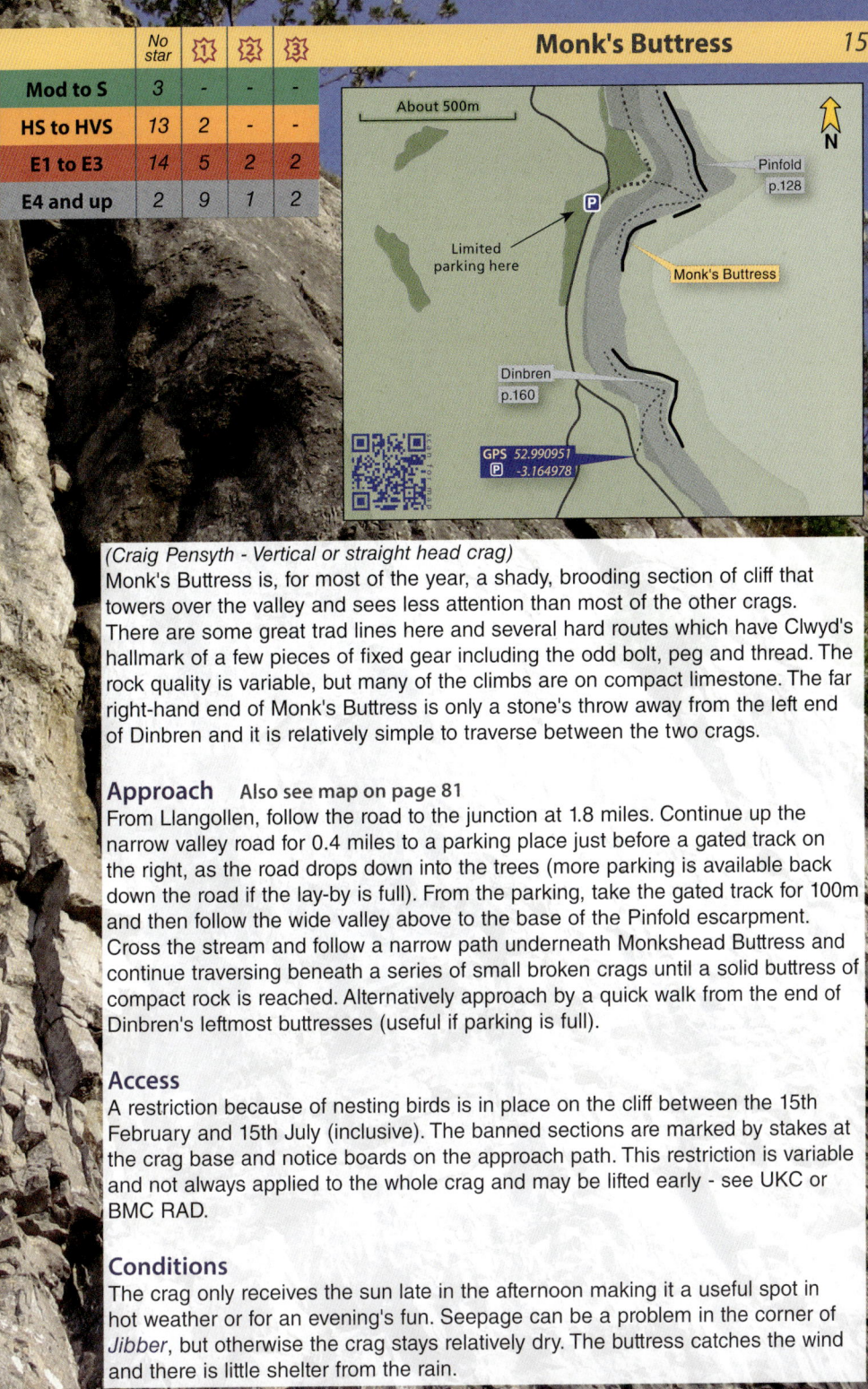

(Craig Pensyth - Vertical or straight head crag)
Monk's Buttress is, for most of the year, a shady, brooding section of cliff that towers over the valley and sees less attention than most of the other crags. There are some great trad lines here and several hard routes which have Clwyd's hallmark of a few pieces of fixed gear including the odd bolt, peg and thread. The rock quality is variable, but many of the climbs are on compact limestone. The far right-hand end of Monk's Buttress is only a stone's throw away from the left end of Dinbren and it is relatively simple to traverse between the two crags.

Approach   Also see map on page 81
From Llangollen, follow the road to the junction at 1.8 miles. Continue up the narrow valley road for 0.4 miles to a parking place just before a gated track on the right, as the road drops down into the trees (more parking is available back down the road if the lay-by is full). From the parking, take the gated track for 100m and then follow the wide valley above to the base of the Pinfold escarpment. Cross the stream and follow a narrow path underneath Monkshead Buttress and continue traversing beneath a series of small broken crags until a solid buttress of compact rock is reached. Alternatively approach by a quick walk from the end of Dinbren's leftmost buttresses (useful if parking is full).

Access
A restriction because of nesting birds is in place on the cliff between the 15th February and 15th July (inclusive). The banned sections are marked by stakes at the crag base and notice boards on the approach path. This restriction is variable and not always applied to the whole crag and may be lifted early - see UKC or BMC RAD.

Conditions
The crag only receives the sun late in the afternoon making it a useful spot in hot weather or for an evening's fun. Seepage can be a problem in the corner of *Jibber*, but otherwise the crag stays relatively dry. The buttress catches the wind and there is little shelter from the rain.

Monk's Buttress — Sir Cathcart Area

Sir Cathcart Area

The Sir Cathcart Area is a fine section of the crag that possess some very good climbs on superb rock. The central trio around *Sir Cathcart D'Eath* are well worth a look. The routes on the left have old fixed gear.

Access - No climbing from 15th Feb to 15th July between markers because of nesting birds. This is a variable restriction - see page 155.

1 Black Moments E4 6b
A short pitch on perfect rock. Climb past a thread to a bolt. A long stretch past the bolt gains the top and a tree lower-off.
FA. Gary Gibson, Hazel Gibson 4.5.1992

2 Mainly for Pleasure E2 5b
Climb up to the thread on *Black Moments*, then continue rightwards up the steep slab before moving back left to the tree.
FA. Stuart Cathcart 26.6.1980

3 The Rebel .... VS 4c
Follow the steep flake-crack, which is a little hollow in places.
FA. Stuart Cathcart 29.6.1980

4 Sombre Music E5 6b
Tough climbing up the steep and friable wall reaches an old ring peg beneath the overlap. Pull around this to a bolt and continue on a similar line to the top.
FA. Gary Gibson 15.5.1992

5 Second Chance E1 5b
A steep and sustained exercise up the hand-sized crack.
FA. Stuart Cathcart, Mike Hughes 1.6.1978

6 Suspended Animation E1 5b
An eliminate which is just right of *Second Chance*. Climb the dubious-looking flake system, passing a tiny sapling at half height.
FA. Doug Kerr, S.Wilkie 9.9.1985

7 Grand Laddie .... VD
Squirm up the curving chimney.

8 Amocco Cadiz .... HVS 4c
The tottering groove.
FA. Stuart Cathcart, Malcolm Cameron 17.3.1981

9 Only a Gesture E1 5a
The open groove is a lot more solid than its neighbour but still requires care. Avoid the temptation of escaping left too early.
FA. Stuart Cathcart, Frank Bennett 28.5.1980

10 Topology .... VD
The wide gully has immaculate rock on its right flank but poorer rock on its left.

11 Cotteril's Found Another Toe
.... E5 6c
Technical climbing on excellent compact rock. Move up to a peg and bolt, then make a long stretch to the base of a flake-crack and second peg. Finish easily up the flake to a lower-off.
FA. Gary Gibson 15.5.1988

12 Façade E2 5b
From the small cave, make a committing move left into a slim hanging groove that soon leads to easier ground.
FA. Stuart Cathcart, Malcolm Cameron 25.4.1980

13 Pierrepoint Pressure ... 7b+
A powerful sequence gains the hanging scoop. Follow this rightwards to a good foot-ledge, then tackle the rounded rib exiting left at the top.
FA. Gary Gibson 15.5.1992

14 The Hype .... HVS 5a
Start immediately right of a large ash and yew trees beneath a thin crack.
1) 5a, 24m. Climb the thin crack to a grassy niche, then step right onto a rib and climb to the bottom of a steep crack which leads to the terrace and belay.
2) 5a, 15m. Move right for 5m then pull around a blocky overhang to finish up a short groove.
FA. Stuart Cathcart, Gerald Swindley 16.8.1977

Sir Cathcart Area — Monk's Buttress

15 Beryl .... **VS 4c**
1) 4b, 22m. Zig-zag up the wide crack to the terrace and belay below a short steep corner.
2) 4c, 10m. Tackle the corner to the top.
FA. T.Williams, J.O'Niel 1969

16 Tamsin **E3 6a**
Good but slighty fluttery climbing. Enter the smooth yellow-flecked groove from the left (peg), and move right with difficulty to a jug. Climb up to a large ear-shaped flake, then continue up easier ground, stepping right to a lower-off beneath the bushy cornice.
FA. Doug Kerr, Paul Evans 2.2.1985

17 The Race is On **E3 6a**
Start right of *Tamsin* underneath the left edge of an overlap. Pull past a faded thread to reach a steep flake-crack and follow this (thread) to join the finish of *Tamsin*.
FA. John Moulding 10.2.1984

18 Catch Me if You Can. **E5 6a**
Start below a thin crack sprouting from an overlap at 3m. Pull into the crack and climb it to a junction with *Sir Cathcart D'Eath* (hard to place nuts in lower overlap). Move left with difficulty and climb direct to the lower-off.
FA. Gary Gibson, Doug Kerr 18.1.1992

19 Sir Cathcart D'Eath.. .... **E3 6a**
One of the better lines in the valley. Follow the steep leftwards-trending flake/crack, past a thread and peg, to jugs. Launch up the groove which soon eases until a traverse left can be made to good small wires in a curving overlap. Climb to the lower-off past a small knobbly ledge and flake above.
FA. Stuart Cathcart, John Dee 4.5.1981

20 Screaming Lord Sutch **E5 6a**
An excellent pitch that combines the best bits of the neighbouring routes. Climb *Sir Cathcart* to a jug, then pull up and right, past a bolt in the steep wall, to join *Another Red Line*.
FA. Gary Gibson 20.4.1992

21 Another Red Line... .... **E4 6a**
Superb technical climbing. Move up the wall, (threads) to a good ledge. Climb up onto the left arete (thread) and pull around it into a steep groove that leads to the top past a peg and thread.
FA. Gary Gibson 11.2.1984

22 Vladimir and Olga **E3 5c**
Climb the shallow groove and thin crack just right of *Another Red Line*, clipping a common thread with that route, to reach a ledge. Continue past an overlap and climb direct to a tree.
FA. Gary Gibson, Adam Hudson 12.2.1984

23 Iceburn........... .... **E5 6a**
Start by a small sapling. Climb boldly leftwards to reach a pinch on the rounded arete which is used to gain entry into the steep groove (peg). Move up to a blank-looking bulge and overcome this to reach an easier groove leading to a tree.
FA. Gary Gibson 25.2.1984

24 Up the Veil **E4 6b**
Powerful climbing past two old bolts gains a large vegetated flake. Climb this, past a dead yew tree, and up an easy groove.
FA. Gary Gibson 20.4.92

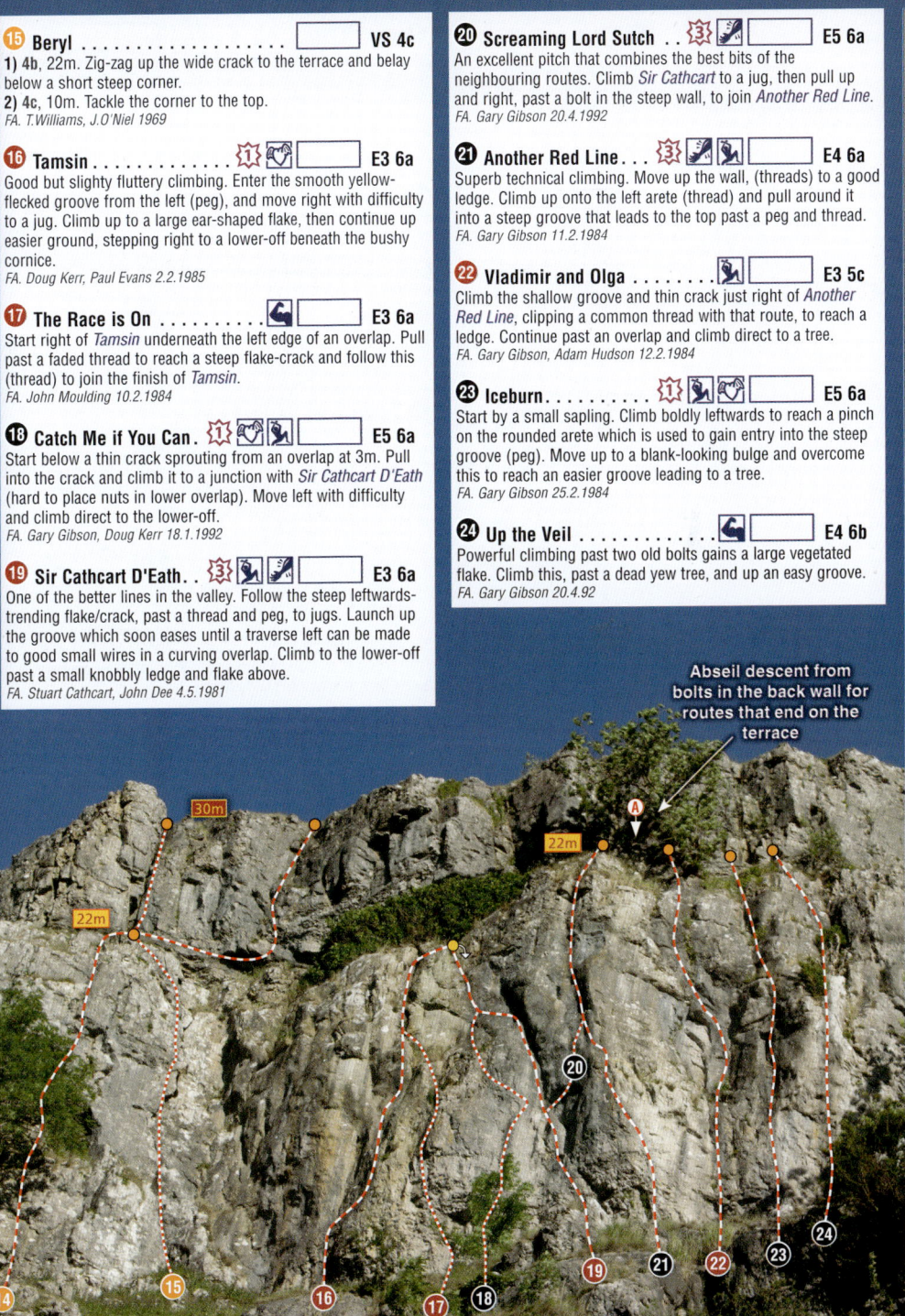

Monk's Buttress — Jibber Area

Jibber Area

The central section of the crag is dominated by the large, left-facing corner of the brilliant trad crack experience *Jibber*. To the right is a less impressive tree-covered wall.

Access - No climbing from 15th Feb to 15th July between markers because of nesting birds. This is a variable restriction - see page 155.

1 The Mantilla E3 5c
Climb a steep crack to a ledge, then step left into a corner. Climb this, then move right over a bulge to the terrace.
FA. Stuart Cathcart, John Dee 14.8.1981

2 Adam's Mistake E3 5c
Climb direct to the whitebeam tree then continue up a thin crack in the grey wall behind the tree (thread) to the terrace.
FA. Gary Gibson 3.4.1984

3 Post Mortem of a Football Team
.... E3 6a
An alternative finish to *Adam's Mistake*. Move right onto the grey wall (bolt) then climb direct over a bulge to the terrace.
FA. Gary Gibson 3.4.1984

4 Kinsman .... HS 4a
1) 4a. 24m. Climb the vegetated groove to the terrace ledge then walk left along this to a tree belay where the overhangs end.
2) 10m. Climb the broken groove containing a yew tree.

5 Cat in a Rat Trap E3 6a
A good varied route. Climb past a thread to reach the traverse break of *The Evader*. Move right to a block overhang and pull around this to tackle the steep snaking crack leading to a tree.
FA. Gary Gibson 25.2.1984. Alternative start added 5.1992

6 The Evader .... VS 4c
Climb the corner (peg) to the block overhang and traverse leftwards along the break to twin vertical cracks beneath a bulge. Pull through the bulge and finish up the open groove.
FA. Stuart Cathcart, Frank Bennett 28.5.1980

7 Life E1 5b
Good technical climbing but high in the grade. Follow *Evader* to the block overhang, then pull over to a good ledge as for *Cat in a Rat Trap*. Move rightwards across the yellow wall to gain a high groove that is followed to a yew tree on the terrace.
Photo on page 154.
FA. Stuart Cathcart, Mike Hughes 18.9.1979

8 Edgeley E5 6b
Excellent climbing, with an exposed and technical finish. Climb the slim white buttress to gain the base of the arete beneath a bulge. Continue steeply up the arete (peg and bolt).
FA. Gary Gibson 20.4.1992

9 Jibber E1 5b
Superb, well protected climbing up the steep corner-crack. There is a lower-off on the right.
FA. Stuart Cathcart 13.4.1980

10 Breaking the Reality Effect
.... E3 6a
A technical pitch based on the slabby arete. The bottom 3m has the odd loose hold but the rock higher up is perfect. There is a jammed wire, thread, peg and a lower-off.
FA. Gary Gibson 11.2.1984

11 Ginger Crack .... HVS 5a
The steep crack is loose, vegetated and not recommended.
FA. Stuart Cathcart 3.4.1980

12 Malevolence .... HVS 5a
The crack and broken wall leading to the whitebeam tree are better than appearances suggest.
FA. Stuart Cathcart 4.4.1980

For routes that end on the terrace abseil off

The Forgotten Buttresses — Monk's Buttress

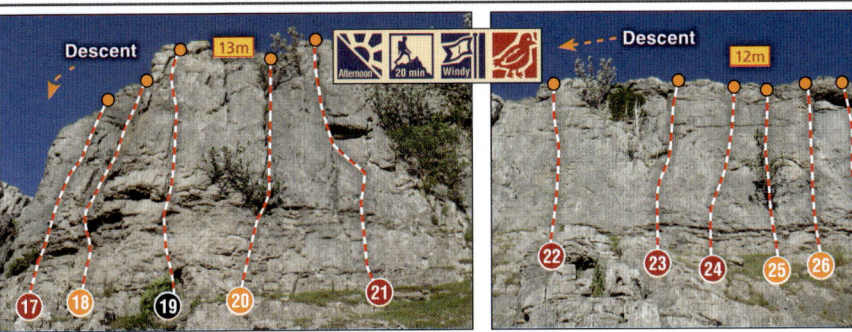

13 Madonna Kebab E1 5a
The short wall past a thread to grassy ledges and a thin crack.
FA. S.Whalley, L.Taylor 1984

14 Smooth Hands .... S 4a
The wide slabby crack above the tree. Big gear needed.
FA. Stuart Cathcart, Malcolm Cameron 25.4.1980

15 Desperado E5 6a
A short, challenging pitch on immaculate water-worn limestone.
FA. Stuart Cathcart 8.4.1980 (solo)

16 Little Deal .... HS 4b
The groove right of *Desperado* has some loose holds.

The Forgotten Buttresses

Right of the Jibber Area are a couple of short sections of the crag with a number of rarely climbed routes on them.

Access - No climbing from 15th Feb to 15th July between markers because of nesting birds. This is a variable restriction - see page 155.

17 Cloven Hoof E1 5b
The disjointed groove system with a low peg.
FA. Stuart Cathcart 15.5.1981

18 Codify .... VS 4c
The yellow-flecked, square-cut groove is loose.
FA. Stuart Cathcart 15.5.1981

19 Memorable Stains .. E5 6b
The steep finger-crack in the bulging white wall past a thread.
FA. Gary Gibson 15.5.1992

20 Gigolo .... HVS 5b
Pass the lower tree and climb the technical crack and wall.
FA. Stuart Cathcart, John Dee 17.4.1981

21 Thick as a Brick E2 5c
Climb the overlap and energy-sapping rounded crack.
FA. Stuart Cathcart, John Dee 17.4.1981

22 As Monk as a Skunk E1 5b
Climb directly up the compact wall passing a horizontal break.
FA. Ian Dunn 31.8.1987

23 Lightly Salted E1 5a
The left-hand side of the wall right of the tree.
FA. Gary Gibson 27.3.2012

24 Coal not Dole E1 5b
Climb up the wall to pass a small overlap (thread) and break.
FA. Simon Cardy, Mike Snell 1984

25 Soft Delight .... HVS 5a
The wall passing a slight bulge.
FA. Gary Gibson 27.3.2012

26 Just a Sprinkling .... HVS 5a
The crack.
FA. Gary Gibson 27.3.2012

27 Hard Crust E5 6a
The centre of the excellent blank face.
FA. Gary Gibson 27.3.2012

28 Dusting Over E1 5a
The crack to a break in the upper overhang.
FA. Gary Gibson 27.3.2012

29 Dig Deep .... HVS 5a
The right-hand of two cracks, finishing over a small overlap.
FA. Paul Harrison, Simon Cardy 1984

30 Depth Charge .... VS 4c
The crack on the far right of the wall.
FA. Gary Gibson 27.3.2012

A few hundred metres right of, and below, the main crag is -

31 A Touch of Spice E4 6a
Good moves and rock. Climb the centre of a square wall to a hidden pocket. Micro-wires protect the crux in its upper reaches.
FA. Ryan McConnell 18.6.2013

Dinbren

	No star	☆	☆☆	☆☆☆
Mod to S / 4+	8	2	-	-
HS-HVS / 5-6a+	30	4	1	-
E1-E3 / 6b-7a	34	36	7	4
E4 / 7a+ and up	15	20	23	16

Dinbren is Clwyd's premier sport crag and presents a long unbroken escarpment of limestone looking out over Castell Dinas Bran, Llangollen and the distant Berwyn Mountains. Dinbren has been a popular venue with both visitors and locals alike since the late 1970s, and today has become a well-known destination with an equal split of sport and trad lines spread out on its left and right wings. The main draw at Dinbren is its high density of sport routes, most of which are endurance in style and although not very long, are of a high level of intensity and quality. Most of the sport routes are in the 6b to 8b+ grade range and well equipped. Although less popular, the trad routes at Dinbren should not be overlooked by those searching for some superb challenges on generally excellent rock, the very best being in the low to mid E grades. The rock on the whole is excellent grey water-worn limestone which is well featured with cracks, flakes, overlaps and rounded horizontal breaks. The crag environment is exceptional, offering sunny climbing and magnificent panoramic views.

Approach   Also see map on page 81

From Llangollen, follow the road to the junction at 1.8 miles and turn sharp right. Dinbren is on the left. Follow the road for 200m to parking on the left. Take a rising path leftwards to gain a wide scree gully and walk up it to the base of the crag at the divide between the left and right wings. Each wing is easily accessed from here.

Dinbren 161

Conditions

Dinbren is very exposed to the wind and during strong westerlies this is not the place to head for. However, in light rain it's possible to climb on the steep areas of the crag. Seepage does occur after prolonged rainfall but it is not persistent and dries after a couple of days. In summer, temperatures can be very high but shade can be found on the Right Wing in the morning. Cold, still and clear days in winter can be surprisingly pleasant.

GPS 52.990951 -3.164978

About 500m

- Pinfold p.128
- Monk's Buttress p.154
- Dinbren

- Dynah Moe Hum Area p.182
- Harmony Area p.184
- Descent Area / Descent p.188
- Combat Zone Area p.190
- Hydrogen Area p.192
- Buccinator Area p.194
- Right Wing - Lower Tier p.195

Dinbren Left Wing - Lower Crag

Left Wing - Lower Crag
This short tier of rock is situated below the main level of the cliff. The rock is generally of good quality and there are a few reasonable routes that are worth seeking out.

Approach - It can be reached from below the route *Hell Hole* on the Back in Black Area by walking left (facing the crag) for 50m to locate a descent line.

The first four micro-routes on the Lower Crag are on a very short buttress of clean rock just left of the main section.

1 Tuber . . . . HVS 5a
The vague groove at the left edge of the buttress.
FA. John Randles, Sean Roberts 29.5.1998

2 Solar Power E1 5b
Delicate climbing up the centre of the short wall.
FA. John Randles, Sean Roberts 29.5.1998

3 Battery Power . . . . HS 4a
The right-hand line of weakness up the wall.
FA. John Randles, Sean Roberts 29.5.1998

4 Ash Crack . . . . HS 4a
Climb the crack to the ash tree, exiting on the right.
FA. John Randles, Sean Roberts 29.5.1998

5 Paper Smile . . . . HVS 5a
Delicate climbing up the slim groove above an awkward start.
FA. Doug Kerr 30.8.1985

6 The Thin Wall E3 6a
The best route on the Lower Crag is fierce, technical and good value for a route of this length. Climb up the centre of the wall, passing a peg and a rotten stuck wire.
FA. Doug Kerr, L.Clarke 30.8.1985

7 Magenta Sunrise E4 6a
A harder and more technical version of *The Thin Wall*, passing a purple bolt.
FA. Gary Gibson 27.6.1993

8 Goblin Girls . . . . HVS 5a
Excellent climbing up the hanging groove and crack.
FA. Paul Harrison, Simon Cardy 27.10.1984

9 Laughing Gnome . . . . VS 4b
Climb the slabby groove to reach a thin crack. Follow this finishing just to the left of the ivy.
FA. John Randles, Sean Roberts 29.5.1998

Lots of sun | 10 min | Windy

Left Wing - Lower Crag — Dinbren 163

10 Yew Tree Wall .... VS 4c
Climb to a yew tree, then move right beneath the branches, finishing up the wall on good holds.
FA. John Randles, Sean Roberts 29.5.1998

11 Rock Thief .... VS 5a
Hand traverse leftwards under the large overhang then, make a difficult move to reach a crack-line that is followed to the top, passing some loose holds.
FA. John Randles, Sean Roberts 29.5.1998

The next routes are around 15m to the right.

12 Tangram E1 5b
A good route with a tricky start up a blunt arete. Start at the foot of the buttress and climb diagonally left across the white wall, moving back right at half height where the arete narrows.
FA. Paul Harrison 6.4.1984

13 May Day .... HS 4b
Climb the open groove exiting to the right.
FA. John Randles 29.5.1998

14 Willy Waits for No Man ..... HVS 5a
Good climbing up the slabby wall finishing over a slight bulge on good pockets.
FA. C.Silverstone, P.Wilson 7.1991

15 Stein Line .... VS 4c
Steady climbing up the crack in the centre of the wall.
FA. C.Silverstone, P.Wilson 7.1991

16 Pulling up the Daisies E3 6a
A hard start to a ledge. Finish direct up the wall.
FA. C.Silverstone, P.Wilson 19.6.1992

17 Birds Cry .... VS 4b
A steep pitch up the corner and crack above the right-hand end of the undercut base, to reach a large ash tree. Pull past this, and a dead yew tree, to reach the top.
FA. John Randles 29.5.1998

18 Fanny Magnet E1 5a
Climb directly up the arete of the buttress, right of the detached pillar.
FA. P.Whalley, C.Silverstone 19.6.1992

19 Shepherd's Delight .... VS 4c
Climb the crack in the slabby groove, passing over a slight bulge, to reach and finish up a thin crack in the smooth wall.
FA. John Randles, Mark Hill 19.6.1998

To the right of Shepherd's Delight there are a number of small buttresses nestling under the main crag. Scattered amongst these craglets are nine short climbs of variable quality ranging from Severe to HVS - see UKC Logbook database for details.

Dinbren — Back in Black Area

Back In Black Area

A fine, quiet section of the crag with some great sport routes and a few trad lines. The left-hand side consists of a superb wall with some enticing small roofs, grooves and scoops. To the right, a huge low-level ivy-clad roof is the dominating feature. This end of the crag can pick up a breeze which is a bonus in warm weather.

Descent - Most of the sport lines have lower-offs. For those routes that top-out, walk right (looking out) to where the cliff fades and drop down to the cliff base.

1 Hell Hole .... M
At the far left of the crag is a small hidden 'hole'. Squirm up this and then either return to the path or continue up *Hell's Chimney*.

2 Hello Arete .... HVS 4c
The left arete of *Hell's Chimney* has a loose start.
FA. Stuart Cathcart (solo) 12.5.1980

3 Hell's Own Variation .... VD
Climb halfway up *Hell's Chimney* then move onto the left wall to finish.

4 Hell's Chimney .... Diff
The wide chimney, with the leaning block in it, is a surprisingly popular venture for beginners.

5 Tongue Pie .... HVS 4c
An interesting little route. Start inside *Hell's Chimney*, then traverse right above the lip of the overhang to reach a thin crack near the arete. Finish up this.
FA. Paul Harrison 25.3.1984

The quality and difficulty level rises spectacularly on this next section.

6 The Sound and the Fury 8b
An impressive climb featuring some intensely powerful moves through the bulges leading to a crux snatch right for a poor side-pull. The bolts are very hard to clip.
FA. Sam Cattell 29.8.2012

7 It's Yours .... 7b+
A route of contrasting halves. Power through the bulge on undercuts, then avoid the temptation to step into *Punishment of Luxury*. Instead pull up on tiny crimps and a painful pocket to good jugs. Tenuous climbing leftwards, requiring precise footwork, leads to the lower-off.
FA. Gary Gibson 27.6.1993

8 Punishment of Luxury E4 6b
Butch cranking up the thread-decorated pocketed crack soon eases. Can be taken direct or by moving in from the left.
FA. Stuart Cathcart, Phil Waters 14.8.1984. FA. (Direct) Steve Boydon.

9 Elite Syncopations 8a
A fine direct line up the buttress. Move up out of the alcove with difficulty and continue without much respite to join *Back in Black* at its good hold. Finish up *Back in Black*.
FA. Rob Mirfin 13.9.2003

10 Elite Deviation . . 2 8a
The link joining the powerful crux of *Elite Syncopations* into the technical crux of *Bolt from the Blue*. The sport grade assumes that the wires are in place on *Bolt from the Blue*.
FA. Dave Ayton 6.7.2010

11 Back in Black . . . . . 3 7b+
A brilliant line featuring sustained and strenuous manoeuvres on excellent rock. Move up to a juggy rail and then left up the curving line of flakes to a good hold and semi-rest. Powerful moves up the headwall gain a distant undercut, from where one final hard pull reaches better holds that lead slightly left to finish. *Photo on page 80.*
FA. John Moulding 27.7.1989

12 Bolt from the Blue . . 2 E6 6c
A good way up the wall with a technical crux sequence. A few wires are needed but they are easy to place. It is **7b+** as a sport route with the wires in place. Follow *Back in Black* to its good hold. Hard moves up and right are rewarded with better holds beneath an overhang and good gear. Final tricky moves out left through the overhang gain the top.
FA. John Moulding, John Codling 1.4.1984

13 Line of Fire . . . . 1 6c+
Climb up to huge holds above the C-shaped flake. Move up to some flakes and make a long hard reach rightwards to enter the hanging groove, which is followed through the roof to the top.
FA. Steve Allen 30.11.1983

14 Train to Hell . . . . . . 2 7c+
A good and challenging route with interesting and contrasting climbing. Climb up through the lower bulge to a good hold. Move up with difficulty and balance leftwards to reach undercuts beneath the hanging flake. Pull up to the flake and follow it easily to a final airy pull through the capping roof.
FA. John Moulding, Simon Cardy 7.4.1987. FFA. Rob Mirfin 9.2005

15 Statement of Ewes
. . . . 2 7c+
A good link-up that takes in the best climbing on this section of the crag. Climb *Train to Hell* to the good hold over the lower bulge, then pull up with difficulty and undercut furiously rightwards to join and finish up *Cured*.
FA. Rob Mirfin 15.5.2005

16 Cured . . . . 1 7b+
Climb up to the undercut flake from the right, then move left to small crimps and make a BIG move for a distant edge. Pull into the vague groove and climb the problematic wall above, through the capping bulge to a lower-off.
FA. Gary Gibson 21.5.1988

Lots of sun | 8 min | Windy

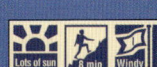

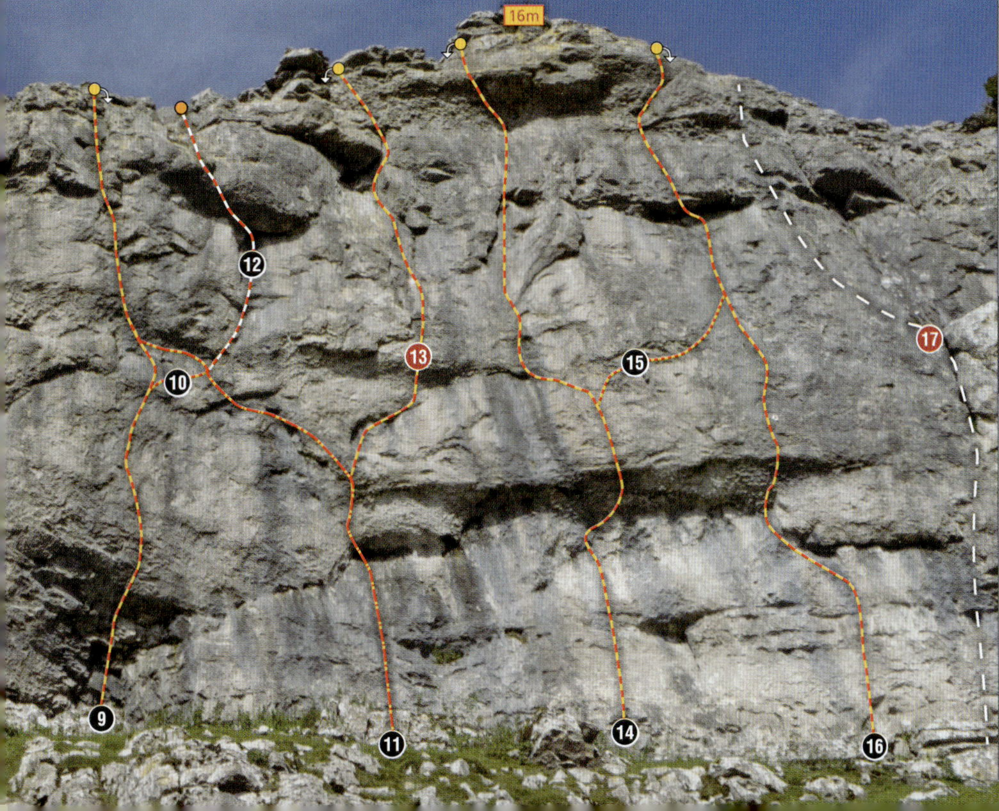

Ruthin Area
Devil's Gorge
Maeshafn
Pot Hole Quarry
Minera Quarry
World's End
Craig Arthur
Twilight Area
Pinfold
Monk's Buttress
Dinbren
Trevor Area
Pandy Outcrop
Llanymynech
Pontesford

Dinbren — Back in Black Area

17 Sticky Toffee .... 6c+
A pleasant way up this wall after a burly start. Make a difficult initial pull to reach a big jug on the right. Move up to the base of the flake-crack and pull up to stand on this. Tiptoe leftwards then climb the technical wall with a tricky final move.
FA. Lee Proctor 9.5.2010

18 Stiff and Sticky E3 6a
Slightly superseded by the previous route. Climb *Sticky Toffee* to the standing position on top of the flake-crack. Continue directly above with easier climbing up the line of weakness. Either belay at the top or move left to reach the lower-off on *Sticky Toffee*.
FA. John Codling, John Moulding, F.Stevenson 1984

19 Ring Piece .... 7b+
A poor route with a very hard bouldery start that leads to easier juggy climbing up large hollow-sounding flakes. The lower-off is quite low.
FA. Rob Mirfin 5.5.2010

Back in Black Area — **Dinbren** — 167

⑳ Fine Feathered Fink .... 7b+
Good powerful climbing on side-pulls and undercuts. It is easy to get wrong handed at the start.
FA. Gary Gibson 21.5.1988

㉑ Gwennan ..... 8a+
This route has lost a hold and has not been reclimbed hence the grade is unconfirmed - formerly 8a. A strenuous route with one very hard move. Use a cunning heel/toe jam to reach a small crimp in the bulge, from where a quick dynamic snatch gains a good jug. Pull up and follow better holds to reach and finish up *Fine Feathered Fink*.
FA. Rob Mirfin 12.8.2003

㉒ The Fog E6 6b
Vicious finger pockets in the steep bulging crack prove a test of not only strength, but resistance to pain. Judicious use of the small yew tree gains the crack (thread and two pegs). At the top of the crack there is a good medium wire from where a final stiff pull gains easier ground and the lower-off. Climbed with gear in place it is **7b+**.
FA. Steve Boydon 1985

㉓ Misty Vision E6 6b
The right-hand finish to *The Fog* is a much better finish, assuming enough skin is left on the fingers after the crux of *The Fog* itself! Undercut the flake-line rightwards before making a final pull through the bulge to a lower-off. Well protected with wires. If climbed with gear in place it is **7b+**.
FA. Steve Boydon 1985

There are two impressive open projects over the ivy roof. The right-hand central line through the roof is particularly striking.

Leftism - p.168

16m

Extreme Ways - p.168

Project

Climb High Area

Climb High Area

An outstanding section of cliff with some excellent rock packed with high quality lines. The thin technical wall climbs on the right contrast well with the more strenuous lines in the centre.

1 Dr. Gonzo **E3 6a**
A classic struggle up the overhanging crack passing bolts and a thread, to an easier wall above. Move right at the top to the lower-off. Can be used as an easier way to start the next route.
FA. John Moulding, John Codling 13.12.1983

2 Extreme Ways . . . . . 3★ **7c**
A very good pumpy climb that is more sustained than most of the routes at Dinbren. Start just left of *Cubase*. Climb direct to join the right-hand side of the *Dr. Gonzo* roof crack. Pull around the roof and traverse leftwards on dwindling footholds to reach a good undercut, then climb the overhanging prow above to a lower-off. Very photogenic! *Photo on page 21*.
FA. Lee Proctor 14.6.2009

3 Leftism . . . . Top 50 **8b+**
Start up *Extreme Ways* before heading further left above the low roof and then up to a lower-off. Currently the hardest pitch in the area. *Photo on page 179*.
FA. Rob Mirfin 30.6.2015

4 Cubase . . . . 1★ **7c**
A hard three-move boulder problem leads to much easier climbing above the low overhang.
FA. Rob Mirfin 11.8.2002

5 Lullaby . . . . **7a+**
A reasonable route with a hard start that soon gives way to easier climbing above the lower bulge.
FA. Gary Gibson 23.7.1989

6 The Dinbren Sanction . . . 1★ **6b+**
A nice ameanable route for this part of the crag. Bridge up the groove and wall above, exiting slightly rightwards.
FA. Steve Boydon 5.1985

Lots of sun | 8 min | Windy

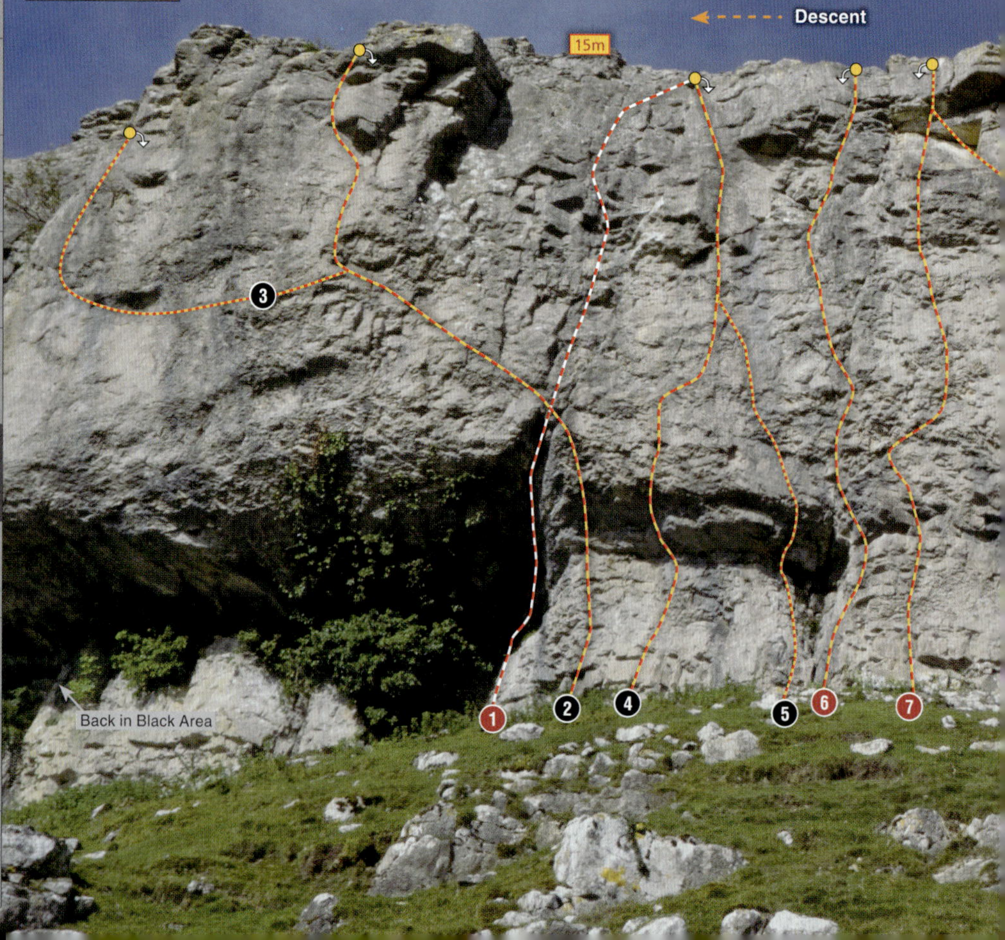

Ruthin Area
Devil's Gorge
Maeshafn
Pot Hole Quarry
Minera Quarry
World's End
Craig Arthur
Twilight Area
Pinfold
Monk's Buttress
Dinbren
Trevor Area
Pandy Outcrop
Llanymynech
Pontesford

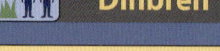

Climb High Area **Dinbren**

7 Cold Turkey 6c
A stiff and surprisingly strenuous climb.
FA. Gary Gibson 25.12.1986

8 Poor Old Hari Kiri .. 7a
A short hard section involving a couple of smallish crimps and one long move leads to easier climbing on slightly hollow sounding rock.
FA. Gary Gibson 14.3.1993

9 Kamikaze Clone .... 6c+
A short power-packed start characterises this route. Finish at the *Jaspers* lower-off.
FA. John Codling, Paul Harrison, John Moulding 29.4.1984

10 Jaspers ...... 6c+
A hard and powerful start - long reach useful - gains easier yet delicate climbing above.
FA. Gary Gibson 14.3.1993

11 Cookie King....... 7a+
Good climbing with a perplexing start up the groove.
FA. Simon Cardy, Steve Boydon 5.1985

12 Flowers are for the Dead 7c
A good route that traces a rightward-trending line to the left edge of the *Broken Dreams* roof. The start is powerful, the middle delicate and the finish absorbing!
FA. Gary Gibson, John Codling 21.5.1988

13 Counting Sheep . 8a+
Start just left of *Broken Dreams*. Climb up to a good undercut at 5m then head leftwards across the fingery white wall via some fine and improbable moves leading to a tooth-shaped undercut. Climb more easily to the top finishing at the *Flowers are for the Dead* lower-off.
FA. Rob Mirfin 17.7.2010

Dinbren — Climb High Area

14 Broken Dreams 7c
An excellent varied climb with a memorable finish. Pull onto the wall from the left and move up to undercuts and side-pulls, from where a reach gains a crimp. Move up to the flake system above and follow it rightwards (peg) to enter the niche beneath the capping roof. Pull straight out over the roof to the lower-off.
FA. John Moulding, John Codling 14.5.1988

15 Broken Flowers .... 7c+
A pumpy alternative finish to *Broken Dreams*. Climb *Broken Dreams* to the good holds beneath the groove of *Insomnia*, then undercut strenuously left to join and finish up *Flowers AFTD*.
FA. Rob Mirfin 6.2010

16 Insomnia .. Top 50 8b
One of the best routes at Dinbren. Start up *Broken Dreams* and continue up a hanging groove.
FA. Pete Chadwick 6.2005

17 When Saturday Comes 7c
A good route requiring strong fingers. Climb up to a line of undercuts and, where these end, make a hard move past a glued-on hold to a distant edge. Finish up *Broken Dreams*.
FA. Gary Gibson 13.8.1994

18 I Punched Judy First .... 7b+
A powerful start, tenuous mid section, and difficult finish up the wide crack give this route bags of character. Low in the grade.
FA. Gary Gibson, John Codling 8.7.1987

19 Technicolour Yawn ..... Top 50 7a+
Pull out of the recess and blast up the wall on pockets, crimps, undercuts and side-pulls, to reach the base of a crack that is climbed more easily to a lower-off on the right.
FA. Steve Allen, John Codling, John Moulding, J.Lockett 1984

20 Walking with Barrence 7b
Superb climbing with a technical thin lower half and super butch finale to finish at the *Technicolour Yawn* lower-off.
FA. John Moulding 8.1987

21 In Search of Someone Silly .... 7a+
Climb the lower wall on good but hidden holds before moving up to stand on sloping holds beneath some flake-cracks. Move left with difficulty to join *Walking with Barrence*.
FA. Gary Gibson 7.1.1984

Climb High Area — Dinbren 171

22 Traction Trauma 6c+
Superb rock. Start up *Climb High* and then follow a thin left-trending line to better holds and the lower-off. *Photo on cover.*
FA. John Codling, John Moulding 3.12.1983

23 Do Walls Have Ears 7a+
From the top bolt on *Traction Trauma*, move right and tackle the thin and very technical wall and bulge above to a lower-off.
FA. Gary Gibson 14.3.1993

24 Climb High Top 50 7a
A classic of the crag. Pull onto the wall and trend leftwards before making a move right to the base of a vague groove. Climb the groove to reach a rounded break and then perform the mother of all rockovers to attain a standing position in the break. Tiptoe right and finish up a flake. *Photo on page 15.*
FA. Stuart Cathcart, Phil Waters, D.Barker 9.1983

25 Climb High Direct E5 6b
After the rockover, climb up and slightly leftwards through the slight bulge to the top.
FA. Lee Proctor 5.2009

26 Dreadlocks 7a+
From the large flake on *Alison* climb the fingery, blind wall above to the rounded break. Move left and nonchalantly cruise the *Climb High* crux to finish. A few wires are needed at the start.
FA. John Codling 16.12.1983

27 Alison E1 5b
The best E1 at Dinbren. A difficult start gains the huge juggy flake. Place some good wires then move right into the corner and bridge up this with a testing move to reach the top. *Photo on page 12.*
FA. Stuart Cathcart, John Dee 12.5.1980

28 Gemma's World E2 5b
An eliminate. Climb *Alison* until a step right can be made to join the easier and bolted climbing on *Gemma's World Direct*.
FA. Stuart Cathcart, John Dee 26.4.1980

29 Gemma's World Direct 6c
Climb the rightward curving line to join *Gemma's World*.
FA. John Codling, Phil Gibson 1.4.1984

30 Hot Lips 7a
Start up *Gemma's World Direct* before moving right around the arete to join and finish as for *Out of Body Experience*. Originally started up *Gemma's World*. Best to second when retrieving gear.
FA. John Codling, John Moulding, Fred Crook 1984

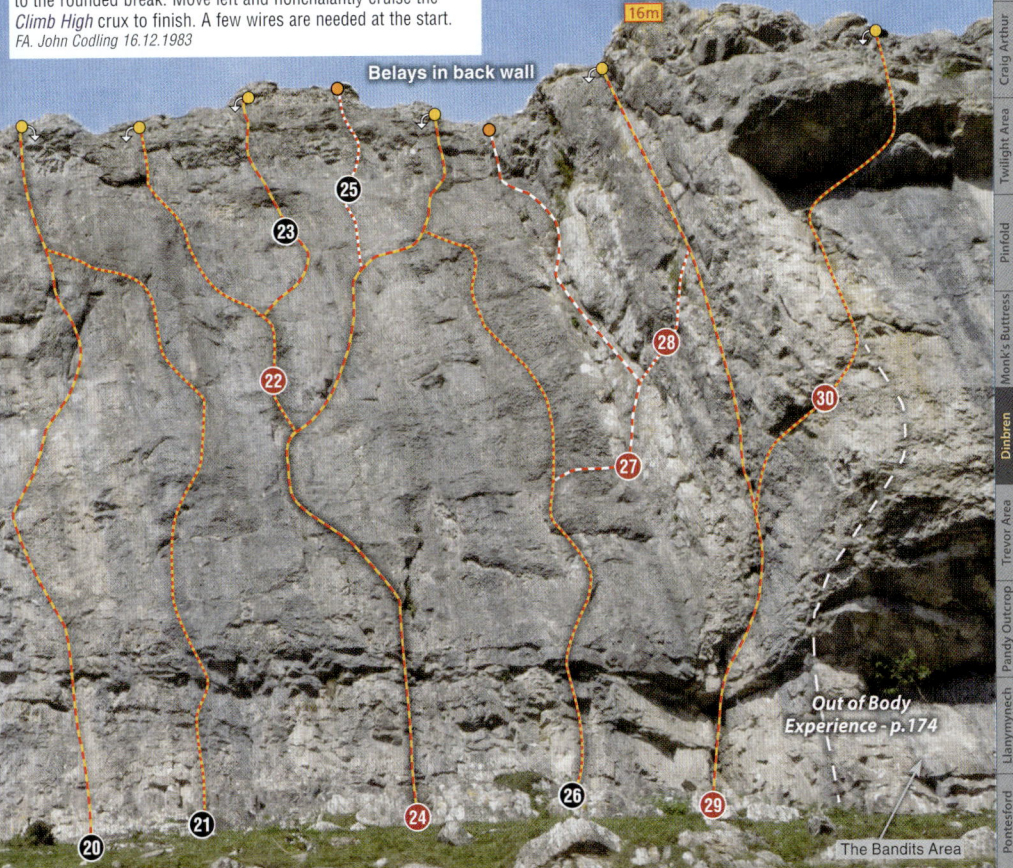

Julian Heath on one of the early sport-style climbs established at Dinbren - and still one of its best *The Bandits* (7b+) - *page 174*. Many of the harder climbs put up on Clwyd limestone in the 1980s and 1990s were climbed in a redpoint fashion, but often used a mixture of bolts, threads and nuts for protection. Most of these lines have now been fully bolted. Photo: Keith Sharples

Dinbren — The Bandits Area

The Bandits Area

The premier section of crag for higher grade quality sport lines. The right-hand side has a few lines on poorer rock. *The Bandits* is one of the best routes in the area.

⛔ **Access** - Although not a formal restriction, the area around *Silent Spirit* on the right-hand side of this wall frequently has ravens nesting early in the year. Please avoid this route if you see any nests.

❶ Out of Body Experience
.... 7c+
A good route with some cool moves. From the start of *Hot Lips*, climb the left side of the roof to reach a good hold on the arete. Move powerfully rightwards using a crafty heel/toe hook and finish direct over the capping roof. *Photo on page 27.*
FA. Rob Mirfin 6.2010

❷ No Kneed .... 8a+
A brilliant and improbable line through the widest part of the roof to join *Out of Body Experience*. The meat of the climb is centred on an uncompromising knee bar at the lip of the roof that is both difficult to get into and hard to leave.
FA. Ally Smith 29.2.2014

❸ Binary Finary 8b
A sustained hard route. Tackle the steep bulging wall to the left of *The Bandits* using small and slightly painful holds. The third clip is hard to make and the route is a little run out above.
FA. Rob Mirfin 5.8.2005

❹ The Bandits .... Top 50 7b+
One of the best sport routes at Dinbren. A powerful start, fingery middle, and easier but energy sapping finish make for a fantastic outing. *Photo on page 172.*
FA. Gary Gibson 13.6.1988

❺ The Rivals .... 7c+
The desperate lower wall is climbed using small side-pulls and tenacity to reach a good hold by the second bolt. Easier above.
FA. Gary Gibson 14.5.1988

There is a bolted project here.

The Bandits Area — Dinbren — 175

6 El Zapatistas ... 8b
A baffling move low down gains poor undercuts. Continue up the finger searing wall to reach a small overlap. A hard rockover gains a good rest below the roof which proves to be a stubborn final barrier to success.
FA. Rob Mirfin 8.2005

7 The Orgasmatron 8a+
A very hard f7C boulder problem gains the undercut flake. The wall and bulge above are climbed much more easily on immaculate rock. The route was originally climbed with an aided start at 7a and has also been climbed by moving in from *El Rincon* at 7c+.
FA. John Codling 26.8.1986. FFA. Rob Mirfin 5.2010

8 El Rincon .. Top 50 8a
A fine route with some challenging moves on continuously poor footholds. Move up with difficulty to a reasonable crimp. Energy sapping moves on side-pulls gain the base of the bulge and better handholds. Pull strenuously up the vague groove to a tenuous rockover, after which the difficulty eases.
FA. Gareth Scott 23.6.2002

9 Highway 8a
A good climb. Boulder out the initial wall to a good hold, then move up and tackle the steep bulge above using shallow pockets, dimples and some slopy holds. No sneaking off-route for a rest at this grade. *Photo on page 33.*
FA. John Dunne 6.2002

10 El Loco E5 6a
Hand traverse boldly leftwards to an inverted pocket. Make a committing move to the crack system and the first good wires. Follow the crack to an old bolt below a bulge, then move left to a peg and make a difficult move to finish.
FA. John Moulding 15.2.1984

11 Going Loco E6 6b
Start up *El Loco*, cross *Highway* and finish up *El Rincon*.
FA. Steve Mayers 4.1989

12 Rhiannon E5 6a
Not shown on topo. Connect *Hot Lips* with the finish of *El Loco*. Usually climbed in three short pitches to reduce rope drag by belaying under the bulge of *Hot Lips* and on a bolts to the right of *The Rivals*.
FA. Steve Boydon, John Moulding 1985

Dinbren — The Bandits Area

> **Access** - Although not a formal restriction, the area around *Silent Spirit* on the right-hand side of this wall frequently has ravens nesting early in the year. Please avoid this route if you see any nests.

⑬ Silent Spirit. . . . . **HVS 5a**
A poor route that is becoming loose and overgrown. Climb the right-trending ramp-line past a whitebeam tree. Probably best to finish at the lower-off of *Con-Dem-Nation*.
FA. Stuart Cathcart 15.3.1978

⑭ Con-Dem-Nation . . . . . . **6c+**
A short pitch with a hard and powerful start.
FA. Lee Proctor 20.5.2010

⑮ Resist and Exist. **6b**
Very popular - the most climbed route at the crag. The route still packs a punch and can feel quite awkward and strenuous on first acquaintance.
FA. Paul Harrison, Doug Kerr 18.11.1984

⑯ Where's the President's Brain **6b+**
Another popular and often top-roped line that starts up *Resist and Exist*. The direct start makes it slightly harder (**6c**) but the main difficulties are gaining and exiting the technical crack higher up. It is best to pre-clip the initial bolt on the direct version. *Photo opposite*.
FA. Simon Cardy, Steve Boyden, Paul Harrison 3.6.1984

⑰ Swansong **E2 6a**
The left-hand corner of the bay has a perplexing start which has stumped several good climbers.
FA. Stuart Cathcart, Dave Johnson 16.6.1979

⑱ Yale . . . . **HVS 5a**
A good exercise in bridging, and one of the better sub-extreme trad routes at Dinbren.
FA. Stuart Cathcart 15.3.1988

Jonathan Cain nearing the finish of the popular *Where's the President's Brain* (6b+) - *opposite* - at The Bandits Area. Photo: Patricia Novelli

Dinbren Fire and Ice Area

Fire and Ice Area

Steep bulging starts and thin technical upper walls typify the style of climbing here. Some of the undercutting is rather brutal, although thankfully fairly brief. The left side is a steep wall of good rock with a well-defined corner on its right. The trad lines are well worth checking out. The right-hand side offers routes with powerful low overhangs and then more technical and fingery upper walls. This area tends to be more sheltered if a wind is blowing.

① Melody 6c
An excellent intricate route up the rounded arete clipping the bolts to the right on *Lucky be Damned*. Originally a bold E4.
FA. Gary Gibson 19.2.1984

② Lucky be Damned ..... 6c+
A bolted line just right of the shallow arete followed by *Melody*.
FA. Gary Gibson 27.3.2012

③ So Lucky E3 6a
Climb direct to the large yew tree via an undercut flake. From the tree move left and finish as for *Lucky be Damned*.
FA. Gary Gibson 25.2.1984

④ Big Mouth Strikes Again 7a
Climb the flat wall left of *A Different Kind of Hypertension*. A tricky start leads to good holds at mid height from where a perplexing move (think laterally) gains better holds. Finish slightly rightwards at the top.
FA. Gary Gibson, Hazel Gibson, Paul Harrison 24.4.1988

⑤ A Different Kind of Hypertension E3 5c
Good wall climbing, passing a fixed nut and an old thread, to an awkward finish rightwards through a small bulge. It is possible to lower off from the *Hyperdrive* belay.
FA. Gary Gibson, Hazel Carnes 25.2.1984

⑥ Hyperdrive E3 6a
The groove is the best route of its grade at the crag. Climb the first few feet of *A Different Kind of Hypertension* before embarking on some committing moves into the groove (peg). Tricky moves up the groove lead to a second peg. Finish direct to a lower-off. There is a direct start which pushes the grade up to **E4 6a**.
FA. Stuart Cathcart, Rick White 28.8.1979. FA. (Direct start) Gary Gibson

Rob Mirfin on the Clwyd's hardest sport route to date *Leftism* (8b+) - *page 168* - on the Climb High Area at Dinbren. This route along with many of Rob's other first ascents have boosted the number of top-standard routes since the last guidebook was published. Photo: Dave Rose

Dinbren — Fire and Ice Area

7 Bolt the Blue Sky 7b
Blast up the steep wall to reach a massive jug, then follow the vague arete above to the top.
FA. John Moulding, John Codling 31.5.1987. FA. (Direct start) Lee Proctor

8 Showing Mystery Bruises ...... 7a+
A real bicep buster involving some very strenuous and reachy climbing on undercuts.
FA. Gary Gibson 23.7.1994

9 Baby Crusher 7b
A good climb that has a surprisingly delicate and technical crux after a butch start. Undercut rightwards to attain a standing position on the protruding block/ledge. Climb the wall above to reach the bottom of the overhanging crack. Easier climbing up this leads to the lower-off.
FA. John Moulding, John Codling 31.5.1987

10 Dyperspace 7c
If there was a 'fun' symbol this route would get it! Gain the hanging block on *Baby Crusher* direct by some super-cool moves. Easier for the tall.
FA. Rob Mirfin 2000

11 This Vision Thing 7b
A hard route requiring a long stretch at the start to reach the base of the orange bulge. Pull up rightwards before moving back left with difficulty to gain the base of a small groove. Finish at the *Fat Boys* lower-off.
FA. Gary Gibson 26.6.1993

12 Fat Boys ...... 7a+
Take a deep breath then blast up the bulging wall using undercuts, crimps and layaways.
FA. John Codling, Gary Gibson, John Moulding 14.5.1988

13 The Planet ...... 7b+
A short and intense sequence that still manages to drain the power out of your arms before the belay is reached. The bottom half is quite strenuous and blind.
FA. Gary Gibson 29.2.1992

14 Fire ...... 7a+
A good and popular route. From the third bolt on *Ice*, step left and climb the wall above, to the base of a yellow groove. Finish easily up this.
FA. John Codling, John Moulding 22.9.1984

Fire and Ice Area — Dinbren

⑮ Ice .... 3 · 7b
A Dinbren testpiece. Pull powerfully up to gain the undercut, then step awkwardly right to more undercuts and a good finger-jug. Pull straight up with a long move to access the hanging groove, which is followed delicately rightwards.
FA. John Codling 23.8.1986

⑯ Blinking Lights .... 1 · 7c
A direct start to *Ice*. A bouldery start leads to a good jug by the third bolt, followed by the technical upper section of *Ice*.
FA. Kiaran Ratcliffe 14.6.2015

⑰ Hot Stuff .... 1 · 7a
A popular and fun climb with a steep start. Pull through the initial bulge into the base of the prominent groove. Move up the arete/wall left of the groove until it is possible to step left to join *Ice*. *Photo on page 35*.
FA. Doug Kerr, Andy Remedios 11.4.1988. FA. (New finish) Lee Proctor

⑱ Silly Games .... 7a+
Fingery climbing up the wall to the right of the deep groove.
FA. Gary Gibson, Hazel Gibson 22.5.1988

⑲ The Solar System ..... 1 · 6c+
The short bouldery route to the left of *Amadeus*. Power through the undercuts then make a long move to edges. Finish with ease.
FA. Dave Rose 20.7.2015

⑳ Amadeus .... HVS 4c
The wall and crack left of *Soap*.
FA. Stuart Cathcart 15.3.1978

㉑ Ice on the Motorway E5 6a
A high-level traverse of the Fire and Ice wall which starts up *Silly Games* and traverses left at around the fourth bolt level to finish up the overhanging crack of *Baby Crusher*.
FA. John Codling, Gary Gibson 8.7.1987

Dinbren — Dynah Moe Hum Area

Dynah Moe Hum Area

A short but well-positioned wall of undercut rock with a selection of testing pitches ranging from the powerful to the bold. The sport lines are very popular but no pushover.

1 Soap .... VD
Often used as a descent route.
FA. H.J.Tinkler, John Hesketh 1962

2 SPC .... VS 4c
A pleasant little climb on good rock.

3 Humble Hog E1 5c
A tricky start leads to better holds and good protection.
FA. Alex Williams 19.2.1984

4 Ripped Apart by Badgers 6c
A tight but independent line that has a thin start.
FA. Chris Rose 2015

5 Dynah Moe Hum ... E4 6b
A highball boulder problem on good rock.
FA. John Moulding 2.6.1984

6 Out With the New E3 6b
Boulder up to the overlap and reach for a good jug, then pull over the bulge to the top.
FA. Gary Gibson 8.5.1988

7 The Homecoming 7a
A short unforgiving route on undercuts.
FA. Gary Gibson 29.9.2011

8 Waiting for Bayley .... 6c+
A hard micro-route route with some worthwhile climbing.
FA. Rob Mirfin 30.8.2003

9 Inaugural Goose Flesh .. 6c+
Boulder through the initial overlap to the first bolt, then make a long move to reach a good hold up and right of the second bolt. Finish direct to a lower-off.
FA. John Codling, Gary Gibson 21.5.1988

Dynah Moe Hum Area — Dinbren — 183

10 Just Another Route Name 6c
From the first bolt, move right to undercuts and then up to small edges. Make a long reach left to better holds and the finish of *Inaugural Goose Flesh*.
FA. Gary Gibson 10.5.1988

11 Heinous Undercling .... 7a+
Difficult climbing up the bulging wall. Hard to onsight.
FA. Gary Gibson 8.5.1988

12 Just Another Undercling . 6c
Start on a set of crimps right of the roof and move left onto jugs. A testing move off an undercut to a crimp leads to a jug up and right. Undercut through the overlap to finish on smooth pockets.
FA. Gary Gibson 29.9.2011

13 Sarcophagus E2 5b
Climb the wall 2m left of *The Varlet* trending leftwards to gain a thin crack.
FA. Stuart Cathcart 12.5.1979

14 The Varlet .... HVS 5a
The left-trending crack leads to an awkward exit.
FA. Stuart Cathcart 12.5.1979

15 Backs to the Wall 7a
A leftwards-trending line to gain a hidden peg, above a small overlap, before the lower-off. The second bolt is difficult to clip.
FA. Gary Gibson 8.5.1988

16 Deadly Nightshade E2 5b
The blunt arete has an awkward start.
FA. Stuart Cathcart 14.5.1979

17 Trailer Trash 6b
A pleasant climb featuring an awkward beginning. A bouldery start reaches some very nice holds which lead to fine technical wall climbing above. *Photo on page 17*.
FA. Ryan McConnell 23.5.2012

18 Driller Thriller .... 6b+
Climb direct up the easy wall, passing a large hollow-sounding block. Tackle the bulge above and move slightly past the lower-off to gain the full tick and grade.
FA. Gary Gibson 22.5.1988

Old Scores - p.186

Harmony Area

Dinbren — Harmony Area

The Harmony Area at Dinbren has a trio of three-star trad pitches on some of the crag's best rock. Here, Craig Bailey pulls over the final overhang of *A World of Harmony* (E2 5b) - *page 187* - the most popular of the three. Photo: Keith Sharples

Dinbren — Harmony Area

❶ Old Scores E4 6a
Start at a left-facing flake and follow it to the bulge. Make a difficult move into the V-groove (hidden thread). Climb the groove to a peg, then move left through the roof.
FA. Gary Gibson 27.3.1984

❷ Pep Talk .... HVS 4c
The steep broken wall into the hanging groove.

❸ The Royal Arch E3 6a
The first of the five classic Right Wing E3s. Climb the leftwards-curving arch for 8m until a vague rightward traverse line is reached. Arrange protection then move right to a good pinch. Thin moves lead to a slot above and good wires. Climb direct to the roof then traverse left slightly until it is possible to pull into the scoop above.
FA. Stuart Cathcart, Gerald Swindley 30.8.1979

Harmony Area
Great rock and strong lines make this one of the best sections for trad climbing at Dinbren. *A World of Harmony* is a fine, if short-lived, excursion.

❹ Blue Nine E5 6b
A route requiring a cool approach. Follow the leftwards-slanting line, right of the start of *The Royal Arch*, to gain a good jug at 5m. Finish up *The Royal Arch*.
FA. John Moulding 4.6.1988

❺ Waltz in Black E4 6a
A varied and intricate route that starts below a small left-facing flake. Rock onto the top of the flake and clip the thread on *World of Harmony*. Move left to a peg and a good flake hold. Move up and right on small footholds to a rounded ledge and second thread. Finish directly through the roof.
FA. Gary Gibson, Adam Hudson, Fred Crook 6.3.1984

Afternoon — 8 min — Windy

Driller Thriller - p.183

13m

Dynah Moe Hum Area

Harmony Area **Dinbren** 187

6 A World of Harmony. `Top 50` — E2 5b
A fantastic climb on perfect rock with a thin start. Place some small wires then clip the thread from the right. Move up to better holds and good protection beneath the bulge. Pull rightwards to gain the hanging crack and follow this to the top.
Photo on page 184.
FA. Stuart Cathcart, Gerald Swindley 30.8.1979

7 Caught in the Crossfire
.... — E4 6a
The wall right of *A World of Harmony* is climbed direct passing a solitary old bolt which soon feels a long way below.
FA. Gary Gibson, Adam Hudson, Fred Crook 6.3.1984

8 Death on my Tongue......... — E3 5c
The curving crack has a few tricky moves.
FA. Stuart Cathcart, Gerald Swindley 30.8.1979

9 Shadowplay .... — E2 5c
An eliminate up the wall left of the corner, passing two threads.
FA. Gary Gibson, Hazel Carnes 25.2.1984

10 Let it Rip .... — VD
The green corner.

11 Return of the Gods........ — E2 5b
Climb the steep crack in the wall right of the corner using a few creaky holds. Good protection.
FA. Stuart Cathcart, Bryan Philips, Dave Barker 30.8.1979

12 Synapse Collapse ..... — E3 5c
An exciting route which feels exposed. Start on the left of the arete (as for *Return of the Gods*). Climb to the base of the crack, then move around the arete (threaded peg). Continue traversing across the exposed wall to a white scoop and poor peg. Finish direct on hollow-sounding flakes.
FA. Simon Cardy, Steve Boydon 5.1985

Dinbren — Descent Area

Descent Area

Two small sections of crag split by the well concealed descent gully. The left side is steep and the right vertical and compact.

❶ In the Heat of the Day E4 6b
A direct start to *Synapse Collapse* (page 187) taking the crack and bulge right of the arete, past a few loose holds.
FA. Gary Gibson 15.5.1988

❷ The Wasp Factory .... 7b+
A powerful start on side-pulls and undercuts leads to a difficult and fingery move to get established on the upper grey wall.
FA. John Codling, John Moulding 27.7.1989

❸ Big Youth .... HVS 5a
The crack and flake system. A good route on which to practice hand-jamming technique. The rock is a little loose near the top.
FA. Stuart Cathcart 14.8.1981

❹ Thanks to Ellis Brigham . E3 5c
Surprisingly hard climbing taking the left-hand crack system.
FA. Stuart Cathcart, John Dee 2.8.1981

Descent Area **Dinbren**

❺ Lecherous Pig E3 6a
Start up *Thanks to Ellis Brigham*, but climb into the right-hand crack and tackle the technical wall above the bulge.
FA. Paul Harrison, John Moulding 6.6.1984

❻ Summer Solstice E1 5b
The final line before the descent gully. Climb the flake and crack system, moving right near the top to belay in the gully.
FA. Stuart Cathcart, John Dee 2.8.1981

❼ German for Art Historians E1 5b
A good little route that follows the thin crack system and pocketed wall, starting 4m up the descent gully.
FA. Barry Barrett, Adam Hudson, Fred Crook 6.3.1984

❽ Sugar Hiccup E3 5c
A committing climb taking the wall and overlaps right of *German for Art Historians*.
FA. Adam Hudson, Gary Gibson, Fred Crook 6.3.1984

❾ Five O'Clock Shadow .... HVS 4c
The corner system above the start of the descent gully.

❿ Arm Worms E4 6a
The deep hanging crack in the arete.
FA. Steve Boyden, Paul Harrison, John Moulding 30.5.1985

⓫ Quick Flash 7a
A good climb on perfect rock. The first bolt is high but the climbing is relatively easy. From an undercut on *Arm Worms*, move right to a crack then balance rightwards to a small undercut. A long move gains rounded holds. Rock up to crimps beneath the bulge and climb this to a hidden lower-off.
FA. Gary Gibson 10.5.1988

⓬ Loosing Grasp E2 5b
Climb the thin crack to the left of the large rowan tree.
FA. Stuart Cathcart, Rick White 12.10.1979

Dinbren — Combat Zone Area

Combat Zone Area

The trio of left-curving overlaps is the distinctive feature of this steep and attractive wall.

❶ Wonderwall 7a
An excellent technical wall climb on immaculate rock feels a little bit spicy and is only slightly spoilt by the close proximity of the ash tree.
FA. Ryan McConnell, Chris Silverstone 18.7.2011

❷ Wood Treatment E3 5c
Resist the temptation to climb the tree and instead climb the bold wall behind the tree direct to a thread and the top.
FA. Gary Gibson, Adam Hudson 6.3.1984

❸ The Nit Nurse E1 5b
Climb direct to a thread at the overlap. Pull over this into the crack above, passing a second thread.
FA. Fred Crook, Ian Barker 3.1984

❹ The Phoenix .... S 4a
Climb past the tree.

❺ Astrola .... VS 4b
Start beneath a dead yew tree. Climb the wall, trending rightwards to reach a good ledge. Finish direct to the left of a whitebeam tree.
FA. Stuart Cathcart, Rick White 12.10.1979

❻ The Scutters E1 5b
Climb the groove and corner right of *Astrola*, finishing to the right of the whitebeam tree.
FA. Stuart Cathcart, Rick White 12.10.1979

❼ The Stukas E4 6a
An eliminate. Clip the ringbolt on *Fighting Spirit* before stepping left to climb the thin crack above.
FA. Gary Gibson, Doug Kerr 18.1.1992

Combat Zone Area — Dinbren

8 Fighting Spirit 7a
Start by a large pocket at chest height. The wall above is climbed by a series of blind technical moves to a lower-off.
FA. Gary Gibson, Doug Kerr 18.1.1992

9 Combat Zone E3 5c
The second Right Wing classic E3. Start by the large triangular flake and make a difficult move up and right into the curving overlap (thread). Balance leftwards to gain the thin crack (peg) and finish direct.
FA. Fred Crook, Ian Barker 3.1984

10 Evil Woman E3 5c
The 'evil' companion to *Combat Zone*. Start to the right of the triangular flake and climb the hanging corner and steep wall to reach the curving flake-crack above and right of *Combat Zone*. Follow this taking the bulge above direct. Committing!
FA. Stuart Cathcart, Dave Whitlow 24.8.1981

11 Mustang Sally 7b
A short sport route with one very hard move.
FA. Gary Gibson 23.5.1992

12 Ripping Yarns 6b
A circuitous line following the flake and arete.
FA. Gary Gibson, Doug Kerr 26.1.1992

Dinbren — Hydrogen Area

Hydrogen Area

The steep smooth wall of perfect rock is home to a couple of stern quality wall climbs in the form of *Raging Storm* and *Hydrogen*.

1 Filth Faze .... VS 4c
The loose, broken crack-line beneath the whitebeam tree.

2 Grooved Arete 6b
Climb the arete between *Filth Faze* and *Sally in Pink* via some good and quite cruxy moves. Originally **E1 5c** and a bit of a sandbag!
FA. Ian Barker, Fred Crook 3.1984

3 Sally in Pink .... VS 4b
Probably the best of the easier trad lines at Dinbren, requiring good bridging skills low down. Climb the square groove containing a small yew tree.
FA. Stuart Cathcart, Malcolm Cameron 11.4.1980

4 Captain Scarlett .... 6b+
A pleasant excursion up the clean narrow pillar to the right of *Sally in Pink*. Thin at first and then on better holds.
FA. Gary Morgan, Rob Watt 18.9.2015

5 Crimson Dynamo E2 5c
Climb direct to two parallel cracks at half-height and finish past a whitebeam tree. Difficult to protect at the start.
FA. Ian Barker, Fred Crook 3.1984

6 Colour Games E1 5b
Climb the crack to reach some good flake holds, then finish up the short compact slab above.
FA. Stuart Cathcart 3.1984

7 Red Storm Rising E5 6b
A hard direct on *Raging Storm*.
FA. Gary Gibson 5.9.1993

8 Raging Storm E3 5c
The third Right Wing classic E3. Climb the compact wall beneath the rightwards-curving overlaps (small wires) to gain a curving crack. From the top of the crack make a hard move right to reach a line of good flake-holds and then climb direct passing a small overhang at the top.
FA. Stuart Cathcart, Dave Whitlow 24.8.1981

Hydrogen Area — Dinbren

9 Hydrogen E3 5c
The fourth Right Wing classic E3 is a difficult companion to *Raging Storm*. From the small wire placements on *Raging Storm*, make a long move rightwards to reach better holds, then follow a line of flakes to the top.
FA. Stuart Cathcart, Dave Whitlow 24.8.1981

10 Ellabella 6c
Good technical wall climbing on clean solid rock up the face between *Hydrogen* and *The Devil's Advocate*.
FA. Gary Morgan, Robbie Watt 23.8.12

11 The Devil's Advocate ... E3 5c
Climb the thin crack in the bulging wall right of *Hydrogen*. Small wires are essential.
FA. Stuart Cathcart, Gerald Swindley 16.6.1979

12 Tower of Babel .... VS 5a
After a difficult start, climb the left arete on good holds to reach the 'summit' top-out.
FA. Stuart Cathcart 9.8.1979

13 Babel Face .... HVS 5a
The shallow groove.
FA. Ian Barker, Fred Crook 3.1984

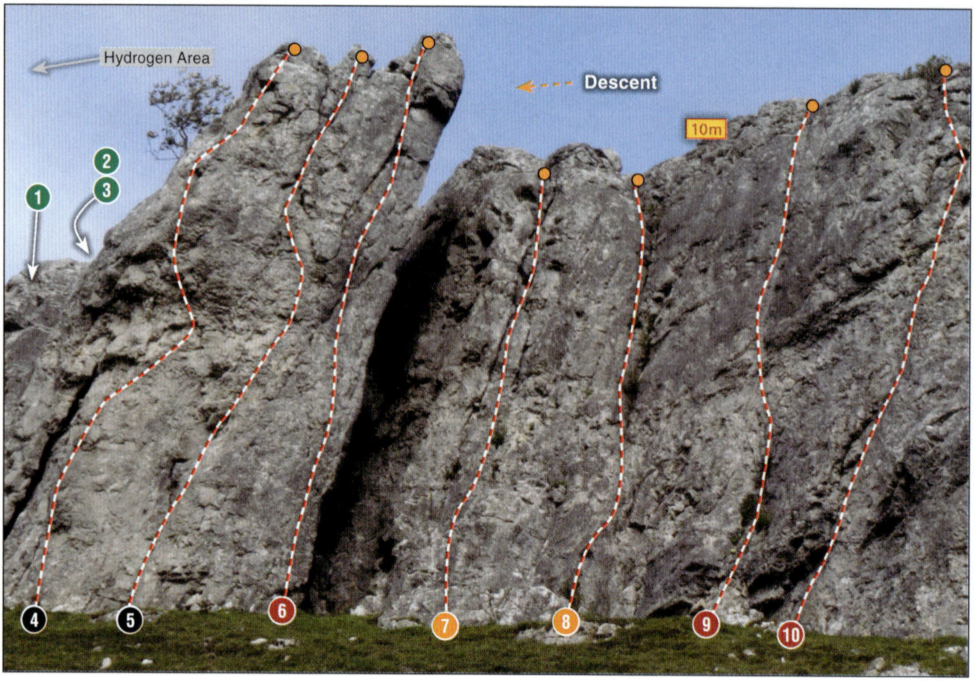

Dinbren — Buccinator Area

Buccinator Area
The final area of note on the Right Wing has one outstanding pitch - *Buccinator* - which tackles the thin crack on the vertical wall right of the Babble Tower.

The first route is on the wall behind the tower.

① Antilla .... S 4a
The vegetated groove on the wall next to the tower.

The next two lines are on the leftside of the tower - lines not shown on topo.

② Babbling Arete .... S 4a
The left arete of *Babbling Tower* is worth seeking out.
FA. G.Pastifield, K.Davies 13.10.1991

③ Babbling Tower .... VD
Tackle the large crack on the front of the tower.

④ Babble on is Burning E4 6b
A difficult route starting up a wide crack and then moving right and over a bulge, passing an old bolt.
FA. Gary Gibson 12.9.1993

⑤ Electra Glide E4 5c
A serious and rarely repeated route up the hanging groove in the front face of the tower.
FA. Stuart Cathcart, Tom Curtis 9.6.1979

⑥ Dawn of Desire E3 5b
A serious route tackling the right arete of the tower.
FA. Stuart Cathcart, Tom Curtis 9.6.1979

⑦ Shaken Not Stirred .... HS 4a
The broken groove, passing a peg.

⑧ Chabris .... VS 4c
The short corner is quite awkward.

⑨ Buccinator E3 5c
A deceptively difficult route and the final Right Wing classic E3. Climb the thin crack, passing two pegs.
FA. Stuart Cathcart, Dave Whitlow 6.8.1981

⑩ Cheeky Pie E3 5b
Climb the rightward-trending flake, and the groove above, to finish left of a dead yew tree.
FA. Doug Kerr 26.1.1986

⑪ Gentle Violence E3 5c
The slabby wall and bulge.
FA. Stuart Cathcart, John Dee 6.8.1981

⑫ Violent Ratcliffe E4 6a
The slabby wall and bulge passing two bolts with a difficult move off a sloper.
FA. Gary Gibson, Jim Shaw 12.9.1993

⑬ Castella .... VD
The blocky groove is loose and best avoided.

⑭ Hamlet .... HS 4b
Start up *Castella* and then move right into a square groove.

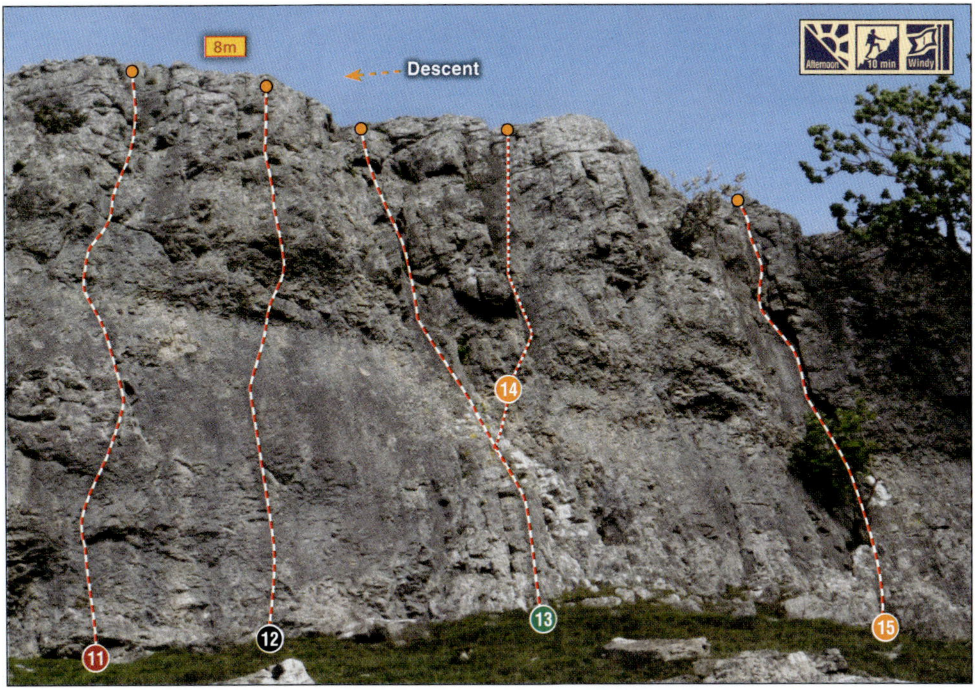

Right Wing - Lower Tier Dinbren

Right Wing - Lower Tier

The long line of low crags beneath the Hydrogen Area on the Right Wing has a few rarely repeated and quite loose climbs, but the route *Pickpocket* is worth seeking out. All climbs are best approached by breaking out right from the main approach path.

15 First Graces . . . . HS 4b
Layback up the short flake.
FA. Stuart Cathcart 24.4.1980

16 Subtopia E1 5b
The short wall past a peg.
FA. Doug Kerr, S.Conion 30.9.1985

17 Ice Run E1 5b
Climb the flake-crack past a thread.
FA. Doug Kerr, S.Conion 23.9.1985

18 Stagnation . . . . HS 4b
The groove past a dead tree.
FA. Doug Kerr, S.Conion 30.9.1985

19 White Lightening E1 5c
The right-hand route of the buttress past a thread.
FA. Doug Kerr, S.Conion 23.9.1985

The next routes are a further 100m along the crag.

20 Fingers . . . . HVS 4c
The short wall and shallow groove.
FA. Doug Kerr, D.Woolgar 11.9.1985

21 Thumbs . . . . HVS 5b
The vegetated groove above a tricky start.
FA. Doug Kerr, D.Woolgar 11.9.1985

22 Pickpocket  7b
At the far right-hand end of the middle tier is a large yew tree. Immediately before this is a short bulging arete of quality limestone. Climb the easy lower wall then tackle the difficult bulge to a lower-off. Good bouldery climbing.
FA. Ryan McConnell 5.2012

Trevor Area

Trevor Quarry, Independence Quarry, Ruabon Quarry

Nearing the finish of the diagonal ramp of *Over the Wall* (6a+) - *page 206* - at the Compact Wall, Trevor Quarry. The Trevor Area provides a wealth of easily-accessed sport pitches in the grades from 4 to 6 and has superb views out towards the Berwyns mountains beyond Llangollen.

Trevor Quarry

Trevor Quarry has a great set of low-to-mid-grade sport routes spread along its length and is now the most popular climbing destination in the area. There will be few days of the year when there is nobody sampling its various delights. The long established venue of The Quarry itself has a fine vertical wall of fingery sport routes, but it is the line of quarried bays and walls that run westward from here that have become extremely popular. This section of Trevor Quarry has a concentration of routes, often of a technical nature, which are well-bolted, nearly always dry, and have flat grassy bases with a magnificent vista. There is good bouldering close by at The Monument Boulders and around Trevor Quarry itself - for information go to UKClimbing.com.

	No star	★	★★	★★★
up to 4+	7	13	1	-
5+ to 6a+	41	36	1	1
6b to 7a	12	12	5	1
7a+ and up	-	1	-	-

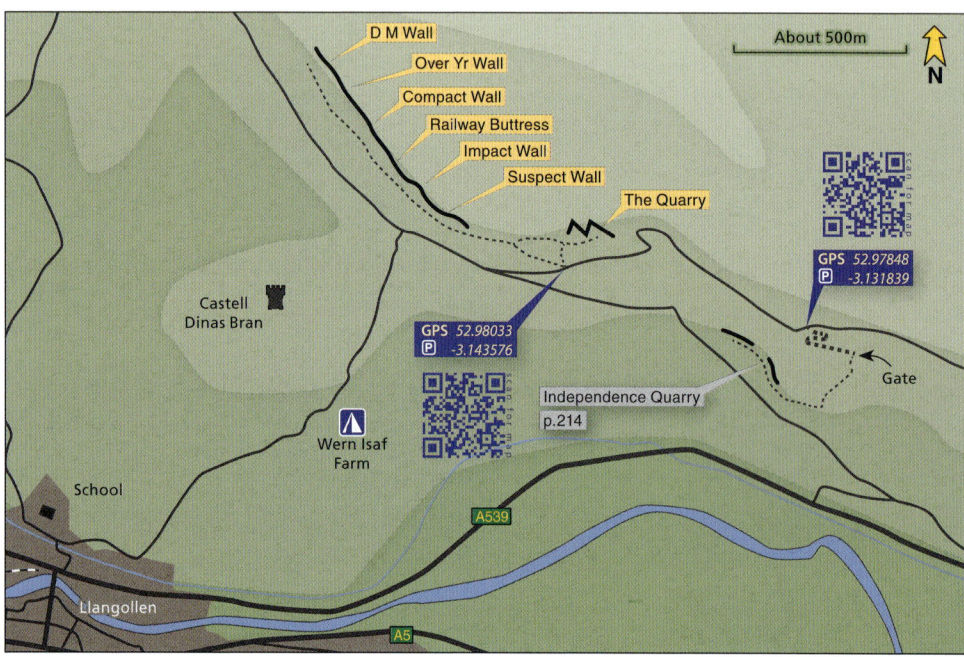

Approach   Also see map on page 196

Approaching from Llangollen, follow the road to the junction at 1.8 miles and turn sharp right. Dinbren Crag is on the left. Follow the road past Dinbren and Castell Dinas for 1.4 miles and park in a lay-by on the left, just before a sharp left-hand bend. The Quarry is directly above the parking. The rest of the walls are reached in five to ten minutes by walking up the easy-angled path leading left out of the parking area.

Conditions

The sectors running from the Suspect to D M Wall are all quick drying and take little seepage. They receive the sun from late morning and are fairly sheltered from the wind but not from the rain. The Quarry itself also dries very quickly but does seep during wet periods. It gets lots of morning sun, is nicely shaded later in the day, and is a good spot to escape the heat during summer. The east-facing wall offers some shelter from strong westerly winds, but not rain.

Trevor Quarry

Access
An agreed climbing restriction due to nesting birds has been in place on the crags northwest (left) of, but not including, the Compact Wall. Recently this hasn't been enforced and it may be lifted completely in the future - check UKC or the BMC RAD for the most recent information.

The landowner below the left-hand (north) end of the crag is becoming increasingly concerned about group usage. Please be aware of this and keep noise and general disturbance down to a minimum.

Lara Debenham nearing the top of the slim corner on *Disappearing Act* (5a) - *page 211* - at Trevor Quarry. Photo: Craig Bailey

Trevor Quarry — D M Wall

D M Wall

This wall has the longest pitches at Trevor Quarry and provides a good number of worthwhile climbs. The climbing tends to be just off of the vertical and fairly technical. There is a horizontal band of shaley rock that crosses the face at about two-thirds height. This band of loose rock is easily passed with care on all but a couple of the routes.

Approach - The wall is the furthest from the parking but is easily accessed from the path that runs beneath the other sectors.

Access - Variable restriction, not applied in recent years - see page 199. No climbing from 15th Feb to 15th July between markers because of nesting birds.

❶ Co-ed in the Coed 5a
A good pitch. Climb the wall to a big ledge and then tackle the shallow twisting groove above.
FA. Gary Gibson 3.11.2007

❷ Maevanwy 6a
An exciting pitch that builds to a good technical sequence high up. Climb up to the final section of wall where a thin sequence directly through the narrow overlap gains a deep pocket. Going right to avoid the crux lessens the grade to a **5c**.
FA. Gary Gibson 3.11.2007

❸ Ogre in the Ogof 5a
Good climbing but unfortunately the rock that has the lower-off in has become unstable, to avoid using it a lower-off ring is in place on the final bolt.
FA. Gary Gibson 3.11.2007

❹ Scratching the Surface . . 5a
Climb to a narrow corner and ascend it with difficulty. Cross the overhang at the break on the left and finish up the wall.
FA. Gary Gibson 3.11.2007

❺ Sgrech yr Hebog 5c
The best route on the wall. Climb the delicate open groove to the break and finish more easily up the wall and corner.
Photo on page 209.
FA. Joss Thomas, John Norman 22.6.2007

D M Wall Trevor Quarry

6 Raptor Rap 5a
Start up *Sgrech yr Hebog*, move right and climb the groove all the way to the break and finish as for *Sgrech yr Hebog*.
FA. Joss Thomas, John Norman 22.6.2007

7 Merlin Magic 5b
Climb to a high first bolt and then follow the rib with interest to the break. Climb up onto the wall above the break and then head up left to the lower-off.
FA. John Norman 29.6.2007

8 Cwm Buy a Thrill 5c
A good climb but the break below the top wall is VERY unstable.
FA. Gary Gibson 11.12.2007

9 The Last Llath 5a
Climb to a tricky move past the initial bolt and then continue to the loose band. Pass the band and avoid a hollow-sounding block above on its right before finishing up the smooth wall.
FA. Gary Gibson 15.11.2007

10 The Full Nine Llaths 5a
Climb to the loose band and pass it just to the left of the tree. Climb the short corner and wall above to finish.
FA. Gary Gibson 15.11.2007

11 Dim Parcio 4a
A good long pitch. Pad up to the first bolt and continue to the final overhang. Either pull around the overhang on suspicious looking rock to the lower-off or use the lower-off just to the right at the top of *Welsh Fargo*.
FA. Gary Gibson 12.11.2007

12 Welsh Fargo 5a
Climb to a bulge and pass it on the left. Continue to the break and then head up the rib left of the flake-crack to a lower-off in the bulge.
FA. Gary Gibson 12.11.2007

13 Slow, Araf, Slow 6a
A varied pitch featuring a delicate crux. Climb the lower wall crossing a flake-crack. Finish over the upper bulge on good holds.
FA. Gary Gibson 12.11.2007

Trevor Quarry — Over Yr Wall

1 Cwm Over Yr 4a
The first route on the left side of the walls. Follow the slab and shallow arete above the horizontal break.
FA. Gary Gibson 11.12.2007

2 Yr, Yr, Yr . . . . 6a+
Climb to the break and then make a puzzling sequence to attain and finish past the overlap.
FA. Gary Gibson 11.12.2007

3 A Rare bit of Welsh 5c
Climb the short awkward wall to the horizontal break and finish rightwards up the face via some nice moves.
FA. Gary Gibson 11.12.2007

4 Dai Laughing 5a
The wall to the horizontal break accesses the rib above.
FA. Gary Gibson 24.1.2008

5 Bath in the Taff . . . . 6a+
Climb the low-angled face and then the technical groove in the upper wall.
FA. Gary Gibson 24.1.2008

6 The Valley's Initiative 5b
Climb the twisting shallow groove to the horizontal break and overlap. Taking care with the rock, pull over the overhang and finish up the groove and wall above.
FA. Gary Gibson 24.1.2008

7 Cwm all ye Faithful 5a
A reasonable line up the face and wall just right of the mid height overhang.
FA. Gary Gibson 25.12.2009

The next four lines all have poor rock at mid height.

8 Cwms the Farmer . . . . 6b+
The easy slab and tough overlap.
FA. Gary Gibson 22.1.2010

9 Help, Help me Rhondda . . . . . . 6a+
Follow the left-hand side of slab and overlap.
FA. Gary Gibson 25.12.2009

10 Do or Dai 6b
The overhang is the hardest and loosest section of the route.
FA. Gary Gibson 25.12.2009

11 Cwms the Snow, Man! 5a
Take the slab and rib to the horizontal break. Finish via the overhang and shallow rib.
FA. Gary Gibson 25.12.2009

12 Free Wales 4a
Right of a vegetated patch above the mid-height break, climb the easy-angled wall and shallow rib to finish.
FA. Gary Gibson 13.2.2008

13 The Welsh Wizard 4c
The bolted line to the right is similar to *Free Wales*.
FA. Gary Gibson 13.2.2008

14 A Dim View of Things 6a
Start left of two trees below an overhang and climb the left-hand side of the overlap and shallow rib above.
FA. Gary Gibson 28.12.2008

15 Canal Canol 5c
Climb the overhang and face.
FA. Gary Gibson 28.12.2008

Over Yr Wall **Trevor Quarry** 203

Over Yr Wall

A long low wall with a series of lines that is slightly spoiled by a metre high band of loose rock that cuts across the face. However much of the climbing above and below the band is worthwhile and well bolted.
Approach - The wall is furthest from the parking but is easily accessed from the path that runs beneath the other sectors.

Access - Variable restriction, not applied in recent years - see page 199. No climbing from 15th Feb to 15th July between markers because of nesting birds.

16 Over Yr, on my Heddlu 5b
Gain the base of the borehole strike with difficulty and then continue to a large ledge and easy finish.
FA. Gary Gibson 25.12.2008

17 Christmas Gone Crackers 6a
Climb direct to the mid height ledge. Finish just left of the vague arete and without using the loose looking crack on its left via a tough sequence. A very tight line that is easier if the loose rock is used.
FA. Gary Gibson 25.12.2008

18 Adrafelin What? 4c
A nice pitch but the lower-off is directly above a perched block.
FA. Gary Gibson 25.12.2008

Trevor Quarry — The Fudd, Dog and Furry Walls

The Fudd, Dog and Furry Walls

A series of low walls that run into each other and provide a concentration of fairly popular lines. This is a very pleasant spot to climb and hangout.

Approach - The walls are easily accessed from nearby Compact Wall.

Access - Variable restriction, not applied in recent years - see page 199. No climbing from 15th Feb to 15th July between markers because of nesting birds.

1 Fuddily Enough .... VS
A trad line on the left of *Fudd For Thought* bolted line.
FA. Gary Gibson, Phil Gibson, Roy Thomas, Hazel Gibson 9.7.2005

2 Fudd For Thought 5b
The bolted line up the wall to the left of the main section of cliff.
FA. Gary Gibson, Phil Gibson, Roy Thomas, Hazel Gibson 9.7.2005

3 All Fudd Up 6a
The far left-hand line has a tricky finish.
FA. Gary Gibson, Phil Gibson, Roy Thomas, Hazel Gibson 9.7.2005

4 Would I, Should I, Fudd I 6c
An intense and reachy sequence.
FA. Gary Gibson, Phil Gibson, Roy Thomas, Hazel Gibson 9.7.2005

5 Fudd Off 6b
Good moves up the wall just left of the central crack.
FA. Gary Gibson, Phil Gibson, Roy Thomas, Hazel Gibson 9.7.2005

6 Elmer J. Fudd .... VS 4b
The left-leaning central crack.
FA. S.Baker, N.Stanford 2.4.1988

7 The Fuddites 6b
The wall between the two cracks.
FA. Gary Gibson, Phil Gibson, Roy Thomas, Hazel Gibson 9.7.2005

8 Betty Bop Rides Again .... VS 4c
The right-hand widening crack-line.
FA. Alec Williams, Simon Williams 3.10.1987

9 Chocolate Fudd .... 6a+
Good moves up the narrow wall.
FA. Gary Gibson, Phil Gibson, Roy Thomas, Hazel Gibson 9.7.2005

The Fudd, Dog and Furry Walls — Trevor Quarry

10 Doggy Shag .... VS 4b
Climb direct up the cracked wall on flaky holds to reach a flat-topped hold and the *Hot Dog* lower-off.
FA. Gary Gibson 13.2.2008

11 Hot Dog 4a
A cleaned line just right of the tree.
FA. Sheila, Ellie Dixon 12.7.2005

12 Dogmatic 6a
Take a direct line through the shallow groove with tricky moves.
FA. Joss Thomas, Daz Haycock 15.8.2009

13 Deputy Dog 4c
Climb up the wall directly past the borehole.
FA. John Norman, Andy Jones 16.11.2006

14 Dogs of War .... 6a+
Climb up just right of a small tree and over the hard bulge.
FA. John Norman, Tim Davies 3.2.2007

15 K9 .... 5a
The last route on the wall shares a lower-off with *Dogs of War*.
FA. John Norman, Tim Davies 3.2.2007

16 Crocs 5c
The short but worthwhile wall.
FA. Gary Gibson, Phil Gibson, Roy Thomas, Hazel Gibson 9.7.2005

17 Alligator's Crawl .... HVS 5a
The thin crack-line.
FA. Gary Gibson, Phil Gibson, Roy Thomas, Hazel Gibson 9.7.2005

18 Snakes in the Grass 6b
The wall and rib. Climb 1m right of the bolt on the lip of the break.
FA. Gary Gibson, Phil Gibson, Roy Thomas, Hazel Gibson 9.7.2005

19 No Reptiles 6a
A good wall climb.
FA. Gary Gibson, Phil Gibson, Roy Thomas, Hazel Gibson 9.7.2005

20 Super Furry Frogs .... 6a+
A thin start leads to a tricky bulge.
FA. Gary Gibson, Hazel Gibson 13.7.2005

21 Horny Toad 6c
Similar climbing to *Super Furry Frogs*.
FA. Gary Gibson, Hazel Gibson 13.7.2005

22 Hornier Toad 6b
This one features hard moves at the break.
FA. Gary Gibson, Hazel Gibson 13.7.2005

23 Long-legged Lizard from Liverpool 6a
A nicely sustained wall climb.
FA. Gary Gibson, Hazel Gibson 13.7.2005

Trevor Quarry — Compact Wall

Compact Wall
A fine section of the quarry that has a superb wall of excellent rock with a number of fingery and sustained routes. The base of the crag is very pleasant and good for picnicking.

Access - Although there is a climbing restriction information board in front of this wall there is no bird restriction here.

1 Thorn in My Side .... VS 4b
Climb the groove up the left edge of the wall passing a small sapling. Move up to the top of the wall then scuttle rightwards to finish at the *Iron Curtain* belay.
FA. Simon Williams, C.Roberts 7.5.1988

2 Iron Curtain E2 5c
The arete and shallow groove. Not bolted.
FA. Doug Kerr, D.Reynolds 16.3.1986

3 Borderline .... Top 50 6a+
Technically interesting but never desperate. Climb direct to the third bolt then move right to finish.
FA. Doug Kerr, D.Reynolds 16.3.1986

4 Margin of Error 6c
Climb direct up the wall above the orange scar.
FA. Doug Kerr 5.6.1986

5 Traction Control .... Top 50 6c
The best route on the wall is sustained and technical requiring precise footwork and strong fingers.
FA. Lee Proctor 6.5.1999

6 Checkpoint Charlie 6b
A good pitch that concentrates its difficulties low down.
FA. Doug Kerr, M.Saunders 5.6.1986

7 Lost Control 6b
A hard start but easier above.
FA. Gary Gibson 11.6.2005

8 Over the Wall .... 6a+
A rising right-to-left diagonal all the way to the *Borderline* belay. An early finish at the *Checkpoint Charlie* belay gives a slightly easier and popular variation. *Photo on page 196*.
FA. Doug Kerr, D.Reynolds 16.3.1986

9 The Great Escape ...... 6a+
A good little pitch with an awkward move past a borehole.
FA. Simon Williams, C.Roberts 17.7.1989

Compact Wall — Trevor Quarry

⑩ I Met a Man from Mars .... 6a+
A good start but an unsatisfactory finish on the upper wall. Climb direct to the high ledge, passing the sloping overlap on its left. Continue above the ledge to a high lower-off.
FA. Simon Williams, C.Roberts 7.5.1988
FA. (Extended finish) Lee Proctor, Gareth Scott 2004

⑪ Boreholderline 6a
Climb past the borehole and bulge.
FA. Gary Gibson 11.6.2005

⑫ Pot Noodle, Don't Leave Home Without One .... VS 4b
An unappealing route up the slabby wall, passing a suspect flake, to reach the ledge. Continue up the easiest line above the ledge to the top of the wall.
FA. Simon Williams, C.Roberts 9.4.1988

⑬ Left Handed Fool .... VS 4b
Climb the prominent steep crack behind the sycamore tree moving right onto the arete to finish. Stake belay.
FA. John Norman 22.8.2006

⑭ April Fool .... VS 4b
Climb the arete at the right edge of the wall, moving left at the break to a shallow groove, which is followed to the top.
FA. Simon Williams, Alec Williams 1.4.1990

⑮ Catch the Pigeon 4c
Tackle the wall past a small hawthorn tree and over the break to a tricky finish on the wall above.
FA. John Norman, Joss Thomas 13.10.2006

⑯ Prof Pat Pending 6a
Climb the brown speckled groove. An eliminate that stays right of the bolts low down. Shares a lower-off with *Ant Hill Mob*.
FA. John Norman, Joss Thomas 14.4.2007

⑰ Ant Hill Mob 5b
The short steep wall on good holds with a difficult start.
FA. John Norman, Joss Thomas 13.10.2006

⑱ Try to Understand, Understand? .... 6a+
A mid height traverse of the wall starting up *Iron Curtain* and finishing up either *I Met a Man from Mars* or *April Fool*. Not shown on topo.
FA. Doug Kerr, M.Saunders 5.6.1986
FA. (Extended version) Simon Williams, C.Roberts 22.9.1989

Impact Wall - 50m

Trevor Quarry — Impact Wall and Railway Buttress

Impact Wall and Railway Buttress
Two small sections of cliff - with both trad and sport lines.
Approach - The walls are easily accessed from nearby Suspect Wall or the lower path from the parking.

1 Full Impact 6c
The short blank wall with three bolts, right of small tree.
FA. Gary Gibson, Hazel Gibson 20.6.2005

2 Opening Impact 6b
The short clean wall to a lower-off.
FA. Gary Gibson, Hazel Gibson 20.6.2005

3 Impaction 5a
The wall and rib with a grassy break midway.
FA. Gary Gibson, Hazel Gibson 20.6.2005

4 Sudden Impact 4a
Good climbing at the grade up the wall and arete.
FA. Gary Gibson, Hazel Gibson 20.6.2005

5 Impact Imminent 6b
The sustained wall up the right-hand side of the arete.
FA. Gary Gibson, Hazel Gibson 20.6.2005

6 No Evasion 5a
A difficult wall leads to the arete right of the corner.
FA. Gary Gibson, Hazel Gibson 20.6.2005

7 Yummy Brummy .... 3+
Line 10m to the left of Railway Buttress itself.
FA. John Norman 21.6.2007

8 Dimmock Crack .... HVD
The corner and flake-crack 2m right of *Yummy Brummy*.
FA. John Norman, Jen Cliffen 9.5.2008

9 James the Red Engine ...... S 3c
The arete left of the corner eases quickly after a stiff starting rockover onto the arete.
FA. Simon Williams, C.Roberts 9.4.1988

10 The Fat Controller .... S 4a
The corner-crack to finish direct over a small overlap.
FA. Simon Williams, C.Roberts 9.4.1988

11 The Boiler House .... S
Ascend a chimney to the overhang. Turn the overhang on the right and climb the steep wall to a good ledge. Step left onto the nose to finish.
FA. John Norman, Joss Thomas 26.3.2007

12 Thomas the Tank Engine .... S 4a
The slim groove just right of the tree and the wall above.
FA. Alec Williams, C.Osborne 9.4.1988

13 Ivor the Engine .... HS 4b
Move up a corner and step right to another slim groove.
FA. C.Osborne, Alec Williams, C.Roberts 9.4.1988

14 Puffing Billy .... HS 4b
The thin crack up the wall to the right of a bush at 4m.
FA. Alec Williams, C.Osborne 9.4.1988

15 The Thin Controller .... VS 4a
A poorly-protected pitch following the hairline crack.
FA. Simon Williams, C.Roberts 9.4.1988

Finishing the delicate groove of the excellent *Sgrech yr Hebog* (5c) - *page 200* - on the D M Wall. The D M Wall has some of the longest and best pitches at Trevor Quarry.

Trevor Quarry — Suspect Wall

Suspect Wall

The first wall of decent rock along from the quarry has a set of interesting technical sport pitches, often with hard moves past the mid-height roof or with a fierce start. Care is needed with the rock in places. The Suspect Wall gets lots of sun from midday and is not prone to seepage. Climbing on sunny calm days in winter is a possibility.

Approach - Follow the path left from the parking and the wall is easily accessed behind a ridge that runs between the path and the escarpment.

❶ Prime Suspect 4a
A popular route that has a tough start up a short wall above a ledge, followed by easier but still interesting moves to finish.
FA. Gary Gibson, Phil Gibson, Roy Thomas, Hazel Gibson 9.7.2005

❷ Innocence 5c
A good route up the rib/groove and wall above.
FA. Gary Gibson, Hazel Gibson 25.6.2005

❸ Crime Scene 6b
The narrow face just right of the rib leads to technical moves over the bulge and onto the wall above.
FA. Gary Gibson, Hazel Gibson 25.6.2005

❹ Suspectus . . . . 6a+
The brown overhanging groove to a small corner high up.
FA. Gary Gibson, Hazel Gibson 25.6.2005

❺ Suspect Device . . . . 6a+
Climb up the low-angled rib to the overhang and make a fingery pull through it on the left and finish up the headwall. Making a direct pull over the overhang is **6c**.
FA. Gary Gibson, Hazel Gibson 25.6.2005

❻ Suspect Criminal 6b
A good pitch up the shallow rib and impressive upper wall. The second clip above the bulge needs a sling.
FA. Gary Gibson, Hazel Gibson 25.6.2005

❼ Under Suspicion 6b
Climb the wall to a steep, white, overhanging upper section. The rock is much better than first appearances suggest.
FA. Gary Gibson, Phil Gibson, Roy Thomas, Hazel Gibson 9.7.2005

❽ SND 4a
Climb the tricky groove to the overlap and shared lower-off with *Cluedo*.
FA. John Norman 15.12.2007

❾ Cluedo 5c
An attractive steep grey wall of fine rock that has a technical and worn start. High in the grade.
FA. Gary Gibson, Phil Gibson, Roy Thomas, Hazel Gibson 9.7.2005

❿ Forensic Science 5a
The blunt rib leads to the overlap. Move rightwards onto upper wall to finish.
FA. Gary Gibson, Phil Gibson, Roy Thomas, Hazel Gibson 9.7.2005

⓫ Forever the Suspect . . . . 6a+
Nice climbing up the thin calcite wall past a rock scar.
FA. Gary Gibson, Phil Gibson, Roy Thomas, Hazel Gibson 9.7.2005

⓬ Haven't got a Clue 6a
An off-vertical wall of good rock with a testing start. High in the grade.
FA. Gary Gibson, Phil Gibson, Roy Thomas, Hazel Gibson 9.7.2005

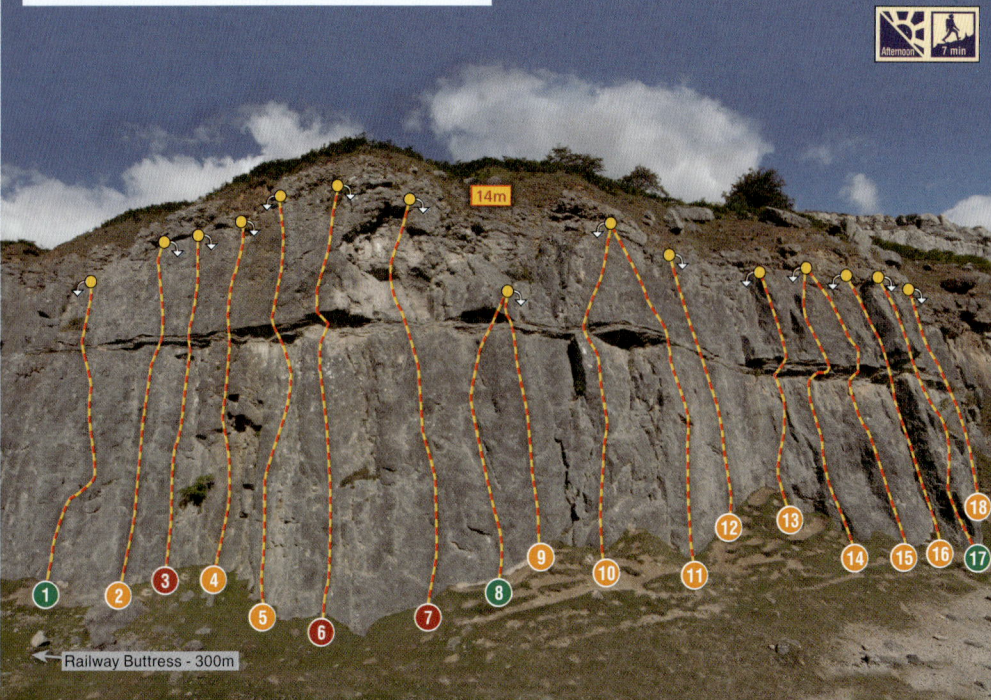

Railway Buttress - 300m

Suspect Wall — Trevor Quarry

13 Proven Guilty 5c
A straightforward steep wall leads to a difficult pull over the roof. Finish easily above.
FA. Gary Gibson, Phil Gibson, Roy Thomas, Hazel Gibson 9.7.2005

14 Plea for Leniency .... 6a+
The wall and small roof has suffered from a rockfall and is now harder than the original line.
FA. Gary Gibson, Hazel Gibson 25.6.2005

15 No Remittal 6a
Climb the thin slabby wall to an overhang and make a powerful move over it to gain an easier finish. *Photo on page 4.*
FA. Gary Gibson, Hazel Gibson 25.6.2005

16 Disappearing Act 5a
The good-looking corner on the right-hand side of the wall is a fine little route. *Photo on page 199.*
FA. John Norman 27.12.2007

17 Clue, So? 4c
Lovely climbing up the arete past a rock scar. One of the better and most popular climbs at the grade in the area.
FA. Gary Gibson, Phil Gibson, Roy Thomas, Hazel Gibson 9.7.2005

18 Amateur Sleuth 5c
A tricky and fairly steep wall is negotiated on sloping holds that lead to easier ground left of two grass ledges.
FA. Gary Gibson, Phil Gibson, Roy Thomas, Hazel Gibson 9.7.2005

30m to the right are the next lines on a tall slim buttress with graffiti at its base.

19 Who's Sam 4a
The start of the route is marked by the declaration of love for Sam! Climb a small protruding rib and the steeper upper wall.
FA. Gary Gibson, Phil Gibson, Roy Thomas, Hazel Gibson 9.7.2005

20 Sam's the Man 6b
A white corner and the big overhang above. The move through the overhang is a bit of a stopper.
FA. Gary Gibson, Phil Gibson, Roy Thomas, Hazel Gibson 9.7.2005

21 A Leaf out of Sam's Book .... 6a+
Watch out for the rose bush! Climb the blunt arete and black slabby wall above the overhang.
FA. Gary Gibson, Phil Gibson, Hazel Gibson 13.4.2007

22 Sam-Sam, the Pan Man 6b
A bouldery outing up the rib and overlap finishing via an arete and overhang.
FA. Gary Gibson, Phil Gibson, Hazel Gibson 13.4.2007

23 Sam-Sam Alert .... 6a+
The wall above a ramp via a hard move past the first overhang.
FA. Gary Gibson, Phil Gibson, Hazel Gibson 13.4.2007

Trevor Quarry — The Quarry

The Quarry

The quarry has two contrasting walls - the less steep south wall which has some easier and mid-grade routes, although these are not strenuous or particularly technical, the lack of protection calls for a steady leader. The vertical east wall has a number of prominent horizontal breaks running across it. These breaks are linked by thin cracks and smooth walls that offer good climbing which can feel bold at times on the trad lines. A few of the lines have now been bolted.

Approach - A short walk up the slope from the parking.

1 Quicksilver .... S 4a
The short slab just right of the corner with a large tree at its base. Climb direct or access the slab from the tree. A poor route.
FA. C.Silverstone (solo) 12.11.1992

2 Big Phlash .... VS 4a
Start on some ledges below a small square-cut corner just above the wide break. Climb direct to the small square-cut corner. Climb this then move right and finish up a broken corner and small overhang. Bold.

3 Long John Silver ...... VS 4b
A much better finish to *Big Phlash*. At the square-cut corner move left and up the bald wall.
FA. C.Silverstone (solo) 12.11.1992

4 Blue Flash .... VS 4b
A bold line up the slab between *Gold Phlash* and *Big Phlash*.
FA. Doug Kerr, D.Reynolds 16.2.1986

5 Gold Phlash .... VS 4b
Gain the wide break just below a little left-facing corner. Move left and climb the wall to finish.

6 Big Splat. .... HVS 4c
Follow *Gold Phlash* to to the wide break and its small corner. Climb straight up to the top.
FA. C.Silverstone 12.11.1992

7 My Route .... VS 4b
Start beneath the flake that is 2m right of *Big Splat*. Climb up to the break before stepping right and ascending the upper wall.
FA. Aaron Willis 28.4.2006

8 Dino. .... VS 4b
Start beneath a vertical borehole at 5m. Climb past the borehole to the wide break. Move through the overhang at an open groove. Continue up easier ground to the top.
FA. S.Williams, N.Stanford 13.9.1987

9 The Silver Line .... HVS 5a
The big arete. Start up its left-hand side. Take the arete on its edge (good nuts) to where it eases, and finish in a good position. Upgraded because of reported hold loss.
FA. Stuart Cathcart, John Dee 5.1978

10 Line Bashing. .... VS 4b
The traverse of the South Wall, starting from the left, as for *Quicksilver*. Climb to the wide break and then pull onto the wall and follow the narrower horizontal breaks right to an easing midway. Wander right and finish up the arete.
FA. C.Silverstone (solo) 12.11.1992

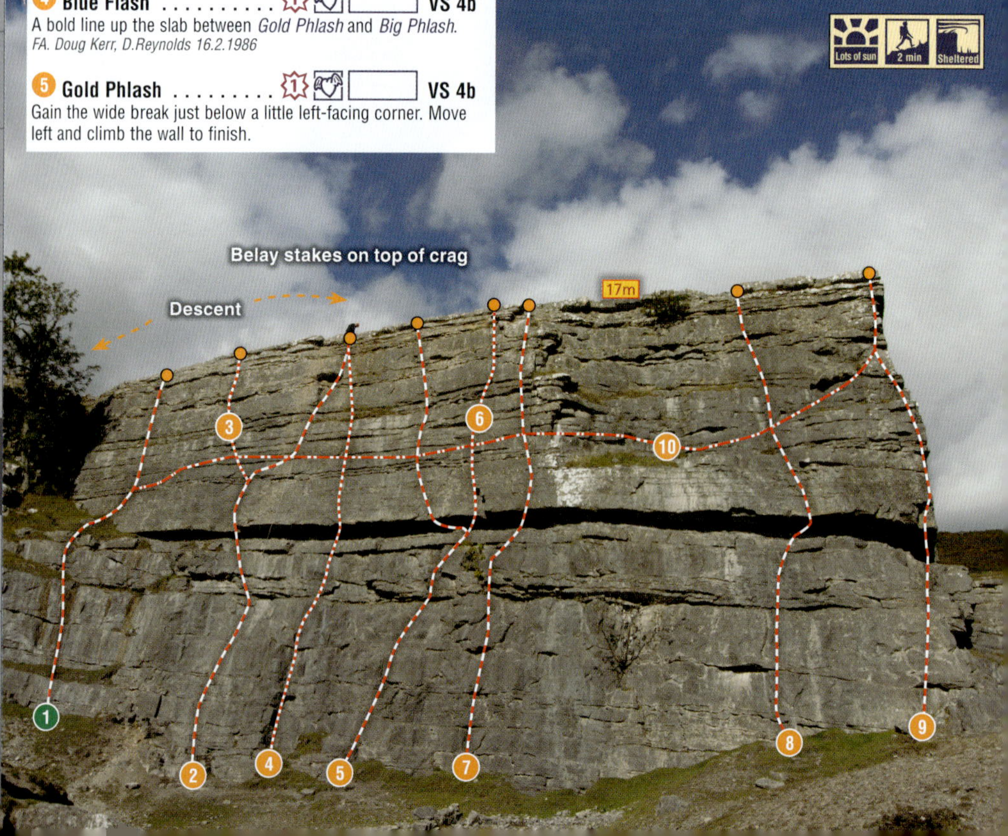

The Quarry — Trevor Quarry

11 Kyani Quatsi E2 5b
Climb to the wide break and move up a small left-leaning corner/groove 3m right of the arete (gear in thin crack to the left). At the next horizontal break, move up to a ledge and then take the crack 3m right of the arete to finish.
FA. Phil Gibson, Gary Gibson 1986 or (as Any Which Way You Can) Dave Baddeley, Darren Boulton 1986.

12 Planet Head E3 5c
Follow *Kyani Quatsi* to the break and then move right to the first rightward-trending thin crack-line. Follow this to the top.
FA. C.Silverstone, A.Picken 7.1992

13 Any Which Way E2 5b
A mini-classic that climbs the line of thin rightward-leaning cracks up the tallest section of the wall. Good protection.
Photo on page 214.
FA. Stuart Cathcart, Malcolm Cameron 11.6.1979

14 Mud Slide Slim 6c
Start just right of the nick in the overhang above the wide break. Pull onto the wall and move up to a small overhang. Make some interesting moves to pass the overhang and gain the next break. More thin and extending moves lead to the top.
FA. Gary Gibson, Phil Gibson 29.12.1986

15 This Way to Clitheroe 6c
A fine piece of wall climbing. Make a stiff pull onto the wall and crank up the shallow horizontal breaks until a hard fingery pull gains a rail. Move right and up to finish.
FA. Gary Gibson, Hazel Gibson 24.4.1988

16 Clevor Trevor 6c
Start up a shallow water-stained groove. Move up the wall to gain a thin crack at the small overhang. Make a series of difficult moves up the crack to reach easier climbing and the top.
FA. Gary Gibson, Phil Gibson 4.5.1992

17 The Last Straw E3 5c
An attractive line that is unfortunately often dirty as it follows a drainage line. The thin crack is tricky to start and becomes increasingly difficult as height is gained.
FA. Stuart Cathcart, Gerald Swindley 15.3.1977

18 Trabucco .... 6c+
Pull onto the wall and climb on sloping breaks to beneath the overhang. Undercut the lip and (perhaps) reach the next hold. Pull up to easier ground.
FA. Gary Gibson, Phil Gibson 29.12.1986

19 White Smear E4 5c
Lovely climbing on fine rock but with no meaningful protection. Move up past the tiny white smear on sloping holds and make a longish reach to pass the overhang and wall above.
FA. Stuart Cathcart, Gerald Swindley 15.3.1977

20 All Over Lancashire E3 5c
The traverse of the East Wall. Start as for *White Smear*.
FA. (Starting in the easy corner) Dave Baddeley, Darren Boulton 1986
FA. (Starting up White Smear) Gary Gibson (solo) 1988

Past the corner is a long, low, slabby side-wall. The blankest section is taken by two lines.

21 Lingen .... VS 4b
The left side of the slabby wall.
FA. Stuart Cathcart (solo) 2.1977

22 Fling .... VS 4b
The right side of the blank slabby wall.
FA. Doug Kerr 13.2.1986

Belay stakes on top of crag — 17m — Descent — Routes on slabby side wall

Lee Proctor on the trad crack of *Any Which Way* (E2 5b) - *page 213* - at The Quarry, Trevor Quarry. The wall to his right now has some good fingery grade 6cs The town in the background is Llangollen and reaching the crag by public transport and a trek up the hill is quite feasible. There is also a campsite between Llangollen and Trevor Quarry.

Independence Quarry

	No star	🟢	🟢🟢	🟢🟢🟢
up to 4+	-	-	-	-
5+ to 6a+	10	3	-	-
6b to 7a	11	13	-	-
7a+ and up	-	-	-	-

The heavily worked but now abandoned Independence Quarry is tucked away on the hillside below the level of the major Trevor crags. The climbable sections of the quarry have been bolted and it now provides a good number of routes in the 6th grade. The quarry is a fairly pleasant spot with a fine outlook and a sunny and relatively sheltered aspect. The rock quality is variable and needs to be handled with care, especially around the horizontal band of shale that runs across all of the lines.

Approach   See map on page 198 and 196

From the main Trevor Quarry parking spots, continue for 750m to a large lay-by on the left just past a left-hand bend. Opposite the lay-by a track winds down hill to a gate. At the gate go right on a path next to a wall to another much smaller gate. Do not go through the gate. Continue on the path downhill until it reaches the floor of the quarry. DO NOT approach the quarry from the narrow single track lane that runs below the floor of the quarry.

Conditions

The climbing sectors face south-west, get plenty of sun and are much more sheltered than the main Trevor Crags. The climbs dry quickly and do not seep very much although it's not possible to climb during rain.

Access

An agreed climbing restriction due to nesting birds at Independence Quarry runs (for all routes) from the 15th Feb - 15th July (inclusive) but may be lifted early. For up-to-date information check UKC or the BMC RAD.

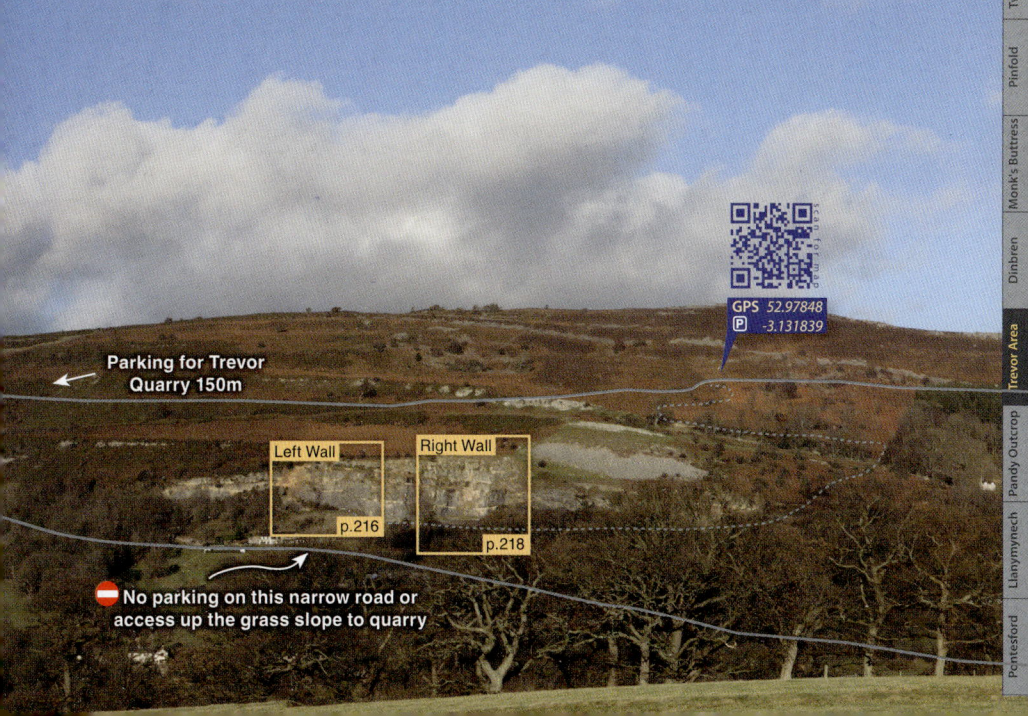

Independence Quarry — Left Wall

Left Wall

A slightly off-vertical wall that is well bolted and with lots of routes in the 6a to 6b range. Some sections of poor rock need to be handled with care.

Access - No climbing (all routes) between 15th Feb and 15th July because of nesting birds.

1 Lipstick 6c
The easy lower wall to a ledge. From here a hard sequence above leads to a lower-off.
FA. Gary Gibson, Hazel Gibson 12.9.2014

2 Lazarus 6b
Tackle a conspicuous flake through the overhang. The interesting lower wall leads to a tough overhang and fingery finale.
FA. John Stringfellow, Dave Vose 28.7.2014

3 Autonomy 6b
Move up a shallow groove and wall to an overhang. Pull through the overhang into a niche and a fingery finish.
FA. John Stringfellow, Dave Vose 28.7.2014

4 Home Rule .... 6a+
Start at a shallow right-facing groove. Sustained technical climbing up the shallow groove and wall leads to the break. Above the break, pleasant easier climbing through an overlap gains a ramp to finish.
FA. John Stringfellow, Dave Vose 28.7.2014

5 Promises .... 6b+
Climb the steady wall to a very hard finish.
FA. Gary Gibson, Hazel Gibson 12.9.2014

6 Better Together 6b
Start at a diagonal borehole. Climb the shallow groove to the break. Pull onto the wall above and another shallow groove that heads to a hard finish.
FA. John Stringfellow, Dave Vose 21.9.2014

7 Rebus .... 6a+
Start at an overhang barring access to a shallow groove. Turn the overhang and move left into the groove and follow it, pulling out right just below the break. Gain the left-trending ramp above and follow this to an exit left to the same lower off as *Better Together*. Variation - move right after pulling onto the ramp and continue up *The Last Bastion*. This gives a long pitch at a consistent grade.
FA. John Stringfellow, Dave Vose 24.8.2014

8 The Last Bastion ... 6c
A long pitch taking the compact grey wall above a grassy ledge, and continuation above the break. A fine route with sustained and interesting climbing, the lower wall being the crux.
FA. John Stringfellow, Dave Vose 21.9.2014

9 Eye to Eye Contact .... 6b+
A good but slightly unbalanced line that has a hard central section.
FA. Gary Gibson 5.9.2014

Left Wall Independence Quarry

10 High Stepper ..... 6a+
A pleasant lower wall leads to a crux on the headwall above the grassy break. *Photo on page 220.*
FA. John Stringfellow, Dave Vose 2.9.2013

11 The Eyes Have It ... 6b
Start at the 'eyes', 3m right of *High Stepper*. Follow a faint groove to a move right onto the rib and up to the grassy break. From the left a difficult move gains the rib on the right, then trend left to lower-off.
FA. John Stringfellow, Dave Vose 2.9.2013

12 The Funnel 6b
Climb the right-hand side of the lower buttress to gain a niche. A tricky move past the break gains the interesting groove above.
FA. John Stringfellow, Dave Vose, Harold Walmesley 28.8.2014

13 The Shute .... 6a+
Take the lower wall to the horizontal break. Above this things become much harder.
FA. Gary Gibson, Hazel Gibson 12.9.2014

14 The Tract .... 6b+
A worthwhile pitch with a hard section and tricky clip above the horizontal break.
FA. Gary Gibson, Hazel Gibson 12.9.2014

15 Conundrum 6c
Climb up steeply through the difficult low overlap.
FA. Gary Gibson 12.9.2014

16 Con Hum-Drum 6b
The bolt-line just to the right of the overlap is not without interest.
FA. Gary Gibson, Hazel Gibson 12.9.2014

17 Technocrat 6a
Around 10m to the right is a slabby rib of good rock. Climb the left-hand line to a lower-off at the horizontal break.
FA. Gary Gibson 21.9.2014

18 Technobrat 6a
The right-hand line also has a lower-off at the horizontal break.
FA. Gary Gibson 21.9.2014

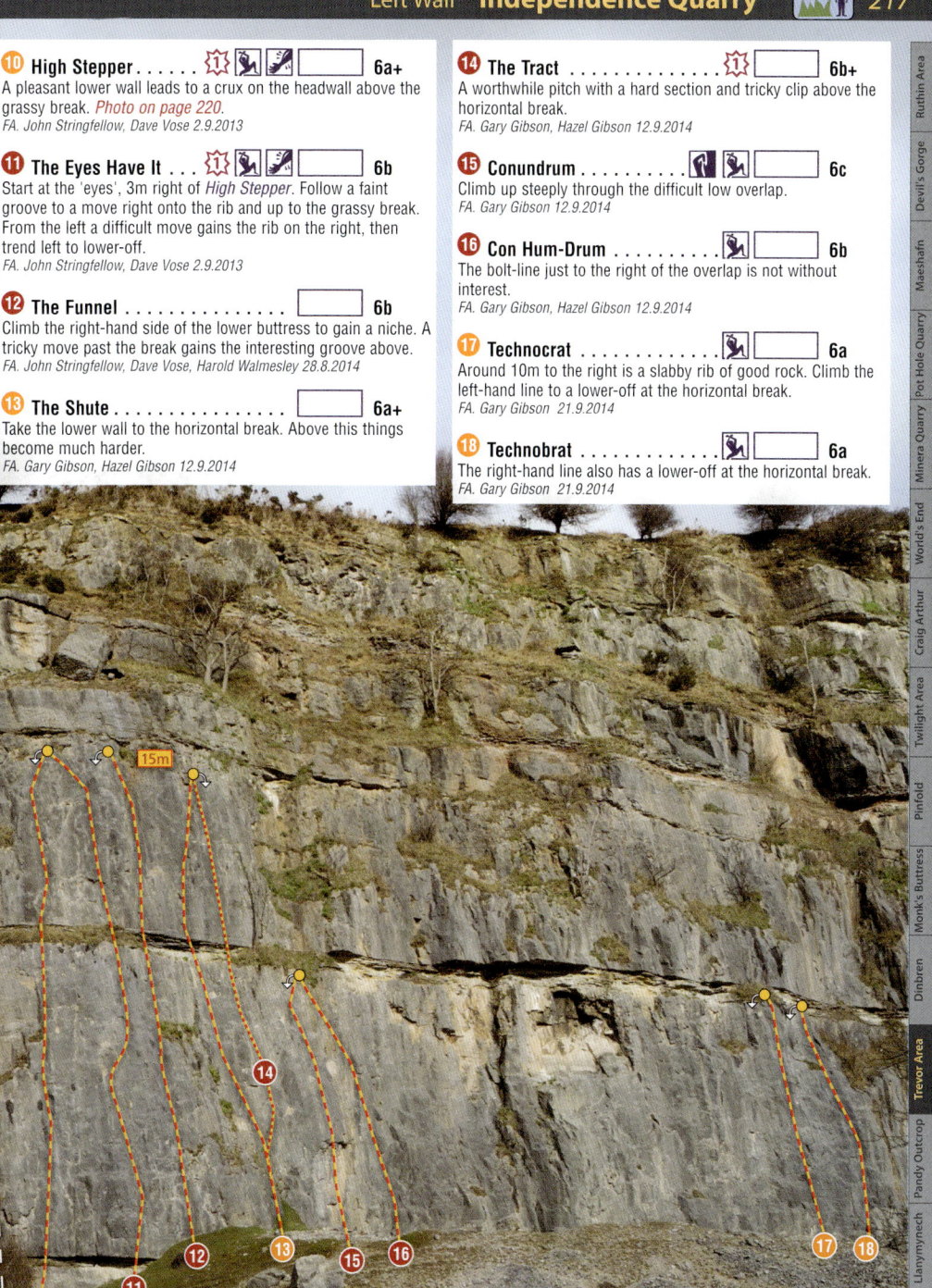

Independence Quarry — Right Wall

Right Wall
The Right Wall has more climbing in the 6s. The large horizontal break has some friable shale in it and some sections of poor rock need to be handled with care on the faces above and below the break.

Access - No climbing (all routes) between 15th Feb and 15th July because of nesting birds.

1 Consider an Evil . . . . 6a+
Climb the shattered wall and difficult overlap to an easier upper groove.
FA. Gary Gibson, Phil Gibson, Hazel Gibson 20.8.2005

2 It Seems So . . . . 6a+
Follow the wall and groove above the horizontal break to a steepish finale on fragile rock.
FA. Gary Gibson, Phil Gibson, Hazel Gibson 20.8.2005

3 Is This as Good as it Gets . . . . 6c+
Climb the short lower wall to the break before a very tough sequence allows entry onto the face via a groove. Finish up the fine rib above.
FA. Gary Gibson, Phil Gibson 20.8.2005

4 No Regard 6b
A tricky move to pass the overlap gains the easier face above. Finish via moves rightwards to a lower-off.
FA. Gary Gibson, Phil Gibson 20.8.2005

5 Beauregarde . . . . 6a+
This climb has suffered a rockfall at the overlap and may be harder.
FA. Gary Gibson, Phil Gibson, Hazel Gibson 20.8.2005

6 Ump and Over 6a
The very shallow rib and pleasant face with a tricky finish that can be dirty.
FA. Gary Gibson, Phil Gibson, Hazel Gibson 20.8.2005

7 Umpalumpa Groove 5a
The crack/groove-line.
FA. Gary Gibson, Phil Gibson, Hazel Gibson 20.8.2005

8 Roald Dahling 6c
Good climbing on the upper wall after a problematic move through the overlap.
FA. Gary Gibson 8.8.2006

9 Verruca Salt 6b
A sustained route that goes past the detached-looking block above the break and continues up the blunt rib above.
FA. Gary Gibson 8.8.2006

Right Wall Independence Quarry

10 Augustus Gloop .... 6a+
The hanging black scoop and wall above. Worthwhile.
FA. Gary Gibson 8.8.2006

11 Into the Fire 7a
Fingery moves to overcome the overlap access the shallow black groove above. A good pitch.
FA. Gary Gibson 8.8.2006

12 Indiana Jones .... 6a+
The wall, cracks and face moving leftwards to a lower-off.
FA. Gary Gibson, Phil Gibson 28.8.2005

13 Indi-Pops 6c
A short difficult line through the overlap to the lower-off just above.
FA. Gary Gibson 8.8.2006

14 The Indi Mix 6c
A brief climb but with some hard moves to pass the overlaps.
FA. Gary Gibson, Phil Gibson 20.8.2005

15 Oh Calcutta 6a
Follow the bolted shallow groove on the left side of the tall grey wall.
FA. Gary Gibson 23.7.2005

16 Independence Day ..... 6b+
A worthwhile pitch featuring sustained climbing and some interesting moves.
FA. Gary Gibson 23.7.2005

17 I Don't Agree .... 6b+
Excellent climbing up the central line of the face on good rock.
FA. Gary Gibson 23.7.2005

18 Independence 6b
Sustained face climbing via a slight rib.
FA. Gary Gibson 23.7.2005

19 The Last Crusade ... 6c+
Difficult and fingery moves above a ledge with a scary clip at the third bolt (this is best done with a pre-placed quick-draw).
FA. Gary Gibson 27.3.2005

20 India 6b
On the far right of the crag is a pleasant groove with an unusual exit leftwards.
FA. Gary Gibson 27.3.2005

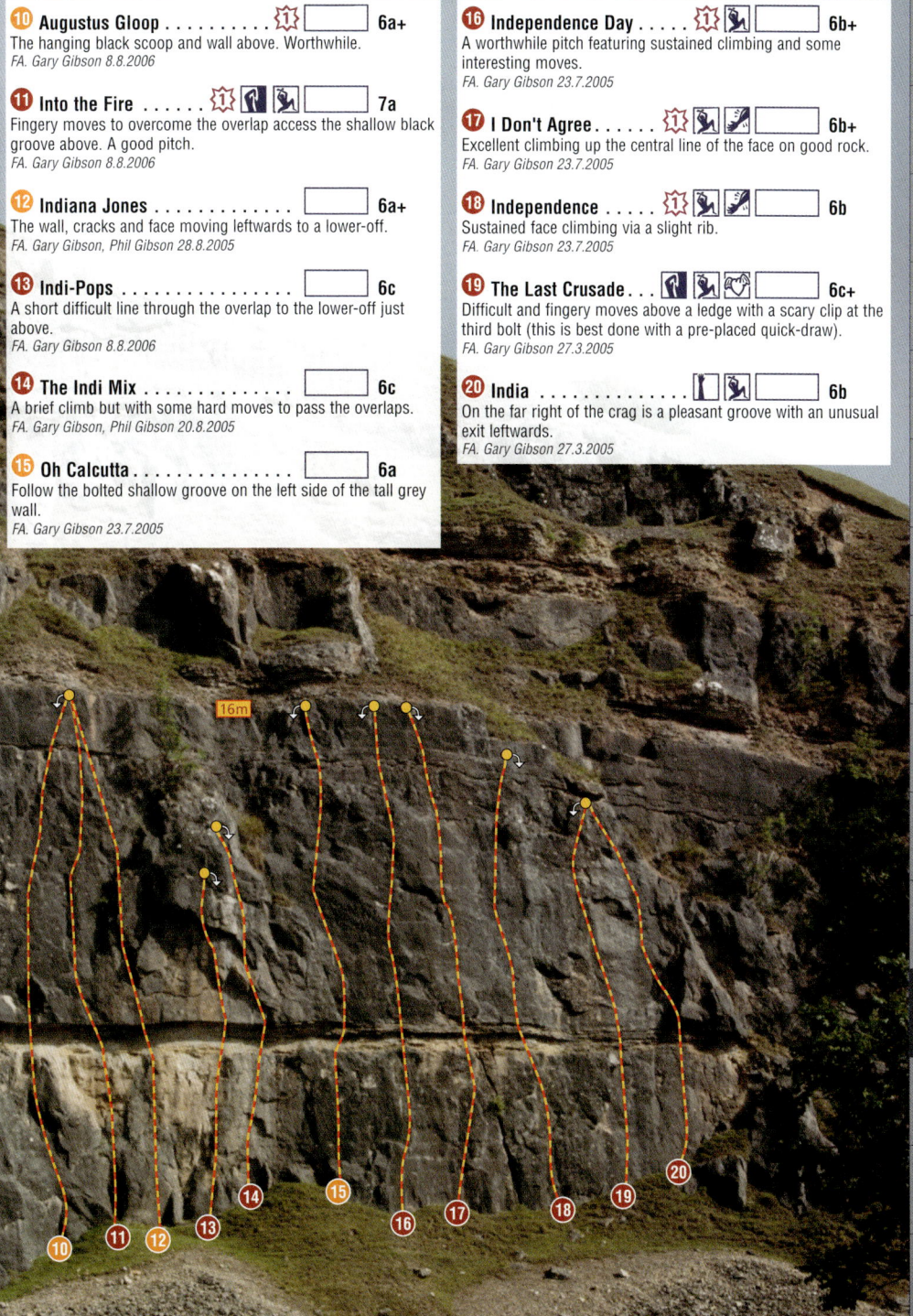

Dave Vose on *High Stepper* (6a+) - *page 217* - on the Left Wall at Independence Quarry. Photo: John Stringfellow

Ruabon Quarry

	No star	★	★★	★★★
Mod to S	-	-	-	-
HS to HVS	-	-	-	-
E1 to E3	-	-	1	-
E4 and up	-	-	1	-

Ruabon Quarry is a short steep venue with a couple of powerful lines on quarried sandstone. This is a local spot that has quick access but in summer, even though it is super steep and rainproof, is heavily shaded by the dense tree canopy and can retain any dampness.

Approach   Also see page 196
From Ruabon, take the B5097 to Pen y Cae for 0.5 miles and park next to a football pitch (next to the traffic calming installation is convenient). Walk along the road for 500m to a bridleway on the right. Go down the bridleway for 120m and the crag is on the right in trees. Avoid trying to park closer to the bridleway since there is little space and the road is narrow.

Conditions
Ruabon Quarry is a steep sandstone wall that might offer some possibilities for climbing in the rain. It is, however, heavily shaded by tree cover in summer and can hold dampness.

❶ **Flyboy** . . . . **7b+**
Starting in the centre of the impressively steep wall, climb via pockets until a wild move may get you through the crux. Very unusual climbing for this area - it overhangs by 4m! A local's 'must do' route!
FA. Ryan McConnell 20.8.2012

❷ **Don't By China** **6c**
Climb the steep arete right of *Flyboy*. A big move at two-thirds height is the crux.
FA. Ryan McConnell 29.8.2012

The Black Wall at Llanymynech Quarry is the preserve of trad pitches. Here Phil Black is tackling the intricate *Black Wall Direct* (E2 5c) - *page 246* - one of a handful of stunning extreme wall climbs.

Outlying Areas

Pandy Outcrop, Llanymynech Quarry, Pontesford Rocks

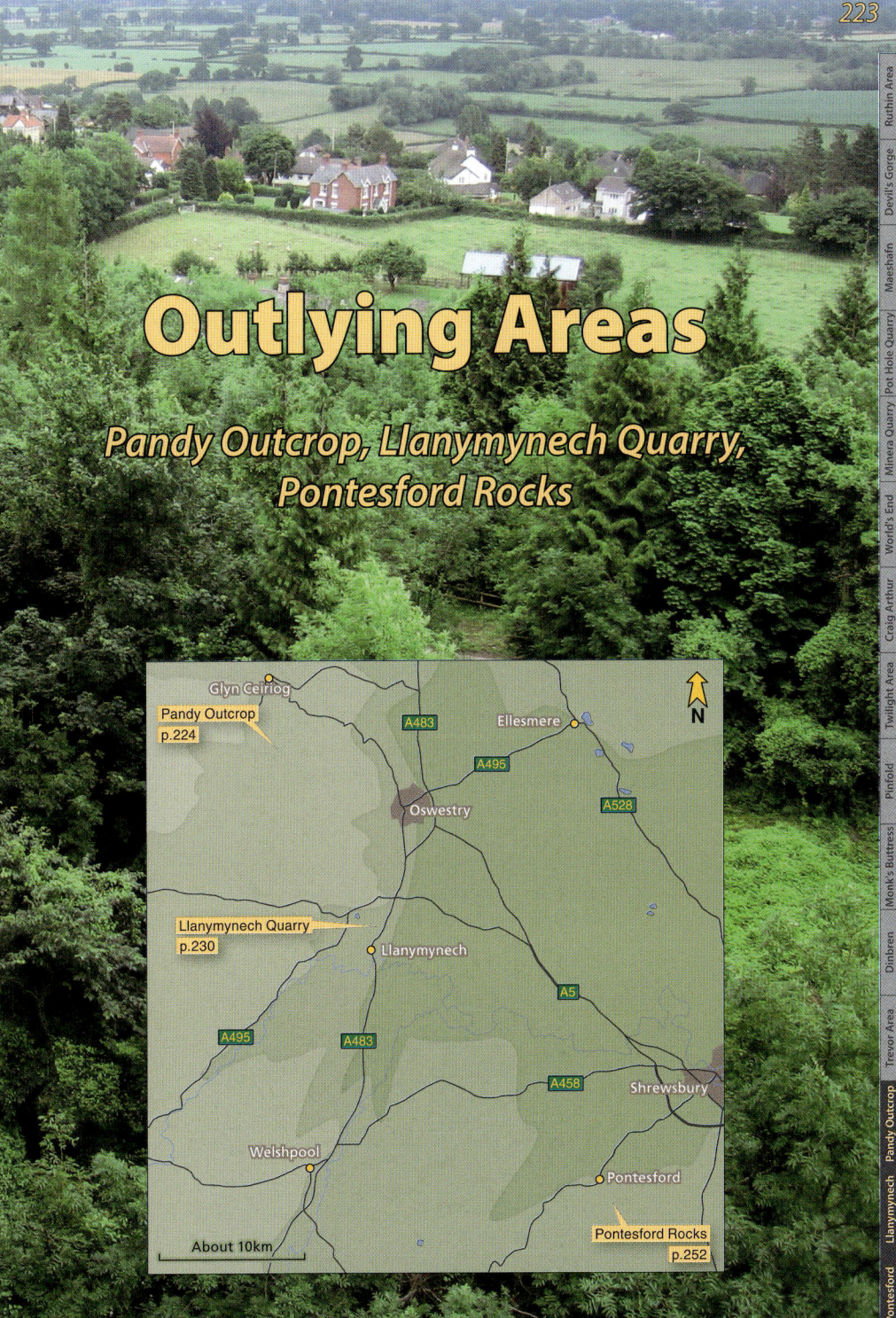

Pandy Outcrop

	No star	⭐	⭐⭐	⭐⭐⭐
Mod to S	6	1	-	1
HS to HVS	1	4	1	1
E1 to E3	1	3	1	-
E4 and up	-	1	-	-

A beautifully located crag that offers a limited number of good single pitch trad lines predominantly in the Severe to VS grade range. The routes are not particularly long but are perched high on the edge of the escarpment with expansive views of the valley below and the hills above. The crag is composed of good solid igneous rock and the climbs vary from steep wall and crack climbs to airy slabs. A great little crag to get away from it all.

Approach   Also see map on page 223

Park in a small lay-by 1km from Glyn Ceiriog (space for three cars). This is just beyond a quarry entrance and opposite a footpath - if the parking is full, park in Glyn Ceiriog. Walk along the road to Pandy and turn right up a lane, opposite the gallery. Walk up here for 500m to a track on the right. Follow the track for 300m to a junction and information board. Take the right-hand track steeply uphill and where the footpath sign indicates a left turn, head straight on up the track. The track opens out into fields and passes a fenced off pond/marsh on the right. Just beyond, enter the woods via a wooden plank on the top of the fence (this is 10m right from the corner of the wood). Walk through the wood and along the top of the cliff to arrive at the descent path that starts above a tiny section of drystone wall.

Conditions

The cliff gets plenty of sun and dries quickly but is high and exposed so is really only a spring to early autumn venue.

Access

The crag is owned by Nantyr Outdoor Education Centre and permission is given for individuals to visit and climb. Please follow the parking and approach notes carefully. Groups should contact the owners before visiting.

Pandy Outcrop

Approaching the upper section of the superb slab climb *Schmutzig* (S 4a) - *page 228* - at Pandy Outcrop. Pandy Outcrop is a fine little crag made up of good solid rock set above a tranquil valley. Photo: Paul Cox

Pandy Outcrop — Cannon Buttress

Cannon Buttress

An unusual section of crag that has a number of jutting prows and aretes separated by some chimney/crack-lines.

Approach - The left-hand lines are reached by a scramble past brambles.

Access - Birds occasionally nest in the cracks. Please keep off the routes close by if this is the case.

1 Hovering on Eternity — E4 6a
Climb the short overhanging arete just right of easy ground. Tough from start to finish.
FA. Stuart Cathcart, Bryan Philips, Dave Barker late 1970s

2 Cannon Chimney — HVD
The traditional chimney passing a chockstone.
FA. Stuart Cathcart, Bryan Philips, Dave Barker late 1970s

3 Bawls Like a Bull — E3 5c
Right of *Cannon Chimney* is an impressive leaning arete. Climb the arete on good holds past a peg.
FA. Stuart Cathcart, Bryan Philips, Dave Barker late 1970s

4 Cannon Left Hand — HVS 5b
Starting as for *Bawls Like a Bull* move up to the crack on the left side of the cannon. Steep but well-protected moves may gain the top of the cannon. Finish up a crack.
FA. Stuart Cathcart, Bryan Philips, Dave Barker late 1970s

5 Cannon Arete — HS 4b
A fine line and a great climb. Start below the cannon itself and ascend the arete and crack on good holds.
FA. Stuart Cathcart, Bryan Philips, Dave Barker late 1970s

Face Value Buttress **Pandy Outcrop** 227

Face Value Buttress
A squat buttress of excellent steep rock with a number of intense lines up it. The routes are very exposed given they are only 10m high.
Approach - Walk up to a huge flat block below the face.

6 ELP **E1 5a**
A slightly artificial line but with some good face climbing. Take the wall to the right of *Cannon Arete* in its entirety. Gear in *Cannon Arete* but the holds are out of bounds.
FA. Stuart Cathcart, Bryan Philips, Dave Barker late 1970s

7 Face Value . . . . Top 50 **VS 4c**
A very good pitch - both exposed and sustained. Climb direct up the front face of the buttress on good holds to meet and finish up a slim groove. *Photo on page 229.*
FA. Stuart Cathcart, Bryan Philips, Dave Barker late 1970s

8 Victims. **E2 5c**
Great rock and holds. Requires some small wires at the start. Climb past a thin crack to a pocket and good hold at 3m. Continue up the wall to finish.
FA. Stuart Cathcart, Bryan Philips, Dave Barker late 1970s

9 Tension Stretcher. . . **E2 6a**
Move up the steep wall to below an overhang and pass it on the left. Continue up the wall above to finish.
FA. Stuart Cathcart, Bryan Philips, Dave Barker late 1970s

10 Lightning Groove . . . . **VS 4c**
From above a gorse bush, make a tricky step left to gain a hanging corner/groove. Climb it and the wall above to the top.
FA. Stuart Cathcart, Bryan Philips, Dave Barker late 1970s

Pandy Outcrop — The Slab

The Slab
An attractive sweep of slab that has a number of good pitches on its cleanest sections. The mossy sections can retain damp after rain.

Approach - The starts are mostly to the left of the heavily vegetated base of the slab.

1 Villeta .... M
Move up to a gorse bush and take the wide crack on the right.

2 Blue Thunder .... HVS 5b
Climb the slab direct to the overhang and pull through it with difficulty using the crack.
FA. Stuart Cathcart, Bryan Philips, Dave Barker late 1970s

3 Splitting the Difference .. HS
A pleasing outing directly up the slab to finish between the two jutting prows at the top of the crag.

4 Gray Face No Space E2 5c
Climb directly up the easy slab to below the prow. Use the centre rib on the bulge to make hard moves to reach onto the face and top.
FA. Simon Cathcart 2.2007

5 Vegetable Crack .... Diff
The wide dog-leg crack lives up to its name.

6 Schmutzig .... Top 50 S 4a
The continuous section of clean slab is followed by this excellent pitch. Move up and make a tricky step right to access the base of the slab. Climb up on good pockets to an easing midway. Continue more easily heading rightwards past diagonal thin cracks to finish. *Photo on page 225.*

The next two lines are overgrown at the time of writing. Not shown on topo.

7 Paper Chase .... VD
Start on the slab directly between the two large sycamore trees. Bear rightwards to the large blocks at mid height and continue up the gully.
FA. Joss Thomas, Wayne Hughes 25.7.2006

Pandy Outcrop 229

8 Llyffant Bach ▢ S 4a
Start by the large sycamore tree on the right. Climb directly up to the overhanging block where a steep pull leads to easy climbing above.
FA. Joss Thomas, Rod Lloyd Jones 27.7.2006

To the right are two more lines - not shown on the topo.

9 Emerald Point ▢ VD
Move up over blocks heading for the start of the slab right of the large corner. Once at the slab, move left to the base of the corner and climb it to the top.

10 Banana Boat ▢ S 4a
From midway down the descent path, cross a grassy gangway and climb the big open groove to a finish over a small roof.

The slab has a fairly popular girdle traverse.

11 Duck Flight ▢ HS 4a
Start as for *Villeta*.
1) 25m. Move up to the small tree and head rightwards to join *Schmutzig* midway. Follow a line of good holds right to a belay on large perched block.
2) 4a, 20m. Gain a horizontal finger-crack on the slab above the belay. Move right to the edge and swing down via a hidden hold into the corner of *Emerald Point*. Cross the slab and gain the groove of *Banana Boat* and finish over its final overhang.
FA. Stuart Cathcart, Bryan Philips, Dave Barker late 1970s

Paul Cox contemplating the finishing groove of the exposed *Face Value* (VS 4c) - *page 227* - at Pandy Outcrop.

Llanymynech Quarry

Llanymynech Quarry has become one of the most popular sport climbing venues in the region and now offers a large number of routes, the best of which are in the mid 6s to 7s grade range. The variety of rock is striking as can be seen in this picture of the Red Wall with climbers on *Mussel Bound* (7a+) on the left and *Poison Ivy* (7a+) - *page 251*.

Llanymynech Quarry

	No star	✪	✪✪	✪✪✪
Mod to S / 4+	3	-	-	-
HS-HVS / 5-6a+	32	9	-	-
E1-E3 / 6b-7a	16	12	13	8
E4 / 7a+ and up	3	6	7	4

The towering grey and red limestone faces of Llanymynech Quarry are home to a large number of fantastic sport pitches, many of which are exceptionally long and often climbable throughout the year thanks to the cliff's sheltered aspect. There is a good depth of quality sport climbing in the 6b to 7b grade span and, as a bonus a handful of excellent trad wall climbs that span the E grade from 1 to 5. The showpieces Nomad, Grid Iron, Black and Red Wall are unmissable when travelling along the road between Wrexham and Welshpool, and sit above a tree covered landscape that was once an active quarry but has now been developed into an attractive nature reserve. As a consequence climbing at Llanymynech Quarry is today an extremely pleasant experience with delightful views out across the River Severn floodplain to the hilltops of The Wrekin and Criggan. There are a number of access restrictions in place - these cover nesting bird sites and access to some of the quarry on ecological and safety grounds - see next page.

Approach
Llanymynech Quarry runs parallel to the A483 that links the towns of Wrexham and Welshpool. Approaching from the north, follow the main A483 into the village of Pant and 100m after the Cross Guns Inn, turn right into Underhill Lane. Follow the lane for 100m onto an unmade section which leads to the parking area after 50m. From the south, follow the main A483 through the village of Llanymynech and, just after the Pant village sign, turn left into Underhill Lane. From the parking area the quarry is easily gained along a path in around 5 minutes.

Conditions
Llanymynech Quarry is an excellent sheltered lowland option if a strong westerly wind is blowing and it is a good place to head for if the higher crags are suffering from bad weather. There is sometimes a bit of seepage, although it is rarely a problem. Climbing is possible in light rain on a few of the Red Wall and Cul-de-Sac quarry lines. The walls dry reasonably quickly after rain and receive plenty of sun throughout the year.

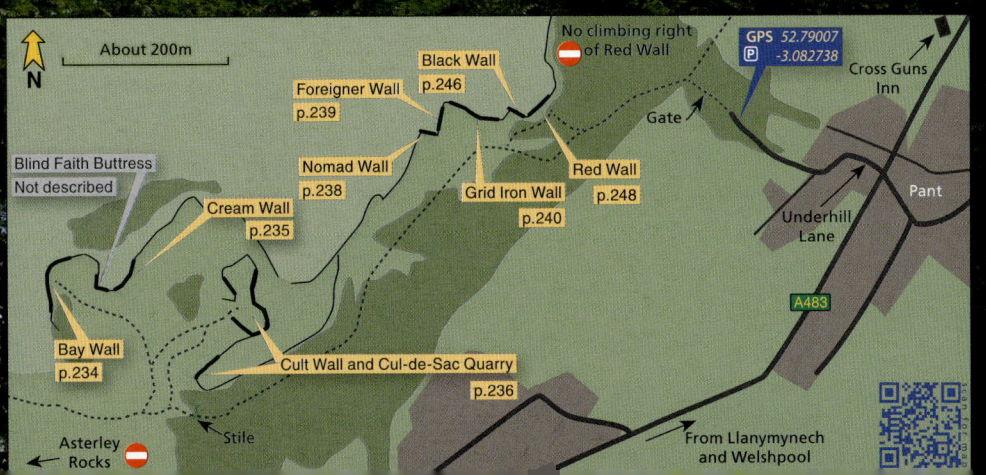

Paul Bolger midway up the sustained *Long John Codling* (7a) - *page 251* - on the right-hand side of Llanymynech Quarry's Red Wall. Climbing on the Red Wall is possible in light rain and is well sheltered from any westerly winds.

Access   Llanymynech Quarry

Access
The site is managed by the Shropshire and Montgomery Wildlife Trusts and there is an agreement with the BMC to allow individual recreational climbers, and club members, to climb at Llanymynech. Nothing in the agreement is legally binding, however failure by climbers to follow the guidelines set out below could lead to a permanent restriction on climbing.

Please pay close attention to the following:

- **Bay Wall**, **Cream Wall** and Blind Faith Buttress (not covered in this guidebook) are on land owned by Montgomery Wildlife Trust and have been identified as being particularly unstable. For this reason the Wildlife Trust cannot allow public access to this area, and signs and fencing are in place to ensure that the Wildlife Trust fully complies with its legal responsibility. Climbers ignoring these signs fully accept the additional risks involved, and that they are then on this land as trespassers. Wildlife Trust staff and volunteers will advise any members of the public that are seen within the fenced area of this fact. Please be polite in your response and leave if asked to do so.

- **A seasonal restriction on climbing is in place on Black Wall and Red Wall to safeguard from disturbance legally protected bird species. This extends from 1st March until June 30th.**

- No climbing is allowed at any time for conservation reasons in the area to the right (east and north) of **Red Wall**. No climbing is allowed at **Asterley Rocks** at any time.

- There are some rare plants below the **Foreigner Wall**. Climbing is not allowed here and the routes maybe de-bolted. The descriptions are only included in this book for completeness.

- The development of new routes may jeopardise the existing access arrangements. No new routes or bolting should be undertaken without prior consultation and agreement with the Wildlife Trusts. Contact the BMC for further details.

- The cliffs and rock faces are inherently unstable and rock falls can occur at any time. In the interest of public safety, especially risks to third parties and other visitors to the site, the Wildlife Trusts reserve the right to prevent climbing at any time if a risk assessment shows there is a significant and immediate threat to public safety.

- The whole site is a SSSI and as such enjoys a degree of legal protection. The rocks are open to the public as nature reserves by the respective Wildlife Trusts. The area has significant conservation, historical and archaeological interest; in particular there are many rare plants along the base of the cliffs which have developed on the thin limestone soils. Climbers should help to conserve the plants and wildlife by not leaving any litter, or by disturbing or removing any soil, vegetation or rock features. This applies equally to the whole site, including the base of cliffs and approach paths, as well as to rock faces.

- The Wildlife Trusts do not take any responsibility for the placement, maintenance or safety of any bolts or other fixed climbing equipment or for the safety or integrity of the rock faces. All climbers have to be aware and accept that the rock face is inherently unstable and no fixed equipment at this site has been tested or inspected. Climbers have to make their own judgement based on experience as to the safety and suitability of any fixed equipment and of the stability of the cliff faces.

Llanymynech Quarry — Bay Wall

Bay Wall
A very sheltered section of quarried wall with some reasonable pitches that can be a little dirty.

Access - This wall is unstable and anyone climbing here does so at their own risk. See page 233.

① **Bayonets Fixed** .... 6a+
The orange-coloured wall to the left of a cave is loose and dirty.
FA. Gary Gibson 9.5.2008

② **Bayeux Tapestry** .... 6c+
Start just right of a cave and climb easily to hard moves.
FA. Gary Gibson 4.4.2008

③ **Bay Watch** .... 6b+
Climb a narrow rib to a steep headwall.
FA. Gary Gibson 4.4.2008

④ **Summer Bay Babe** 6a
Follow the ledges/ramp to a leftward exit at the top.
FA. Gary Gibson, Mark Richardson, Goi Ashmore 24.3.2008

⑤ **Bayonets Ready** 6b
Climb the wall to some powerful pulls near the top.
FA. Gary Gibson, Mark Richardson, Goi Ashmore 24.3.2008

⑥ **Bay City Stroller** ...... 6a+
Interesting climbing up a groove and wall.
FA. Gary Gibson, Mark Richardson, Goi Ashmore 24.3.2008

⑦ **Bay Bee** 6a
Good climbing. From a ledge climb to a slab and rib.
FA. Gary Gibson, Hazel Gibson 4.4.2008

⑧ **Welcome to the Bay** . 6b
One of the wall's best that moves out right from *Bay Bee*.
FA. Gary Gibson, Hazel Gibson 4.4.2008

⑨ **Be My Baby** .... 6b+
Climb up via ledges to gain a puzzling finish.
FA. Gary Gibson 9.5.2008

⑩ **Bye Bye Baby** 6b
Head out right from *Be My Baby* and move up to a tough finish.
FA. Gary Gibson 9.5.2008

⑪ **One Fine Bay** 6b
A low technical slab gains easier but steeper ground.
FA. Gary Gibson 26.4.2008

⑫ **Bay Leaf** 5c
A worthwhile climb with the difficulties at mid height.
FA. Gary Gibson 26.4.2008

⑬ **Bay of Figs** 6a
A long line with a steep ending.
FA. Gary Gibson 26.4.2008

⑭ **About a Bay** 6a
A good long pitch just to the right of *Bay of Figs*.
FA. Gary Gibson 9.1.2010

Cream Wall — Llanymynech Quarry 235

Cream Wall

A tall wall of variable rock. The base is prone to becoming heavily vegetated.

Access - This wall is unstable and anyone climbing here does so at their own risk. See page 233.

15 Better Lait than Never 6b
Follow the left-hand arete of the wall.
FA. Gary Gibson 18.4.2009

16 Screaming Dream .... 6a+
A powerful initial section gains face climbing above.
FA. Gary Gibson 19.2.2009

17 Semi Skimmed .... 6a+
A tough start and finish with easier ground in between.
FA. Gary Gibson, Hazel Gibson 12.4.2009

18 Gold Top 6b
Follow the left-hand line of bolts after a steady start.
FA. Gary Gibson 19.2.2009

19 All Gone Sour 6b
The right-hand line with a technical section low down.
FA. Gary Gibson 19.2.2009

20 The Cat that Got the Cream .... 6b+
Climb the long face behind a tree to a good finish up a headwall.
FA. Gary Gibson 12.4.2009

The route **Past Your Eyes, 6b+** went direct above the fourth bolt on UHT. The top section has fallen down and is unstable - DO NOT climb this route.

21 UHT 6b
At the fourth bolt on *Past Your Eyes* move up right to the second of two bolt-lines and climb it to finish up a hanging groove.
FA. Andy Taylor, Dan Taylor 30.3.2008

22 Never Rub Another Man's Rhubarb
.... 6b
Climb up to meet *UHT* before taking the bolt line on the left to a steep finish.
FA. Gary Gibson, Hazel Gibson 12.4.2009

100m to the right of the Cream Wall is a plantation in a slight amphitheatre.

23 Sasha the Basha 7a
Climb a crack with care to a roof. Head left on edges on the lip of the roof and then move up to gain a standing position above the roof. Move slightly right a to a good hold from where hard moves up and left lead to better holds below a slight roof. Pull over the roof on its right and follow the delightful slab to a lower-off.
FA. Chris Jones, Dylan Burgess 6.11.2006

Llanymynech Quarry — Cult Wall and Cul-de-Sac Quarry

Cult Wall and Cul-de-Sac Quarry

The main attraction here is a leaning wall that is a useful spot for those in need of an intense finger workout. It can be a bit dusty.

Approach - Follow the path underneath the main quarry and after crossing a stile, take a path on the right (Cult Wall is to the right) that leads up into a huge quarried basin. Cul-de-Sac Quarry is at the back of this.

1 Culture and Boutique 6a
The left-hand line. Nice climbing up the face with a tricky finish.
FA. Gary Gibson 2015

2 Eau de Culture 5c
The face.
FA. Gary Gibson 2015

3 No Name 6a
One hard passage up a smooth wall.
FA. Gary Gibson 2015

4 The Cult 5c
Features a difficult long move low down.
FA. Gary Gibson 2015

5 Culture Vulture 5b
A long face.
FA. Gary Gibson 2015

6 Culture Cryptic 5b
The right-hand line.
FA. Gary Gibson 2015

7 Alors! . . . . Diff
The well-worn left-hand wall. Stay on line to avoid loose rock.

8 Ca Va! . . . . VD
The left-hand crack. Can be very dirty at times.

9 Voila! . . . . VD
The left-trending line to a block. Finish direct. Can be dirty.

10 Merde! . . . . HS 4a
Start up *Voila!* and move up to, and past, a square-cut overhang. Finish direct up the horizontally-banded wall. The top-out needs care.

11 Dirty Climb 5b
The wall left of the cave. The hangers go missing at times.
FA. Nick Dixon 7.2005

12 Walker's Walk 6a
The right-leading line out over the tunnel entrance.
FA. Andy Walker 2000s

13 Dream of White Horses, Not . . . 6a
Starting to the right of the tunnel entrance follow the left-trending line of bolts.
FA. Callum Dixon 7.2005

14 Sheila's Route 5c
Climb direct from where *Dream of White Horses, Not* goes left.
FA. Sheila Dixon, Nick Dixon 2003

15 Andy Pandy E4 5c
The unprotected arete on the right of the descent path. Ivy may need removing before an ascent.
FA. Gary Gibson 29.4.1989

16 Flowery Pot . . . . 6c+
The steep line passing a ledge just left of the arete.
FA. Gary Gibson 9.1.2010

17 Slobberlob 7b
The right-hand side of arete. Upgraded due to hold loss.
FA. Gary Gibson 22.4.1989

Cult Wall and Cul-de-Sac Quarry — Llanymynech Quarry

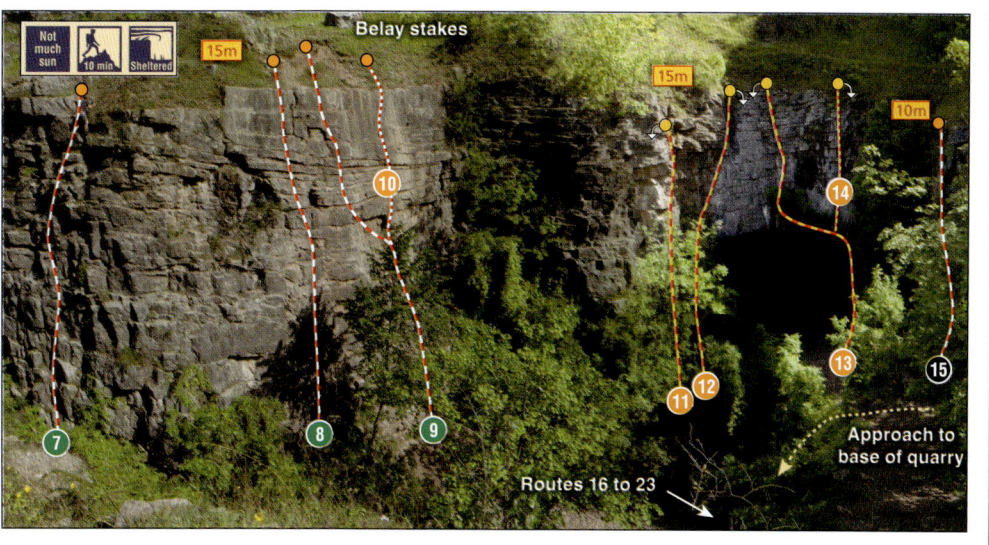

18 Back-Bee Tubin 8a
A bouldery pitch featuring some intense and fingery climbing.
FA. Nick Dixon 2003

19 Little Weed 7c
A fine route up the central crack-line with a tough upper half.
FA. Gary Gibson, Nick Dixon 11.2.1989

20 Spotty Dog 7b
Good moves between the breaks just right of the thin crack of *Little Weed*.
FA. Nick Dixon, Andy Popp 1988

21 Bill and Ben .... 7b+
The bolted wall passing an old peg.
FA. Gary Gibson 29.4.1989

22 C'est Chaud! ...... 7c+
Bolted line left of *Saul's Crack* via some cemented up breaks.
FA. Nick Dixon 2008

23 Saul's Crack .... VS 4c
A steep, dirty and wide crack on the right-hand side of the wall.
FA. Gordon Caine, Dave Cuthbertson 7.1970

Llanymynech Quarry — Nomad Wall

The first route starts down in the hollow below the Nomad Wall.

1 Southern Mountains **6a**
A massive pitch with the hardest climbing at the top and some poor rock below. The route is 50m long and has an intermediate lower-off point. 17 quickdraws needed.
FA. Gary Gibson 2.11.2007

The next set of routes start from a large ledge at 10m, reached by climbing up to the right of the arete from the quarry floor.

2 The Screaming Skull **7b**
A route of great stature that takes the left-hand side of the face and features a delicate central section and a pressing upper wall.
FA. Gary Gibson 29.4.1989

3 Nomad . . . . Top 50 . . . . **7a+**
An excellent direct line up the centre of the wall, packed with plenty of fine moves and a crux in its upper reaches.
FA. Nick Dixon, Adam Brown 1988

4 Unbroken **7a**
A brilliant face pitch on fine rock, once again featuring a fingery and technical upper wall.
FA. Gary Gibson 19.3.2008

Nomad Wall

A huge and intimidating wall that has a number of big climbs on good rock. These routes have now been fully equipped as sport climbs and give some of the finest pitches at Llanymynech.

Approach - The wall is situated in the bay along from Grid Iron Wall. To gain the large belay ledge climb up leftwards from the edge of Foreigners Wall. The wall under the belay ledge was de-bolted, however the bolts on most off the lines are now back in.

Access - Rare plants. See notes on page 233.

5 This Won't Hurt . . . . Top 50 . . . . **7a**
Superb technical and fingery moves interspersed with good shakeouts. The lower half is the most demanding. Finishing directly up the final wall is a fluttery **7b**. *Photo on page 241*.
FA. Gary Gibson 11.3.1989 - Direct 23.8.1989

6 Rabble Rouser . . . . **6b+**
Start just to the right of the trees. Climb the technical right-hand side of the wall, to a wide horizontal-break. Continue up the wall just left of the arete via good breaks to a lower-off.
FA. John Codling, Chris Calow 5.1989

Foreigner Wall — Llanymynech Quarry

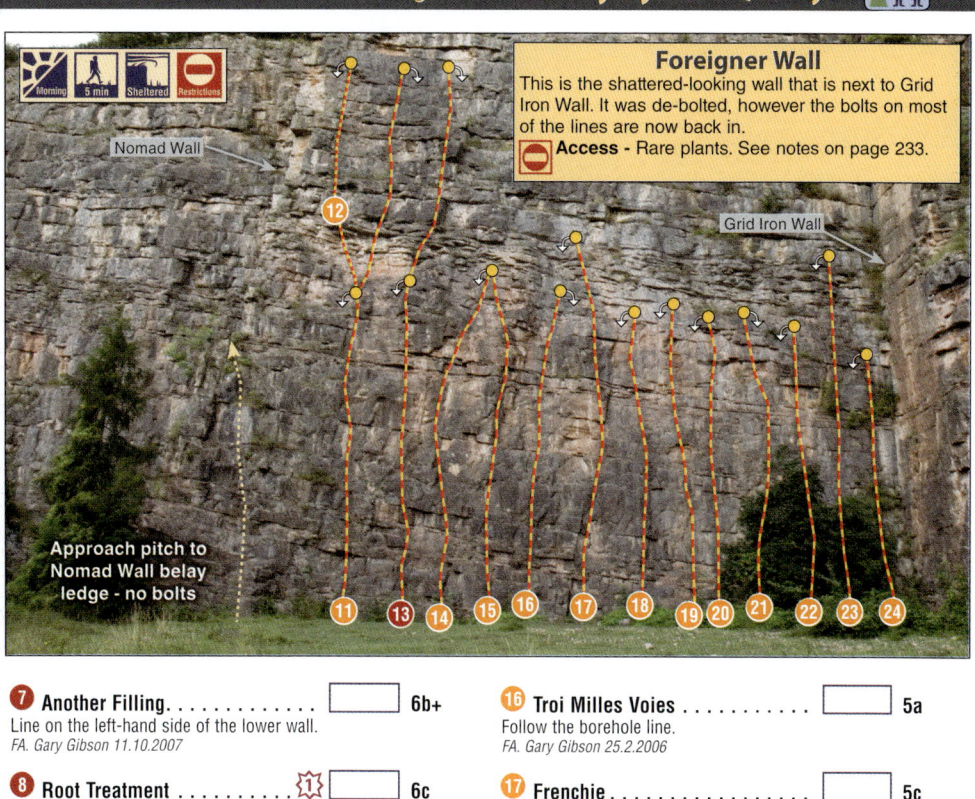

Foreigner Wall
This is the shattered-looking wall that is next to Grid Iron Wall. It was de-bolted, however the bolts on most of the lines are now back in.

Access - Rare plants. See notes on page 233.

7 Another Filling. .... 6b+
Line on the left-hand side of the lower wall.
FA. Gary Gibson 11.10.2007

8 Root Treatment 6c
Take a line up the centre of the lower wall.
FA. Gary Gibson 11.10.2007

9 Pull 'em Out 6a
Good wall climbing.
FA. Gary Gibson 11.10.2007

10 Dentine 5c
Right-hand side of the lower-wall.
FA. Gary Gibson 11.10.2007

11 Journee de Merde .... 6a+
Two pitches 5+, 6a+. Short hard section on the second pitch.
FA. Gary Gibson, Hazel Gibson 22.8.2008

12 Autoroute de Soleil 6a
Head left from belay of *Journee de Merde*.
FA. Gary Gibson, Hazel Gibson 31.7.2009

13 La Ligne Vert 6b
Two pitches 6a+, 6b. A good route.
FA. Gary Gibson 27.1.2007

14 Damn Foreigners 6a
Climb the shallow groove-line.
FA. Gary Gibson, Hazel Gibson 3.2.2006

15 Chaud Show 6a
A well-defined rib to a belay in the alcove.
FA. Gary Gibson 3.2.2006

16 Troi Milles Voies 5a
Follow the borehole line.
FA. Gary Gibson 25.2.2006

17 Frenchie. 5c
Hardest in the central section. Finish over a flake.
FA. Gary Gibson 10.12.2005

18 The Foreign Legion .... 6a+
Start up a rounded grey rib that gains steeper climbing.
FA. Gary Gibson, Hazel Gibson 4.11.2006

19 Too Much Dutch. .... 6a+
Climb the wall beginning on a ledge in a shallow alcove.
FA. Gary Gibson, Mark Richardson 18.11.2006

20 Herman the German. .... 6a+
Good wall climbing.
FA. Gary Gibson, Hazel Gibson, Goi Ashmore 22.9.2007

21 FCUK 5c
Climb the right-hand side of the face passing an overlap.
FA. Gary Gibson 27.1.2007

22 Foreign Muck 6a
Move easily up ledges to steeper and trickier ground.
FA. Gary Gibson 27.1.2007

23 TGV 5c
Longer line up the wall behind tree.
FA. Gary Gibson 5.8.2009

24 Who Fell in the Poubelle 5a
Just left of the corner.
FA. Gary Gibson 17.8.2009

Grid Iron Wall — Llanymynech Quarry

Grid Iron Wall
A massive wall with some huge bolted routes that have a slightly adventurous feel about them. The climbing is not strenuous but often involves thin moves or long reaches between breaks. The routes tend to feel very exposed in their upper reaches. The rock is mostly solid but there are loose sections lower down on the wall, and on the mid height ledges.
Rope Length - Take great care when lowering off; a 70m rope is essential in order to lower back down to the ground unless an intermediate lower-off is used.

❶ Strawberry Tubin 7b
A long and sustained line up the narrow wall that is set slightly forward from the main section of the wall. Low in the grade.
FA. Nick Dixon 5.2005

❷ Jack the Smuggler . . 7a
A great wall climb that has plenty of hard and crimpy moves between good shakeouts at the horizontal breaks. Continuing up the *Smack the Juggler Extension* gives *Juggler the Smuggler* a good variation with no change in grade.
FA. Gary Gibson 11.3.1989

❸ Smack the Juggler . . . . . 6b+
The arete and wall up the right-hand side of the narrow wall has some interesting moves, the trickiest around midway.
FA. Gary Gibson 15.4.1989

❹ Smack the Juggler Extension. 6a
The bolted line above the lower-off of *Smack the Juggler*.
FA. Gary Gibson 27.1.2007

❺ Sack the Stranglers 6c
A reasonable line with a difficult pull over a bulge midway.
FA. Gary Gibson 15.1.2007

❻ A Night on the Town . . . . 6c+
Start up the broken lower wall and open corner that accesses the vegetated ledges under the upper wall. Climb the upper wall just to the right of the vegetated corner - the best bit of the climb.
FA. Gary Gibson 15.4.1989

❼ The Stranglers 6b
Climb to the mid height vegetated ledges via the broken lower wall and open corner/groove. Can be used as an alternative start for either *Gaza Strippers* or *A Night Torchlight Parade*.
FA. Gary Gibson 15.1.2007

❽ Gaza Strippers. . . . . 6b+
Start up the lower wall just right of the corner groove of *The Stranglers* to access the mid height ledges. Take the long and sustained thin crack-line that heads up the upper wall which gives some fine climbing right up to the lower-off.
FA. Stuart Hardy, Andy Popp, Nick Dixon, Adam Brown 1986

❾ A Night Torchlight Parade . . . 6c
A worthwhile right-hand finish to *Gaza Strippers*.
FA. Gary Gibson 31.12.2002

❿ Curfew . . . . 6b+
This long pitch with some good moves gives a memorable outing. The upper section is an amazing wall at the grade.
FA. Gary Gibson 21.2.1989

Chris Calow moving up the lower part of the fantastic wall climb *This Won't Hurt* (7a) - *page 238* - one of a number of great grade 7 outings on the Nomad Wall at Llanymynech Quarry.

Llanymynech Quarry — Grid Iron Wall

11 Grid Iron .... Top 50 — 6c
The best on the wall. A fine piece of climbing from start to finish with the hardest section attaining the strip overhang.
Photo this page.
FA. John Codling 1980s

12 Pew, Pew, Barney, McGrew, Cuthbert, Dibble, Grub ..... 7a+
Good tough moves high up but with some slightly poor rock at the start. Gain the large dirty ledge with care, then make some hard moves up to, and through, the overlap onto the slightly easier upper wall.
FA. Gary Gibson 15.4.1989

13 Incy Wincy Spider ...... 7a+
A similar upper wall to *Pew, Pew*... again with some hard moves to break through the overlap.
FA. Gary Gibson 21.2.1989

14 Hickory Dickory Dock ... 7a
Start up some broken ground before tackling the solid upper wall. There is a hard reach for a break just above the overhang at mid height. *Photo on page 244.*
FA. Gary Gibson 11.2.1989

15 Humpty Dumpty .... 6c+
A good solid pitch just left of the right arete of the wall. Make a steep pull off a raised ledge and climb the gradually steepening wall via some fingery moves between clean breaks culminating in a fine finish.
FA. Gary Gibson 14.3.1989

16 Up the Spout 6b
Nice moves and positions. Climbs the wall and passes the belay of *Bah Bah Black Sheep* to the left.
FA. Gary Gibson 7.1.2006 - extended 9.8.2009

17 Bah Bah Black Sheep ..... 6a+
The far right-hand side of the main wall passing a mid height overhang.
FA. Gary Gibson 10.12.2005

18 Coming of Age 6a
Start on a ledge up and to the right of the base of the main section of the wall. The left-hand line of bolts is a pleasant pitch.
FA. Gary Gibson 7.8.2009

19 49 and Counting 6a
The line of bolts just to the right of *Coming of Age*.
FA. Gary Gibson 7.8.2009

Enjoying the final exposed wall of *Grid Iron* (6c) - *this page*. Photo: Lee Proctor.

The huge walls of Llanymynech offer some of the longest single pitch sport routes in the UK. In this picture Gary Gibson is inching his way up *Hickory Dickory Dock* (7a) - *page 242* - on the Grid Iron Wall.

Llanymynech Quarry — Black Wall

Black Wall

Black Wall is a superb vertical face of good rock that compares favourably with any quarried wall in the country. It has a brilliant set of trad routes that have good but spaced protection, mostly in the form of gear in the horizontal breaks and cracks although there are some pegs. The three central lines are of a reasonable grade, the flanking lines are much more difficult and all incorporate some exquisite vertical wall climbing. Unfortunately the vital fixed gear on the harder lines is now showing its age and an abseil inspection is advised before you attempt any of these routes. The middle three lines tend to see many more ascents and are cleaner and rely on less crucial single gear placements. Most of the rock on Black Wall is solid, dark and sandy limestone with a profusion of horizontal breaks, good pockets and intermittent vertical thin cracks. A band of poorer rock is present at about 3/4 height but here the holds and climbing are less difficult. The wall seeps after heavy prolonged rain and mud can build up in the horizontal breaks leaving some slippery holds. The wall dries very quickly after rain, is sheltered and gets the sun for a good part of the day.

Descent - There is a bolted abseil/lower-off station on the large ledge at the top of Black Wall. Alternatively walk off left (facing in) via a long path along the top of the crag.

Access - No climbing (all routes) from 1st March to 30th June between markers because of nesting birds.

❶ Picking Blackheads E5 6a
A serious route on the left of the face. Start from a hollow and take a direct line past the prominent sandy alcove that is just before the main difficulties.
FA. Gary Gibson 15.4.1989

❷ While the Cat's Away E4 6a
Excellent wall climbing with limited protection and some testing run-outs. Climb up to a peg in a very faint left-trending seam. Technical climbing past another peg, and not much other gear, gains a slim overlap. Easier climbing in the same style finishes this monster pitch. Variation - moving right and finishing up the wall between the finishes of *Black Wall* and *Black Bastard* is a trickier option than the original but direct finish.
FA. Ian Dunn, Nick Dixon 1986. FA. (Variation) Ed Booth 19.11.2014

❸ Black Wall E1 5b
A great pitch that weaves its way up the centre of the face. The climbing is sustained, route finding intricate, and the route is high in the grade. Start on the highest point of the earth mound then step left onto a narrow ledge and make a steep move to get established on the wall. Climb up until a horizontal traverse right, with feet level with a low peg (on *Black Bastard*) can be made, to beneath a line of pockets. Climb these, past an old thread, to a break. Continue direct up the thin wall to a more broken band of rock. Traverse left to a corner and climb this to its top. Move up the next short wall before hand traversing right to the finishing ledge. *Photo on page 6.*
FA. Gordon Caine, E.Austrums 4.10.1970
FA. (Start) Doug Kerr, S.Grove 25.7.1987

❹ Black Bastard E2 5c
The best route on the wall with lots of fine climbing on good rock. Climb to a low peg and move directly up to a thin crack system. Excellent technical climbing up this gains a break. Follow the wall above, past a peg, to the broken band of rock. Head directly up this to below a white-stained crack and then step right to below another crack. Step up to reach the crack and the top.
FA. Doug Kerr, Pete Stacey 1.6.1987

❺ Black Wall Direct E2 5c
A fine combination improves on the original route but ups the grade slightly. Start up *Black Bastard* and continue up the pockets and thin wall of *Black Wall* to link up with the finish of *Black Bastard*. *Photo on page 222.*

❻ Black is Beautiful E5 6b
A fine climb of contrasts on immaculate rock. It is advisable to finish up the last 8m of *Black Bastard* since the upper wall is dirty in the breaks. Very possibly a 6c move for the short.
FA. Doug Kerr 8.8.1987

❼ Churnet Runners E4 6a
Climb steep and slightly dirty rock, past a poor peg, to better rock above. Two marginal pegs protect intricate moves on pockets and crimps that gain easy but loose and dirty ground. To avoid this upper section, a long traverse left from the third peg can be used to gain *Black Bastard* to finish.
FA. Nick Dixon, S.Hardy. Adam Brown 1986

❽ Zeppelin E2 5b
The striking arete offers a stunning line but the start and finish of the route has some very poor rock. There are number of pegs to protect but these are of questionable quality.
FA. Gordon Caine, Dave Cuthbertson (1pt) 25.5.1970
FFA. S.Hardy 1986

Red Wall — Llanymynech Quarry

Alison Martindale on the fine *Dead Man's Fingers* (7a) - *this page* - at the Red Wall, Llanymynech. The Red Wall routes are all well bolted and most give super-sustained gently leaning pitches of around 30m.

Red Wall

This is a huge face with some amazing routes that are far more interesting than the rather featureless and uniform appearance of the rock might suggest. The wall itself is gently overhanging although the climbing is not particularly strenuous.

Access - No climbing (all routes) from 1st March to 30th June between markers because of nesting birds.

❶ Crab Stick 6c
A good introduction to the climbing on Red Wall. Follow the face just to the right of the arete with a tough move to pass the first low bolt. Above this a section of poorer rock is soon passed and is followed by excellent climbing on superb brown rock.
FA. Gary Gibson 29.4.1989

❷ Lobster on the Loose 7a
A worthwhile pitch with contrasting halves. Make a thigh-busting rockover to start, then steep and juggy moves gain the intricate and sustained mid-section. A few more slightly run-out moves lead to a short, steep finish and the lower-off.
FA. Gary Gibson 22.4.1989

❸ Rapture of the Deep 7a
Start below a large overhang with a staple bolt beneath it. Good moves through the overhang gain an awkward wall above. A very blind mid-section on slopers and poor holds feels precarious until the easier finishing moves. High in the grade.
FA. Gary Gibson 22.4.1989

❹ Subterranean Sidewalk .... 6c+
Super-sustained climbing. Passing the second bolt is hard, especially for the short, but the rest is no push over. There is a slight deviation out right just past mid height. *Photo on page 30.*
FA. Gary Gibson 22.4.1989

❺ Dead Man's Fingers . 7a
A fabulous pitch packed with technically intricate climbing. A pressing sequence up the steep wall and small overlap using some boreholes is the hardest section. From the lower-off it is possible to finish steeply up rightwards to gain the lower-off of *The Ancient Mariner*. *Photo on this page.*
FA. Gary Gibson 29.4.89. FA. (Extension) Gary Gibson 3.2.2006

❻ The Ancient Mariner . 7a+
A monster pitch. Increasingly difficult climbing gains a steep wall with a leaning borehole. Perplexing and strenuous moves up this access the easier but pumpy and rounded upper wall.
FA. Gary Gibson 4.3.1989

Red Wall — Llanymynech Quarry

7 Shipperdy Doo-Dah . . . . 7a+
A direct line that has a hard and reachy finish plus some snappy rock in places. Start at a shallow groove in the left-hand side of the low grey ledges.
FA. Gary Gibson 24.12.2005

8 The Deep . . . . 6c+
A good outing that features a fine slab section and easier but steeper moves above on well-hidden holds. Low in the grade.
FA. Gary Gibson, Doug Kerr 15.7.1989

9 I Saw Three Ships . . . . . 6c+
Plenty of fine moves link together nicely and provide a worthwhile pitch. The hard moves are generally on good holds, but the start may be a bit dusty at times.
FA. Gary Gibson 15.12.2002

10 Ship Dip . . . . 6c+
Excellent climbing with one technical section high up. The start may be a touch dirty.
FA. Gary Gibson, Doug Kerr 15.7.1989

11 Mussel Bound . . . . Top 50 . . . 7a+
Good climbing featuring a steep upper third on superb rock. Start up a shallow groove from where steady climbing leads to the final steepening. The bolts are a little spaced on the lower section. *Photo on page 230.*
FA. Gary Gibson 15.7.1989

12 Long John Codling 7a
The long groove system on the right-hand side of the wall is yet another excellent pitch. *Photo on page 232.*
FA. John Codling, Gary Gibson 2.7.1989

13 Clematis . . . . 6b+
The huge corner is a fine line that gives a very sustained route. Can be a little dusty at times.
FFA. Jon de Montjoye 1970s

14 Poison Ivy . . . . 7a+
The centre of the tall narrow wall gives a fine pitch on good rock that has technical moves interspersed with good shakeouts. Low in the grade. *Photo on page 230.*
FA. Gary Gibson 20.9.1989

15 Day of the Triffids 6b
The arete is climbed mainly on its left-hand side.
FA. Gary Gibson 1.1.2010

16 Dead Man's Chest 7a
A diagonal leftward-rising line starting up *Long John Codling* and finishing at the lower-off of *Crab Stick*. 80m rope required.
FA. Gary Gibson 3.2.2006

Pontesford Rocks

	No star	★	★★	★★★
Mod to S	6	7	1	-
HS to HVS	2	4	1	-
E1 to E3	5	-	-	-
E4 and up	-	-	-	-

Pontesford Rocks is an enchanting crag perched on the edge of Earl's Hill Nature Reserve – the 'whale's back hill', just to the south of Shrewsbury. The buttresses are composed of solid and juggy igneous rock that is for the most part set at an accommodating angle. The cliff is located high above an unspoilt and roadless valley, that gives all the lines here a whiff of exposure and lots of charm. A beautiful walk through bluebell woods and gorse dotted fields, followed by a swift pull up a small scree slope gains the base of the crag, from which the three main buttresses are easily located. Pontesford is a playground for the beginner and those seeking some great lower-grade trad routes, although caution is required as protection is not abundant and a steady head is needed on all the lines.

Patricia Novelli enjoying the fine climbing and setting of *Oak Tree Wall Direct* (HVD) - *page 255* - at Pontesford Rocks deep in the Shropshire countryside.

Pontesford Rocks 253

Approach Also see map on page 223
From the A5 Shrewsbury bypass, take the A488 signposted to Pontesbury and after 4.4 miles the village of Pontesford is reached (just before Pontesbury). In Pontesford turn left into a small road signed 'Earl's Hill Nature Reserve'. Follow this for 0.3m to a parking area on the left. Take the path out of the car park and take the left (lower path) where it splits after a short distance. Follow the path through woodland and fields for 0.9km until an information board is reached next to a stile. A small path branches off uphill from here to the base of the crag.

Conditions
All of the buttresses get plenty of morning sun and dry quickly. The cliff is fairly high up and exposed so will be cold in windy weather.

Access
The rocks are under the stewardship of the Shropshire Wildlife Trust. No gardening of routes and keep off of the scree slope. There is usually an agreed climbing restriction due to nesting birds in place between 1st March and 30th June (check on UKC or BMC RAD to confirm it is in place).

Pontesford Rocks — West Buttress

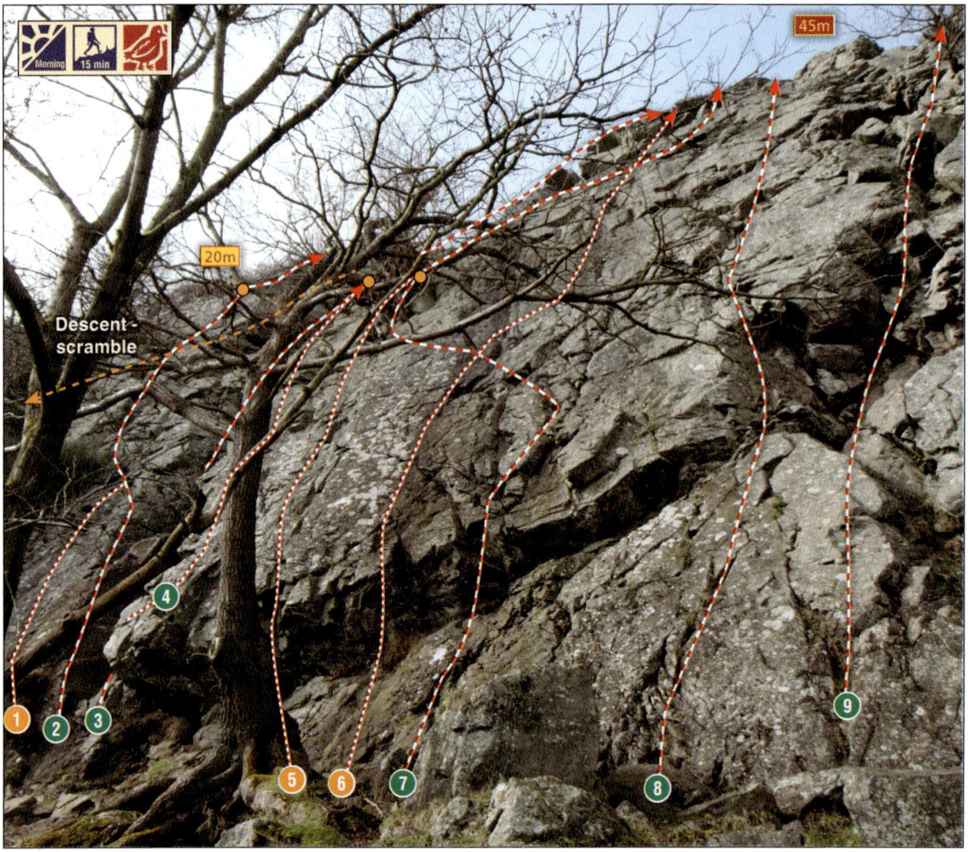

West Buttress

The finest section of Pontesford Rocks has a number of nice multi-pitch routes that are generally on solid clean rock. The top pitches of the routes are all much easier than the initial pitches and are not all shown on the topos.

Approach - Walk up leftwards to a large tree below *Oak Tree Wall Direct*.

Descent - Scramble down to the side of the arete on *West Crack* and then cut across and down *West Wall* from right to left (facing the crag). There is an obvious line when you see it - this is a grade 1 scramble.

The first routes start just to the left of a wide crack.

1) West Wall Direct Start . . . . **VS 4c**
A short variation start up the slab to gain the small ledge on the initial pitch of *West Wall*. A very tight line with easier ground on either side.

2) West Wall . . . . **M**
An excellent climb at the grade - interesting and sustained. Start to the left of the wide crack on the left side of the wall.
1) 20m. Climb up for 5m and move left to gain a small ledge. Continue up to below a large tree and move right around it to gain a large ledge and belay.
2) 35m. Scramble up little buttresses to the top of the crag.

3) West Crack . . . . **M**
The wide chimney crack and long ridge above gives a worthwhile and varied climb.
1) 13m. Climb the wide chimney crack. Belay above.
2) 35m. Finish up the series of aretes on the right.

4) Moonlight Variation . . . . . . **Diff**
The left-hand edge of the wall just to the right of *West Crack* is a good sustained pitch. Finish up the second pitch of *West Crack*.
FA. Walt Unsworth, S.Thomas 1961

5) Eliminate G . . . . **HVS 5a**
Pull through the low overhang with difficulty and continue on small holds to the first belay of *Oak Tree Wall Direct*. Finish as for *Oak Tree Wall Direct*.
FA. R.Tait 1964

West Buttress **Pontesford Rocks** 255

⑨ Stoats Chimney .... M
The broken chimney on the right-hand side of the main section of wall. Follow the chimney past a large boulder and continue over smaller slabs to the top.
FA. Birmingham University 'stoats' c1940s

⑩ Last Post .... VD
Start at a slab to the right of the col.
1) 25m. Climb the middle of the slab, move left and climb a mossy wall and bulge to a tree and belay.
2) 15m. Move down rightwards to an arete and climb it.
FA. R.Tait 1964

⑪ Kit Hill King .... VS 4b
Opinions on grade vary widely from HS to E1. Sustained with steady but bold climbing in places. Climb the slab without much prospect of gear until a break at 7m. From the top of the slab, pull left onto the hanging slab using a large pancake hold and move up to an awkward ledge. Pull direct through the overhang and climb a dirty wall to a thin grassy ledge just right of an oak tree. Move up and left behind the tree to an easy gully and nut belay a little higher. Scramble off right.
FA. Chris Full 20.10.2012

⑫ Wall End Climb .... VD
Good climbing up the slabs to the left of *Grassy Gully*.
1) 20m. Climb up the right-hand edge of the slab to a short wall. Go left to bypass it and climb to a huge tree and belay.
2) 14m. Move up the overlapping slab and then make a stretch left before continuing to a tree and belay on a terrace.
2a) 10m. An alternative pitch at Severe standard is to climb the corner on the right. This is known as the 'The Notch'.
3) 20m. Walk left 7m down the terrace and climb a slab to finish.
FA. Walt Unsworth, J.Fullard 1950s

A number of direct variations on the slab have been claimed but the lines are indistinct and the slab can be climbed anywhere at about VS.

⑬ Finale Groove .... VS 4b
The highlight of this route is the eye-catching square-cut corner/ groove high on the face above the slab.
1) 4a, 21m. Climb the narrow inset slab between the main slab and *Grassy Gully* and make a technical move out left onto the main slab. Continue up the slab and short wall and then move right to a large tree and belay.
2) 4b, 12m. Make some bold moves up and left into the corner/ groove. Climb it and exit left at its top to a tree belay on the terrace, or better a nut belay a little higher. The groove can be gained directly at **4c**.
3) 20m. Walk left 7m down the terrace and climb a slab to finish as for the final pitch of *Wall End Climb*.
FA. A.J.J. Moulam, P.J.Harding 1949

⑭ Awaken .... VS 5a
Follow a narrow slab right to a steep flake. Move up and left via a hard rockover onto the slab. Take the right side of the slab to finish at a tree.
FA. Paul Harrison, N.Harrison 1.3.1979

Grassy Gully is here. A number of routes have been climbed and recorded on the gully walls but have now become overgrown and should not be gardened.

⑥ Surplus Requirements-Not
.... HVS 5a
A bold but escapable pitch. Start between *Eliminate G* and *Oak Tree Wall Direct* directly below a black streak. Make a powerful pull over the low overhang onto the slab and climb boldly straight up left side of black streak, to meet the traverse of *Oak Tree Wall Direct*. Continue up and diagonally right on positive but spaced holds before easier climbing leads straight to a long ledge. Finish up the slab and bulge to good nut belays on flat ledges.
FA. M.J.Hirst, J.S.Whitford 27.3.1993

⑦ Oak Tree Wall Direct HVD
A worthwhile first pitch up the wall. Start by the oak tree at the point where a diagonal break meets the ground.
Photo on page 252.
1) 20m. Move up onto the wall via a small overhang and climb for 7m until a traverse leftwards accesses better holds. Follow the good holds to the oak tree and belay on the terrace.
2) 20m. Walk right along the terrace before taking a slab and bulge to finish.
A variation on pitch one called **Lower Traverse, S 4a** heads left above the overhang to finish up *West Crack*.

⑧ Right-Hand Route ..... VD
A good long pitch. Begin 3m to the right of the point where the diagonal break meets the ground. Move up to the overlap via the slab and pull over it. Move right and climb direct to the top.
FA. Walt Unsworth, E.Adamson 1961

Pontesford Rocks — The Needle

The Needle
Set just in front of the main cliff is The Pontesford Needle. The climbing on The Needle is steep, fairly serious and provides the bulk of the harder routes at Pontesford Rocks. The Needle gets the morning sun but there is some lichen covered rock on the right.

Approach - Walk down to the base of The Needle from below the main cliff.

❶ Indirect Route .... M
Follow easy ground left of *Hawthorne Crack* before heading out leftwards at steeper ground on broken rock. A minor route on poor rock.
FA. Walt Unsworth 1950s

❷ Hawthorne Crack ...... S 4a
Follow the corner/groove to below the overhanging corner-crack. Climb the wide crack which proves to be awkward but can be well protected.

❸ Possum E2 5b
A serious line up the stepped bulges to the right of *Hawthorne Crack*.
FA. Stuart Cathcart, Charlie Leventon 1980

❹ Direct Route .... S 4a
Climb up the broad arete and at 5m move right to below a slim groove in a smooth wall. Climb the groove, which can be green with lichen. The wall on the left of the groove can also be climbed at **4c**.

❺ The Superdirect E1 5a
Where *Direct Route* heads out right, continue direct up steeper and insecure ground.
FA. M.Baxter 1962

❻ Right Hand Wall .... M
A short and poor climb that climbs the narrow ledges just right of the smoother rock taken by *Direct Route*. Often dirty.

East Buttress

The Fifty Foot Wall has been traversed at a low level f5+.

❼ Varsity Buttress .... VS 4b
A good and reasonably popular route that is fairly exposed in places. Start at the left-hand end of the 'Fifty Foot Wall'.
1) 4b, 20m. Climb on polished holds - unprotected - for 4m. Continue by first moving right and then left to the arete. Follow the arete to a tree belay.
2) 20m. Easy climbing on poor rock gains a belay on the left below the nose.
3) 4b, 20m. Gain the scoop on the left face of the nose and move awkwardly right to the arete. Go directly up this to the top. A tough alternative is to climb the short groove and overhang to the right to join the arete.
FA. Birmingham University 'stoats' 1940s

❽ Vive La Wombat E2 5b
Start at a pedestal of rock halfway between *Varsity Buttress* and *Epiglottis*.
1) 5b, 30m. Ascend the grey rounded tower by bold dynamic moves to a pocket and gain the mixed ground above.
2) 5b, 15m. To the right of the traverse of the top pitch of *Varsity Buttress* is a hanging slab, below an roof. Traverse across the exposed slab and pull over the right-hand end of the roof. Finish as for *Trachea*.
FA. Sion Roberts 18.9.1994

East Buttress **Pontesford Rocks**

East Buttress
The East Buttress is the first section of the cliff encountered on the approach path and is now much easier to view since the felling of trees. It has a low wide wall at its base - the 'Fifty Foot Wall' - topped off with a narrow nose separated by some poorer rock and vegetation. Apart from *Varsity Buttress* most of the routes see little attention and will probably be heavily vegetated and have sections of poor rock. The buttress gets the early morning sun but will be cold in windy weather.

Approach - The buttress is at the top of the scree slope on the approach path.

Descent - Either descend the grassy gully - not very pleasant - or walk over and descend as for the West Buttress.

⑨ Epiglottis . . . . **HVS 5a**
The first two pitches are run out and loose but the top pitch is good. Start below two cracks.
1) **5a**, 10m. The steep wall and cracks are fairly pressing.
2) 16m. Continue up vegetated ground to a ledge below the overhanging nose.
3) **4c**, 20m. Climb the thin overhanging crack to a slab and continue to a ledge. Finish up the rib.
FA. (Top pitch) C.Shaw 1960s

⑩ East Climb . . . . **S**
Start at the right-hand end of 'Fifty Foot Wall', two poor pitches leads to an exposed finish above the nose.
1) 10m. Move up the wall and then head right along a ledge and up a slab to a tree and belay.
2) 16m. Continue up vegetated walls to a ledge and tree belay.
3) 20m. Make an exposed and tenuous leftward traverse to join and finish up the rib of *Epiglottis*.
FA. Walt Unsworth, S.Thomas 1961

The following routes start below the nose best reached via the lower pitches of Varsity Buttress.

⑪ Varsity Wall **E2 5b**
The blank wall above the start of the top pitch of *Varsity Buttress*.
FA. Stuart Cathcart, Charlie Leventon 1980

⑫ Trachea **E1 5a**
The short, overhanging and unprotected arete is climbed by big moves on good holds. Short lived but very exposed!
FA. Stuart Cathcart, Charlie Leventon 1980

To the right a number of climbs have been recorded but are now overgrown and should not be gardened.

Route Index

Stars	Grade	Route	Photo	Page
*	6b	21 Steps to Pigeon Street		51
	6a	49 and Counting		242
	VD	A'Cheval		89
*	6a	About a Bay		234
**	7b	About Time		102
*	7a+	Acapulco		115
	E1	Accidents Will Happen		113
*	6c	Acer		43
*	E3	Adam's Mistake		158
	4c	Adrafelin What?		203
	7b+	After Eights, The		152
	S	Agay		124
	E3	Alchemy		151
*	E5	Alex's Crack		64
**	E1	Alison	12	171
	VS	Alive Not Dead		150
*	6c	All Fingers and Thumbs		113
*	6a	All Fudd Up		204
	6b	All Gone Sour		235
	E3	All Over Lancashire		213
	HVS	Alligator's Crawl		205
	Diff	Alors!		236
**	7b	Alpha Track Etch		104
	HVS	Amadeus		181
	5c	Amateur Sleuth		211
	HVS	Amocco Cadiz		156
**	7a+	Ancient Mariner, The		249
	E4	Andy Pandy		236
*	E2	Angel of Mercy		57
	6b+	Another Filling		239
***	E4	Another Red Line		157
	5b	Ant Hill Mob		207
	VS	Antibes		124
	S	Antilla		194
**	E2	Any Which Way	214	213
	E1	Apex		63
*	7a	Aphrodizziness		139
	7b	Apple Crumble		51
	VS	April Fool		207
*	VS	Arete, The		68
	E4	Arm Worms		189
	E1	As Monk as Skunk		159
*	S	As Yew Like It		90
	S	Ash Bole		84
	HS	Ash Crack		162
	VD	Ashgrove		89
*	VS	Ashgrove Prelims		90
	VS	Astrola		190
**	VS	Atlantic Traveller		134
	7a	Atmospheres		138
	VS	Attenuation		118
	6a+	Augustus Gloop		219
	S	Auto-De-Fe		145
*	6b	Autonomy		216
	6a	Autoroute de Soleil		239
	VS	Avenger, The		125
*	VS	Awaken		255
	E4	Babble on is Burning		194
*	S	Babbling Arete		194
	VD	Babbling Tower		194
	HVS	Babel Face		193
*	7b	Baby Crusher		180
*	E3	Baby Frogs with Dirty...		144
***	7b+	Back in Black	80	165
*	6c+	Back Yard Holiday		99
**	8a	Back-Bee Tubin		237
	7a	Backs to the Wall		183
	E2	Badge		104
	E2	Badger Disco		72
*	E5	Bagpus		143
*	6a+	Bah Bah Black Sheep		242
	6b	Balling		127
	S	Banana Boat		229
*	E3	Banana Splits		151
*	7a+	Bananas and Coffee	53	57
*	7b+	Bandits, The	172	174
	E2	Baraouche		65
	E6	Baron Greenback		143
	E3	Basket Case		143
*	6a+	Bath in the Taff		202
	HS	Battery Power		162
**	E3	Bawls Like a Bull		226
*	6a	Bay Bee		234
*	6a+	Bay City Stroller		234
*	5c	Bay Leaf		234
*	6a	Bay of Figs		234
*	E1	Bay of Pigs		127
*	6b+	Bay Watch		234
	6c+	Bayeux Tapestry		234
	6a+	Bayonets Fixed		234
*	6b	Bayonets Ready		234
*	6b+	Be my Baby		234
*	7a	Beastie Boys		46
	6a+?	Beauregarde		218
***	8a	Beetroot and Creatine		55
	HS	Bennetto		132
	VS	Beryl		157
	6c+	Beta Beware		104
	6b	Better Lait than Never		235
*	6b	Better Together		216
	VS	Betty Bop Rides Again		204
*	7a	Big Mouth Strikes Again		178
*	VS	Big Phlash		212
	E3	Big Plop, The		111
*	HVS	Big Splat		212
	HVS	Big Youth		188
	7b+	Bill and Ben		237
**	8b	Binary Finary		174
	VS	Birds Cry		163
*	E1	Bitter Ender		122
*	E2	Bitter Entry		122
*	6b	Bitter Pill, A		100
**	7b	Black and Blue		111
	HVS	Black Ash		90
	E2	Black Bastard		246
	VS	Black Dog		95
***	E3	Black is Beautiful		246
*	E4	Black Moments		156
	VS	Black Out		95
	E2	Black Path		90
**	7b+	Black Poppies		115
**	E1	Black Wall	6	246
	E2	Black Wall Direct	222	246
	HS	Blindfold		72
*	7c	Blinking Lights		181
	HVS	Blister		145
	6a	Blocky Wall, The		79
*	8a	Bloopers and Production...		46
	HVS	Blue Chrome		66
*	VS	Blue Flash		212
*	E5	Blue Nine		186
*	HVS	Blue Thunder		228
	S	Boiler House, The		208
	VS	Bold Poly		133
**	E6	Bolt from the Blue		165
	E2	Bolt in the Snow		120
	7b	Bolt the Blue Sky		180
*	E3	Bone Orchard		134
*	E5	Bootlace Thread		90
*	6a+	Borderline		206
	6a	Boreholderline		207
***	7c+	Born Slippy		55
**	7b+	Brainbox		139
*	E3	Breaking the Reality Effect		158
*	E4	Brewing up with Les Williams		63
*	E5	Brigadier Gerard	83	86
	E2	Brinkman		95
**	7b	Broccoli and Ice-Cream		55
***	7c	Broken Dreams		170
	7c+	Broken Flowers		170
	S	Brown Cracks		95
	VS	Brown Shade of Lime, A		57
*	E3	Buccinator		194
	VS	Buffoon		133
*	7b	Bug Off		132
*	HVS	Bulger, The		68
	E1	Bumble Arete		63
	6c+	Bunter		127
*	E3	Burger King, The		134
	VS	Burning Bush		72
*	E3	Buster Bloodvessel		149
**	E3	Butter Arete		88
**	7b	Butterfly Collector, The		49
	6b	Bye Bye Baby		234
*	7c+	C'est Chaud!		237
	VD	Ca Va!		236
	VD	Cake Walk		78
*	6b+	Calch, The		78
	E4	Calculus		64
	VS	Calefaction		145
**	7c	California Highway Patrol		102
	7a	Calorie Control		122
*	5c	Canal Canol		202
*	7b	Candy		140
**	E2	Canine Meander		74
**	HS	Cannon Arete		226
*	HVD	Cannon Chimney		226
*	HVS	Cannon Left Hand		226
***	8a	Canyonlands		55
*	6b+	Captain Scarlett		192
*	6c+	Caricature		122
	E2	Carter U.C.M.		94
	VD	Castella		194
*	E3	Cat in a Rat Trap		158
	6b+	Cat that Got the Cream, The		235
*	E5	Catch Me if You Can		157
*	6a	Catch the Pigeon (Ruthin E)		51
*	4c	Catch the Pigeon (Trevor Q)		207
*	E1	Cathcart's Got a Brand New...		84
	S	Cato		246
*	E4	Caught in the Crossfire		187
	HVS	Cause, The		94
	E4	Cave Wall		55
	E2	Caveman Wall		95
**	7a	CCR		46
*	E1	Ceba	40	74
*	E1	Celery Stick		147
	HS	Central Groove		122
	VS	Centre Line		144
*	HVS	Centrefold		145
***	8a	Cerberus		55
	VS	Chabris		194
	E2	Chance		84
*	E1	Charlain		106
	5a	Charlie's Podium	121	106
	6a+	Charlotte's Web		106
	VS	Chateau		126
	6a	Chaud Show		239
*	6b	Checkpoint Charlie		206
	E3	Cheeky Pie		194
*	7b	Chilean Moon		115
	E4	Chills of Apprehension		115
	6a+	Chocolate Fudd		204
	E2	Chopper Squad		113
	6b	Christiana		127
*	6a	Christmas Gone Crackers		203
	E1	Christmas Spirit		85
*	6c+	Chrysalis	45	49
*	E4	Churnet Runners		246
*	VS	Chutney		72
*	7b	Cigars of the Pharaohs		86
	HVS	Cima		72
	VS	Clearout, The		118
*	6b+	Clematis		251
**	6c	Clevor Trevor		213

Route Index 259

Stars	Grade	Route	Photo	Page
📷	7a	Climb High	15	171
**	E5	Climb High Direct		171
**	E1	Close to the Edge		86
	E1	Cloven Hoof		159
*	4c	Clue, So?		211
*	5c	Cluedo		210
*	5a	Co-ed in the Coed		200
	E1	Coal not Dole		159
	VS	Codify		159
	E1	Cold Finger		112
*	6c	Cold Turkey		169
*	E1	Colour Games		192
*	HS	Coltsfoot Corner		91
*	HVS	Coltsfoot Crack		91
**	E3	Combat Zone		191
	7a+	Comfortably Numb		57
	6a	Coming of Age		242
	6b	Con Hum-Drum		217
	6c+	Con-Dem-Nation		176
	HVS	Condessa		142
	6a+	Consider an Evil		218
	6a	Constantinople		127
	VS	Continental Chocs		125
	6c	Conundrum		217
*	7a+	Cookie King		169
	6a+	Copenhagen		127
	HS	Copper Pinnacle		89
*	E1	Corner, The		64
*	E1	Cornucopia		90
*	E5	Cotteril's Found Another Toe		156
**	8a+	Counting Sheep		169
	E2	Cousin M		65
	VD	Cow Parsley		118
*	6c	Crab Stick		249
	E1	Crackstone Rib		90
***	E2	Craig Arthur Girdle		112
*	6c+	Crash Diet		122
	HS	Craznitch Crack		86
*	6b	Crime Scene		210
	E2	Crimson Dynamo		192
*	VS	Cristallo		75
*	6b+	Crocodile Shoes		106
	5c	Crocs		205
	5b	Crumples		127
*	HVS	Crypt Tick		146
**	E1	Crystal		87
*	E3	Crystal Ship		89
*	7c	Cubase		168
	5c	Cult, The		236
	6a	Culture and Boutique		236
	5b	Culture Cryptic		236
	5b	Culture Vulture		236
*	6b+	Cunning Plan, A		100
*	7b+	Cured		165
📷	6b+	Curfew		241
*	5a	Cwm all ye Faithful		202
	5c	Cwm Buy a Thrill		201
	4a	Cwm Over Yr		202
	6b+	Cwms the Farmer		202
*	5a	Cwms the Snow, Man!		202
**	7b	Cycle Path, The		133
	E2	Cyclops		60
*	5a	Dai Laughing		202
	6a	Damn Foreigners		239
**	7b	Dance of the Puppets		101
	HS	Dandy Lion		68
**	E5	Dangermouse		144
	E3	Darling Rose		150
	E1	Das Bolt		66
	E3	Dawn of Desire		194
*	6b	Day of the Triffids		251
*	E3	Dead Fingers Talk		89
**	7a	Dead Man's Chest		251
*	6c	Dead Man's Creek		107
📷	7a	Dead Man's Fingers	249	249
	VS	Dead or Alive		150
	E2	Deadly Nightshade		183
	E3	Deadly Trap, The		114
	E3	Death on my Tongue		187
**	6c+	Deep, The		251
**	E4	Delaware Slide		114
*	6c+	Delta Force	1	104
*	E4	Demolition Man		140
	5c	Dentine		239
	VS	Depth Charge		159
*	4c	Deputy Dog		205
	VS	Desist		92
*	E5	Desperado		159
	E1	Deuce Coupe		48
*	E3	Devil's Advocate, The		193
*	HVS	Devil's Alternative		151
***	7c	Devil's Haircut		55
	8b?	Devil's Haircut Extension		55
*	E1	Diagonal Route		75
	VS	Diamond		93
	E2	Diamond Solitaire		93
	6a+	Dick Turpin		43
*	E3	Different Kind of Hypertension,		178
	HVS	Dig Deep		159
📷	E2	Digitron		103
*	4a	Dim Parcio		201
	6a	Dim View of Things, A		202
	HVD	Dimmock Crack		208
*	6b+	Dinbren Sanction, The		168
*	VS	Dino		212
	S	Direct Route		256
	5b	Dirty Climb		236
	7a+	Disappear		120
*	5a	Disappearing Act	199	211
	6b	Do or Dai		202
*	7a+	Do Walls Have Ears		171
📷	HVS	Dog, The	70	74
	VS	Doggy Shag		205
*	6a	Dogmatic		205
*	6a+	Dogs of War		205
**	6c	Don't By China		221
*	E6	Dope on a Rope		89
*	6c+	Dose of Barley Fever, A		133
*	E3	Double Crossbones		114
	E3	Dr. Gonzo		168
*	E4	Dr. Technical		87
**	7a+	Dreadlocks		171
	6a	Dream of White Horses, Not		236
	6b+	Driller Thriller		183
*	VS	Droggo		72
*	HS	Duck Flight		229
	E1	Dusting Over		159
*	7a+	Dying Tonight		135
*	E4	Dynah Moe Hum		182
*	7c	Dyperspace		180
**	VS	E.C.V.		149
	HS	Eagle's Nest Crack		150
	S	East Climb		257
*	4c	Easy Grooves		79
**	6c+	Eating Words		47
	5c	Eau de Culture		236
*	7a+	Echoes		55
	8a+?	Echoes Extension		55
	HVS	Eclipse		118
*	6c+	Eddie Waring Lives On		140
**	E5	Edgley		158
*	E3	Ego	73	75
*	E3	Ego Beaver		87
	HVS	Ego Maniac		48
	HVS	El Crapitan		147
*	E5	El Loco		175
📷	8a	El Rincon		175
***	8b	El Zapatistas		175
	E4	Electra Glide		194
	S	Elephant Crack		68
*	HVS	Eliminate G		254
***	E4	Eliminator		102
**	8a	Elite Deviation		165
***	8a	Elite Syncopations		164
*	6c	Ellabella		193
*	VS	Elmer J. Fudd		204
*	E1	ELP		227
	VD	Emerald Point		229
	HVD	End Flake		91
	HVS	Epiglottis		257
*	HVS	Epitaph		72
*	6b+	Et Tu Brutus		132
*	VS	Evader, The		158
*	E3	Evil Woman		191
*	HVS	Exostosis		145
	VS	Extension		117
***	7c	Extreme Ways	21	168
	6b+	Eye to Eye Contact		216
*	6b	Eyes Have It, The		217
	E2	Façade		156
📷	VS	Face Value	229	227
*	7b+	Fair Trade		57
**	E3	Fall and Decline, The		99
***	E1	Fall Out		89
	E1	Fanny Magnet		163
	E3	Fat and the Filthy, The		43
*	7a+	Fat Boys		180
*	S	Fat Controller, The		208
	5c	FCUK		239
*	7a	Fighting Spirit		191
	VS	Filth Faze		192
**	7c+	Final Solution, The		86
*	VS	Finale Groove		255
*	7b+	Fine Feathered Fink		167
**	HVS	Finer Feelings		84
	6c	Finger Press		112
*	HVS	Fingerbobs (Pinfold)		147
*	E4	Fingerbobs (Twilight A)		127
*	HVS	Fingernail		130
	HVS	Fingers		195
**	7a+	Fire		180
	HS	First Graces		195
	HVS	Five O'Clock Shadow		189
	HS	Flakeless Groove		90
**	E4	Flash Dance		85
*	E5	Flash Harry		85
	VD	Flawse		119
	E1	Flied Lice		146
	HVS	Flighting		130
	VS	Fling		213
**	7a	Float Like a Butterfly		49
	HS	Flotta Arete		60
**	7c	Flowers are for the Dead		169
	6c+	Flowery Pot		236
*	7b+	Flyboy		221
*	E1	Flying Block		64
*	E6	Fog, The		167
*	E1	Follow Me Home		57
	E4	Foolish Pride		143
	E1	Foot Loose and Fancy Free		151
*	7b	Force Majeure		43
**	E3	Forced Entry		122
	6a+	Foreign Legion, The		239
	6a	Foreign Muck		239
	5a	Forensic Science		210
*	6a+	Forever the Suspect		210
	VS	Fossil Finish		87
	7a	Fraction Fictor		142
	HVS	Franco		130
	7c	Fraxinus Excelsior		51
*	4a	Free Wales		202
*	7a+	Freedom Fighters		43
	7b	Freely Slapping Upwards		135
*	E4	Freeway Madness		133
	HVD	Frejus		124

Route Index

Stars	Grade	Route	Photo	Page
	5c	Frenchie		239
	6a	Freshly Dug		115
*	E2	Friction Factor		142
*	E5	Friday the Thirteenth		110
	E1	Frigorific		145
	6c	Fritillary Flake		49
	VS	Frolic		124
**	7a	Front of House		99
	5b	Fudd For Thought		204
*	6b	Fudd Off		204
	VS	Fuddily Enough		204
*	6b	Fuddites, The		204
	6c	Full Impact		208
**	E5	Full Mental Jacket		107
	5a	Full Nine Llaths, The		201
**	HS	Funeral Corner		117
*	7c+	Funky Monkey Pie		138
	6b	Funnel, The		217
*	E3	G.M.B.H		149
	S	Ganjah		95
	S	Gardener's Question Time		90
**	E5	Gates of the Golden Dawn		114
**	6b+	Gaza Strippers		241
	E2	Gemma's World		171
*	6c	Gemma's World Direct		171
***	7b+	Generation of Swine	136	139
	E3	Gentle Violence		194
	VS	Gerald's Dilemma		149
*	E1	German for Art Historians		189
	E2	Get a Grip of Yourself		125
	S	Gift, The		124
*	HVS	Gigolo		159
*	HVS	Gilly Flower		146
	HVS	Ginger Crack		158
*	E4	Glorious Wobblegong		149
**	E2	Go-a-Go-Go		118
*	HVS	Goblin Girls		162
**	7b+	Goin' to a Go Go		118
	E2	Going Bad		86
*	E6	Going Loco		175
*	VS	Gold Phlash		212
	6b	Gold Top		235
	6b+	Golly Gee		153
	6b+	Golly Gosh		153
	6c	Golly Wog		153
	E1	Gone Bad		86
	7b+	Grand Canyon	3	55
	VD	Grand Laddie		156
	HVD	Grass		93
	E2	Gray Face No Space		228
*	6a+	Great Escape, The		206
	HVS	Great Slab Girdle		57
*	6b+	Green Bean		46
*	E4	Green Wall, The		62
	E2	Grey Tripper		57
	6c	Grid Iron	242	242
*	HVS	Grizzly		75
	6b	Grooved Arete		192
	8a+?	Gwennan		167
	E1	H Block		126
	E3	Haco		60
***	8a+	Hades		55
	S	Half and Half		85
	HS	Hamlet		194
*	7a	Hand in Glove		101
	S	Handjam		92
*	E4	Happy Slapper		146
*	VS	Happy Valley		125
*	E5	Hard Crust		159
	E2	Hard Fought		142
	7b	Hard Shoulder		133
	6a+	Hard Start		79
*	E2	Harvey Wall Banger		91
*	6a	Haven't got a Clue		210
	E3	Having a Crack		43
*	S	Hawthorne Crack		256
*	E3	Heart of Darkness		85
***	E5	Heaven or Hell		103
*	7a+	Heinous Undercling		183
	VS	Heist, The		127
	7a+	Hell Drivers		118
*	M	Hell Hole		164
	E4	Hell's Arete		88
	Diff	Hell's Chimney		164
	VD	Hell's Own Variation		164
	HVS	Hello Arete		164
	S	Helme's Highway		118
	6a+	Heloma Durum		145
	6a+	Help, Help me Rhondda		202
	6a+	Herman the German		239
**	7a	Hickory Dickory Dock	244	242
	E4	Hiding in There		68
*	E2	High Impedance		118
*	6a+	High Stepper	220	217
***	8a	Highway	33	175
	HVS	Highway Hysteria		133
	HVS	Hoax, The		112
	S	Holly Tree Wall		94
*	6a+	Home Rule		216
	7a	Homecoming, The		182
	HVS	Horn Dog		72
*	E3	Hornbeam		91
	VS	Hornbeam Wall		91
*	E2	Hornblower		91
	6b	Hornier Toad		205
	E1	Hornwall		91
*	E2	Horny		91
	6c	Horny Toad		205
	7a+	Hot Lips		171
*	7a	Hot Stuff	35	181
	E4	Hot Tin Roof		60
*	E4	Hovering on Eternity		226
*	E4	Howelling for Beaver		43
*	E1	Howling		125
	E1	Humble Hog		182
*	6c+	Humpty Dumpty		242
*	E3	Hungry Days		122
	6c	Hunky Monk		152
*	E3	Hydrogen		193
	HVS	Hype, The		156
*	E3	Hyper Medius Meets Little		127
*	E3	Hyperdrive		178
	E3	Hypertension		93
*	6b+	I Don't Agree		219
*	7b	I Feel Like a Wog		152
	6a+	I Met a Man from Mars		207
***	7b+	I Punched Judy First		170
*	6c+	I Saw Three Ships		251
***	7b	Ice		181
	E5	Ice on the Motorway		181
	E1	Ice Run		195
*	E5	Iceburn		157
	E3	Icicle of Death		95
*	E3	Id		74
*	6b	Impact Imminent		208
	5a	Impaction		208
**	7a+	In Search of Someone Silly		170
	E4	In the Heat of the Day		188
*	6c+	Inaugural Goose Flesh		182
*	HVD	Incompetence		89
*	E4	Incy Wincy Spider		242
*	6b	Independence		219
*	6b+	Independence Day		219
	6c	Indi Mix, The		219
	6c	Indi-Pops		219
	6b	India		219
	6c	Indian Summer		153
	6a+	Indiana Jones		219
	M	Indirect Route		256
**	VD	Inelegance		89
*	6c	Inglorious		149
*	5c	Innocence		210
*	HVS	Insecure		89
	8b	Insomnia		170
	E4	Inspector Gadget		63
*	HS	Inspiration		89
**	HVS	Intensity		86
	HVS	Inter Digital Pause		117
	VS	Interface		119
*	7a	Into the Fire (Independence Q)		219
*	E5	Into the Fire (World's End)		89
	E2	Iron Curtain		206
*	6c+	Is This as Good as it Gets		218
	6a+	It Seems So		218
	7b+	It's Yours		164
	E3	Itsu		66
	HS	Ivor the Engine		208
*	7c	Ivory Smile, An		57
*	S	Ivy Crack		85
*	VS	Ivy Groove		88
	VD	Ivy Tower Chimney		118
*	HVS	J.T.P		88
	E2	Jabberwocky		120
**	7a	Jack the Smuggler		241
	6b+	Jam Spread		115
	S	James the Red Engine		208
*	6c+	Jaspers		169
**	HS	Jennifer Crack		84
***	E1	Jibber		158
	E1	Jittering Tower		122
*	E1	Jocca		63
	HVD	Joker		62
	6a+	Journee de Merde		239
	E4	Jumping Jack Flash		85
	HVS	Jungle Warfare		105
	HVS	Just a Sprinkling		159
	E1	Just a Tad		144
	6a+	Just a Treat		133
*	6c	Just Another Route Name		183
*	6c	Just Another Undercling		183
*	5a	K9		205
*	6c+	Kamikaze Clone		169
*	E5	Keeping Secrets		104
**	7a+	Killer Gorilla		138
***	VS	Kinberg		134
*	E3	King of Fools		143
**	7a	King of the Castle		43
	E2	Kinky		95
	HS	Kinsman		158
	VS	Kit Hill King		255
	6c+	Kitten's Paws		98
*	E1	Knotty Problem		65
	E2	Kyani Quatsi		213
	E2	La Di Da		95
	6b	La Ligne Vert		239
*	7b+	La Porte de l'Enfer		57
	HS	Ladywriter		57
	E1	Land of Fairies, The		126
*	6c	Last Bastion, The		216
	6c+	Last Crusade, The		219
*	E1	Last Fandango		142
	VS	Last Fling, The		124
	5a	Last Llath, The		201
	VD	Last Post		255
*	E3	Last Straw, The		213
	VS	Laughing Gnome		162
	M	Lax		145
*	E5	Laxix		65
	HS	Lay Me Back		148
*	VS	Layback on Me		63
	HS	Layback with Me		92
*	6b	Lazarus		216
*	E3	Le Chacal		99
	6a+	Leaf out of Sam's Book, A		211

Route Index 261

Stars	Grade	Route	Photo	Page
*	E3	Lecherous Pig		189
	HS	Left Edge		91
	VS	Left Handed Fool		207
	8b+	Leftism	179	168
	E1	Legacy		101
*	E3	Lemon Entry		122
	E3	Lemon Kerred		115
*	E1	Lentil Man		147
	VS	Les Elephants		85
	VD	Let it Rip		187
*	6c	Let's See Those Fingers		113
*	7b	Lickin' Lollipops		140
**	E1	Life	154	158
*	E4	Life of Dubious Virtue		150
	E1	Lightly Salted		159
	VS	Lightning Groove		227
	VS	Line Bashing		212
*	6c+	Line of Fire		165
	VS	Lingen		213
	6c	Lipstick		216
	HS	Little Deal		159
	HVS	Little Finger Jam		68
	HS	Little Fingers		127
**	7c	Little Weed		237
	S	Llyffant Bach		229
**	7a	Lobster on the Loose		249
**	7a	Long John Codling	232	251
*	7a	Long John Silver		212
*	6a	Long-legged Lizard from Liverpool		205
	E2	Loosing Grasp		189
*	S	Loran		117
*	6b+	Lost Arrow		50
*	6b+	Lost Boys		50
*	6c+	Lost Cause		50
*	6b	Lost Control		206
*	6c	Lost Innocence		50
*	6c+	Lucky be Damned		178
	7a+	Lullaby		168
**	E1	Lurking in the Long Grass		132
	E1	Madonna Kebab		159
*	6a	Maevanwy		200
	E2	Maeve		61
*	E4	Magenta Sunrise		162
	E3	Main Wall Girdle (Maeshafn Q)		65
	E2	Main Wall Girdle (Pot Hole Q)		75
	E2	Mainly for Pleasure		156
*	E3	Mainstay		143
**	HVS	Major		75
	HVS	Malevolence		158
	7a+	Manakin		120
*	HS	Mango		72
***	E6	Manic Mechanic		110
*	E3	Manikins of Horror	37	101
	E3	Mantilla, The		158
*	E1	Marander		151
	HVS	Margarine Arete		88
**	6c	Margin of Error		206
*	E5	Marie Antoinette		110
	HVS	Marjoun		92
*	7b	Mark of Zorro, The		55
*	HVS	Marnie		150
*	7a	Marsh Flower, The		101
**	7b+	Masquerade		101
	VS	Masungi		125
***	E3	Mathematical Workout		64
	HS	May Day		163
	6b	Meat Head		43
	HS	Megalith		144
**	6c	Melody		178
*	E5	Memorable Stains		159
*	E4	Mental Transition	141	140
***	7b+	Mercury Rising		110
*	6b+	Mercy Mercy Me		140
	HS	Merde!		236
*	4b	Merlin Magic		201
	S	Mestre		75
	6b	Metamorphosis		49
	6b	Metamorphosis Direct		49
	E1	Meth		87
	HVS	Midnight Special		151
	6c	Minnie Minor		146
	E1	Minstrel, The	67	64
	VS	Missing Link		124
*	S	Misty Dawn		125
**	E6	Misty Vision		167
*	HVS	Mitsuki Groove		134
	6c	Mon Miel		100
	VD	Moncrieff		118
	E3	Monkey's Claws		98
	HS	Monumental		133
	E4	Moomba		63
*	Diff	Moonlight Variation		254
	E3	Moving Finger, The		149
	VS	Mr Flay		92
	E3	Mr Wobbler		135
**	6c	Mud Slide Slim		213
	6c	Muppet Show, The		120
**	HS	Murren		75
	E2	Muscle Bound		94
	E1	Muslim		60
	7a+	Mussel Bound	230	251
	7b	Mustang Sally		191
	VS	My Route		212
*	6a+	Narrow Arete		79
	E2	Neon Knights		150
*	E1	Nerd, The		48
	HVS	Nesting Crack		133
	6b	Never Rub Another Man's Rh....		235
	E1	New Bend in My Arm, A		124
	HVS	News		57
	6c+	Night on the Town, A		241
**	6c	Night Torchlight Parade, A		241
*	E1	Nit Nurse, The		190
	5a	No Evasion		208
*	E2	No Grips		124
***	8a+	No Kneed		174
	6a	No Name		236
	6b	No Regard		218
	6a	No Remittal	4	211
*	6a	No Reptiles		205
	7a+	Nomad		238
*	E1	Non Stop		135
	VD	Nose		95
*	E2	Now and Then		106
	E5	Nurse Nurse		87
**	HVD	Oak Tree Wall Direct	252	255
*	HS	Obelisks Fly High		144
**	E6	Oblivion		110
	HVS	Octopus		113
	HVS	Odysseus		61
*	5a	Ogre in the Ogof		200
	6a	Oh Calcutta		219
*	E3	Old Chipatti		147
*	6c+	Old Gunk's Grandad's Pastime		46
*	E1	Old Scores		186
	6c+	Omegod		104
	S	On Line		117
	VS	Once Is Never Enough		72
	E5	One Carlos		130
**	7b	One Continuous Picnic		99
	6b	One Fine Bay		234
	S	Onegin		118
	E1	Only a Gesture		156
**	S	Open Book		88
*	4a	Open Grey Groove, The		79
	VD	Open to Offa's		119
	6b	Opening Impact		208
**	8a+	Orgasmatron, The		175
	E4	Origami Today		143
	E4	Ornamental Art Mark 2		143
**	E5	Osteophyte		134
	Diff	Ouja Chimney		95
**	7c+	Out of Body Experience	26	174
	7b	Out of the Fire, Into the Furnace		135
	E3	Out With the New		182
*	6a+	Over the Wall	196	206
	5b	Over Yr, on my Heddlu		203
**	E1	Overhanging Crack		149
*	HS	Owl Wall		72
**	E3	Oxygen		139
	HVS	Pagoda		125
	HS	Pancake, The		122
	E1	Pant-y-Gyrdl Wall		60
	VD	Paper Chase		228
	HVS	Paper Smile		162
*	VS	Penetration Factor		117
	E1	Pengrail		65
**	7c	People Give Me the Eyes		152
	HVS	Pep Talk		186
	HVS	Phallic Tower		150
	S	Phoenix, The		190
	7a	Physical Transaction		135
***	8a	Pi		102
*	E5	Picking Blackheads		246
*	7b	Pickpocket		195
	VS	Picture Arete		95
*	E4	Pictures of Living		135
*	7b+	Pierrepoint Pressure		156
	E3	Pig Pen		147
	VS	Pinfold Left-hand		149
	VS	Pinfold Right-hand		149
	HVD	Pinnacle Crack		119
	S	Pisa		93
	S	Pitmungo		126
*	S	Planerium		95
***	7b	Planet Claire		138
	E3	Planet Head		213
*	7b+	Planet, The		180
*	S	Plasuchaf Crack		94
	E2	Play to Kill		151
	6a+	Plea for Leniency		211
	E4	Pocket Rocket		149
*	7a+	Poison Ivy	230	251
*	E3	Poison Letter		143
	6c+	Polytextured Finish		133
*	7a	Poor Old Hari Kiri		169
	HS	Portobello Belle		57
	E2	Possum		256
*	E3	Post Mortem of a Football		158
	VS	Pot Noodle, Don't Leave Home		207
**	E3	Pour Lulubelle		102
	Diff	Prejudice		119
	E3	Prel		93
**	7a	Prickly Heat	131	135
	VD	Pride		119
	4a	Prime Suspect		210
**	7c	Private Idaho		138
	6a	Prof Pat Pending		207
*	E3	Progressions of Power		149
	?	Project		78
	6b+	Promises		216
***	E6	Protect and Survive		107
	5c	Proven Guilty		211
*	HS	Puffing Billy		208
	HS	Pugilist		145
*	6a	Pull 'em Out		239
	E3	Pulling up the Daisies		163
*	E1	Pumpkin Seed		147
**	E5	Punch and Judy		107
*	E4	Punishment of Luxury		164
	7b+?	Puppet Symphony		120
**	VS	Puppy Power		63
*	E4	Pussyfooting		60
*	6a	Quartz Slab, The	77	79
*	6b	Quartz Wall		79

Route Index

Stars	Grade	Route	Photo	Page
	7a	Quick Flash		189
	S	Quicksilver		212
	VS	Quill		84
*	6b+	Rabble Rouser		238
	E3	Race is On, The		157
*	HVS	Race Riot		122
**	E3	Raging Storm		192
	E2	Ram Jam		68
	HS	Rama		60
*	S	Rambler		63
*	4a	Raptor Rap		201
**	7a	Rapture of the Deep		249
	5c	Rare bit of Welsh, A		202
	E3	Rasp, The		66
	6b	Ravenous		105
*	6c+	Ray of Hope		132
*	7b+	Rays and Hail		132
	E5	Read My Lips		87
	VS	Rebel, The		156
	6a+	Rebus		216
*	VS	Recession Blues		91
**	E3	Red Flag Day		149
*	E5	Red Storm Rising		192
	7b+	Relentless 108		110
*	6b	Resist and Exist		176
*	E2	Return of the Gods		187
	E1	Return to the Trees		48
*	7a+	Revival of the Latest		107
*	E5	Rhiannon		175
	S	Riboflavin		119
	S	Rich's Robbery		90
	HS	Right Angle		74
*	VS	Right Edge		91
	M	Right Hand Wall		256
**	E2	Right Wall		74
*	VD	Right-Hand Route		255
	7b+	Ring Piece		166
	6c	Ripped Apart by Badgers		182
	6b	Ripping Yarns		191
	HVD	Rising Champ		125
**	7c+	Rivals, The		174
*	6c	Roald Dahling		218
*	E2	Rock a Little		149
*	E3	Rock Special		125
*	VS	Rock Thief		163
	E1	Roger Rabbit		74
*	6c	Root Treatment		239
	VS	Roots		124
	VS	Rough Cut		89
	VS	Route, The		46
***	E3	Royal Arch, The		186
*	E2	Royal Plume		64
*	7b	Rubberbandman		112
*	7c	Rubs and Tugs		102
	Diff	Rumble		92
**	6c+	Runner Bean		46
	HVS	Running Wild		124
**	E2	Running with the Wolf		60
	E2	Russian Roulette		151
	VD	Ruth's Ramble		117
*	6c	Sack the Strugglers		241
**	VS	Sally in Pink		192
	6a+	Sam-Sam Alert		211
	6b	Sam-Sam, the Pan Man		211
*	E1	Sam's Arete		43
	6b	Sam's the Man		211
	E2	Sarcophagus		183
*	7a	Sasha the Basha		235
	VS	Saul's Crack		237
	VD	Sayfari		130
	HVS	Scaremonger		145
	Diff	Scarface Groove		90
*	E3	Scary Fairy		105
**	S	Schmutzig 225		228
	E1	Scrapyard Things		114
	5a	Scratching the Surface		200
	6a+	Screaming Dream		235
***	E5	Screaming Lord Sutch		157
***	7b	Screaming Skull, The		238
	E1	Scutters, The		190
	E1	Second Chance		156
*	E2	Secret, The		64
	VS	Selva		75
	6a+	Semi Skimmed		235
**	E2	Sentinel		132
*	7a	Serengetti		132
*	HVD	Sesto		75
**	5c	Sgrech yr Hebog 209		200
*	E1	Shabby Slab		90
	E3	Shadow		122
*	E2	Shadowplay		187
	HS	Shaken Not Stirred		194
	VS	Shakin' Stevens		125
	E1	Shasavaan		143
**	HS	Shattered Crack 69		68
	5c	Sheila's Route		236
	S	Shelfway		91
	VS	Shepherd's Delight		163
*	6c+	Ship Dip		251
*	7a+	Shipperdy Doo-Dah		251
*	E7	Shoot to Thrill		151
***	E6	Shootin' Blanks		110
***	E4	Shooting Star		86
	VS	Short Trip		147
	7a+	Showing Mystery Bruises		180
	6a+	Shute, The		217
*	7a	Shy of Coconuts		140
	HVS	Sidestep		117
	HS	Sideswipe		72
	HVS	Silent Spirit		176
	6c+	Silhouette 123		122
	7a+	Silly Games		181
*	E1	Silly Lilly		74
*	HVS	Silver Line, The		212
**	E4	Silver Shadow		88
	HVS	Single-handed Sailor		57
*	E2	Sinking, Shrinking, Shrimp		140
***	E3	Sir Cathcart D'Eath		157
*	E3	Sister Moon		146
	E5	Sisters of the Moon		86
*	E2	Sita		62
*	VS	Skullion		118
*	7a	Slap and Tickle		135
	E3	Slapalong		88
	E3	Sleeping Beauty		85
	6c	Slim Faster		122
*	HS	Sling		68
*	7a+	Slippery Caramel		133
*	VS	Slither		85
	7b	Slobberlob		236
*	VD	Sloth		119
*	6a	Slow, Araf, Slow		201
*	6b+	Smack the Juggler		241
*	6a	Smack the Juggler Extension		241
	E2	Smokey Bear		135
***	E6	Smokin' Gun		110
	S	Smooth Hands		159
	5c	Smooth Wall Left		47
	6a	Smooth Wall Right		47
	E3	Smouldering Bouldering		130
*	6b	Snakes in the Grass		205
*	4a	SND		210
	E3	So Lucky		178
	E3	So She Did		65
	VD	Soap		182
	E3	Soft Delight		159
*	E5	Soft Machine, The		143
*	6a	Soft Shoulder		133
	E1	Solar Power		162
*	6c+	Solar System, The		181
***	E3	Solo in Soho		151
	E5	Sombre Music		156
*	E5	Someone Like You		84
*	E3	Sometimes Yes, Sometimes No		133
*	E4	Soul on Ice		84
**	8b	Sound and the Fury, The		164
*	6a	Southern Mountains		238
**	E3	Space Ace		134
	E4	Spaceman in the Whitehouse		134
*	E2	Spastic Spider		140
	E2	Spastic Spider Direct		140
	VS	SPC		182
	E2	Spetsnaz		94
	6b+	Spiderpig		120
*	E2	Splitting Finger Crack		148
*	HS	Splitting the Difference		228
*	7b	Spotty Dog		237
	Diff	Squirm		89
*	7b	Stab in the Back, A		132
	HS	Stagnation		195
	HVS	Starting Block		122
**	7c+	Statement of Ewes		165
*	HVS	Stay Alert Malcolm		127
	VS	Stein Line		163
*	E5	Steppin' Razor		110
*	6c+	Sticky Toffee		166
	E3	Stiff and Sticky		166
*	HS	Sting		84
*	7c	Sting like a Bee		49
*	M	Stoats Chimney		255
	E1	Stoned Roman		132
	E3	Storm Rider		143
*	HS	Straight Edge		91
*	E2	Stratagem		101
**	7c+	Strawberry Tubin		241
	E4	Stress Test		143
	6b	Stringlers, The		241
	E4	Stukas, The		190
*	6c+	Stupid Schoolboyz 42		43
*	6c+	Subterranean Sidewalk 30		249
	E1	Subtopia		195
*	4a	Sudden Impact		208
	E3	Sugar Hiccup		189
	6c+	Sugar Sweet		100
***	E3	Suicide Crack		88
*	7a+	Suite XV1		105
	6a	Summer Bay Babe		234
	E1	Summer Solstice		189
*	7a	Summertime Blues		47
*	VS	Sunday Driver		118
***	7b	Sunnyside Up Mix		115
	VD	Sunset		72
	HVS	Sunspots		93
*	6a+	Super Furry Frogs		205
	E1	Superdirect, The		256
	HVS	Surplus Requirements-Not		255
	E5	Survival of the Fastest 31		107
*	E5	Survival of the Fattest		107
*	6b	Suspect Criminal		210
*	6a+	Suspect Device		210
*	6a+	Suspectus		210
	E1	Suspended Animation		156
	E2	Swansong		176
	HS	Sweet Satisfaction		130
	VS	Swell		145
*	7b+	Swelling Itching Brain		99
	E5	Swiss Drum Roll		153
	HVS	Swlabr		101
*	E3	Swlabr Link		101
	E3	Synapse Collapse		187
	E2	Taerg Wall		85
*	HVS	Talking Fingers		74
*	E1	Talking Legs		74
*	E3	Tamsin		157
	E1	Tangram		163

Crag and Route Index

Stars	Grade	Route	Photo	Page
	7a+	Technicolour Yawn		170
	6a	Technobrat		217
	6a	Technocrat		217
*	E4	Telegram Sam		85
**	7c	Ten		105
*	E2	Ten Percent Special		125
**	7c	Ten Year Banana, The		57
**	7c	Ten Year Fog, The		57
*	E2	Tension Stretcher		227
	VS	Terminal		119
	5c	TGV		239
*	E3	Thanks to Ellis Brigham		188
⬛50	7a+	These Foolish Things	11	114
*	E2	Thick as a Brick		159
	VS	Thin Controller, The		208
*	6c	Thin Grey Wall		79
*	E3	Thin Wall, The		162
**	E5	Thin White Line		149
	E6	Think a Moment		65
*	7b	This Vision Thing		180
**	6c	This Way to Clitheroe		213
⬛50	7a	This Won't Hurt	241	238
*	S	Thomas the Tank Engine		208
	VS	Thorn in My Side		206
	7a	Those Stumbling Words		114
**	E2	Three Dimensions		99
**	7b	Through the Grapevine		140
	HS	Thrutch		62
*	6a	Thumb Print		113
	E3	Thumberline		127
	HVS	Thumbs		195
*	6c+	Thumbs Down		112
	E3	Tick Tock		125
*	E2	Tiger Awaits, The		127
*	E3	Titanium Man		87
*	E2	Tito		102
	HVS	Tizer the Surpriser		122
	VS	To Cut a Long Story Short		119
**	VS	Toccata		151
	E4	Tock Tick		125
	E2	Toe Bitter		146
	HVS	Tongue Pie		164
	E2	Too Many Women		150
*	7c	Too Monk to Funk		152
	6a+	Too Much Dutch		239
	VD	Topology		156
*	HVS	Tosa		72
**	E2	Touch of Class, A		99
*	E4	Touch of Spice, A		159
	VS	Tower of Babel		193
*	6c+	Trabucco		213
	E1	Trachea		257
*	6b+	Tract, The		217
⬛50	6c	Traction Control		206
***	6c+	Traction Trauma	Cover	171
*	7b+	Trade Fair		57
*	6b	Trailer Trash	17	183
**	7c+	Train to Hell		165
*	6a+	Tranche de Vie		112
	HVS	Transient		145
	VS	Tre-Fynnon		75
	6b	Trending		127
***	E6	Tres Hombres		110
*	HVS	Trick, The		84
	E1	Tripe and Landah		87
	5a	Troi Milles Voies		239
	HS	Trophy		144
	6a+	Try to Understand, ...?		207
	HVS	Tuber		162
	E1	Tweak		132
	6a+	Tweeting		127
*	HS	Twilight Chimney		122
*	HS	Twisting Corner		90
*	7a+	U Got Me Bugged		132
	6b	UHT		235
	6b	Uhu		57
	6a	Ump and Over		218
	5a	Umpalumpa Groove		218
*	VS	Un-Aided		75
	E2	Unbladed		122
***	7a	Unbroken		238
	7a	Uncrossed		114
*	6c+	Under My Thumb		112
*	6b	Under Suspicion		210
	E2	Undercurrent		130
**	7c	Underworld		55
	S	Unite		126
	VS	Unknown Crack		146
**	E2	Unknown Feelings		134
	6c	Unmegaladon		144
*	6b	Up the Spout		242
	E4	Up the Veil		157
*	7a+	uthbert, Dibble, Grub		242
**	E2	Vacances Verticales		150
	5b	Valley's Initiative, The		202
	HVS	Varlet, The		183
*	VS	Varsity Buttress		256
	E2	Varsity Wall		257
	Diff	Vegetable Crack		228
*	6b	Verruca Salt		218
*	E3	Vertical Games		84
**	E1	Vetta		75
*	E3	Vetta Variation		75
	E5	Vicious Circles		143
*	E2	Victims		227
	M	Villeta		228
	E4	Violent Ratcliffe		194
	E2	Vive La Wombat		256
	E3	Vladimir and Olga		157
	E4	Voie de Bart		112
	VD	Voila!		236
	S	Volenti		124
	HVS	Vulcer		66
*	VS	Wafer Way		143
**	E2	Waffle and Crackers		146
	6c+	Waiting for Bayley		182
	6a	Walker's Walk		236
***	7b	Walking with Barrence		170
*	VD	Wall End Climb		255
*	7b+	Wall's Have Ears		105
***	E4	Waltz in Black		186
*	HS	Wanderer		68
*	E1	Warp Commander		84
*	6c+	Was it Stew		99
*	7b+	Wasp Factory, The		188
**	E4	Wasters Mall		85
*	VS	Watzmann, The		75
*	7c	Wee Beastie, The		46
*	6b	Welcome to the Bay		234
*	5a	Welsh Fargo		201
*	4c	Welsh Wizard, The		202
*	M	West Crack		254
*	M	West Wall		254
	4c	West Wall Direct Start		254
**	7a	What's Goin' On		140
*	7a+	What's in a Word		57
	6b	When I was a Viking		105
**	7c	When Saturday Comes		170
	HS	Where We Going		57
*	6b+	Where's the President's Brain	177	176
**	E4	While the Cat's Away		246
*	7a	Whilst Rome Burns		132
**	HVS	Whim		88
	E2	Whispering Wall		144
	VD	White Crack		90
	S	White Groove		90
	E1	White Lightening		195
*	E4	White Smear		213
	HS	White Spring		61
	E3	White Wall Traverse		61

Crag Index

Crag	Page
Craig Arthur	96
Denbigh Castle Quarry	42
Devil's Gorge	52
Dinbren	160
Independence Quarry	215
Llanymynech Quarry	230
Maeshafn Quarry	58
Minera Quarry	76
Monk's Buttress	154
Pandy Outcrop	224
Pinfold	128
Pontesford Rocks	252
Pot Hole Quarry	70
Ruabon Quarry	221
Ruthin Escarpment	44
Trevor Quarry	198
Twilight Area	116
World's End	82

Stars	Grade	Route	Photo	Page
	5a	Who Fell in the Poubelle		239
*	4a	Who's Sam		211
*	6c	Wibbly Wobbly World		135
*	VS	Wilkinson Sword Edge		61
	HVS	Willy Waits for No Man		163
**	E2	Windhover		88
*	E3	Winterhill		147
	Diff	Wither		85
*	7a	Wonderwall		190
	HS	Wood Pigeon Crack		118
	E3	Wood Treatment		190
	VS	Wooly Ramble		149
⬛50	E2	World of Harmony, A	184	187
**	E4	World's Edge		84
*	6c	Would I, Should I, Fudd I		204
	E2	Xuxu		150
*	HVS	Y-Corner	129	150
*	HVS	Yale		176
*	7b+	Yankee Doodle Dandy		152
	E3	Ye Old Cod Piece		130
*	E1	Yellow		62
	E3	Yew and Me		86
	VS	Yew Tree Wall		163
	E3	Yo yo yo yo		153
*	HS	Yobo	58	63
	6a+	Yr, Yr, Yr		202
	3+	Yummy Brummy		208
	E2	Zeppelin		246
	VD	Zilla		124

Map and General Index

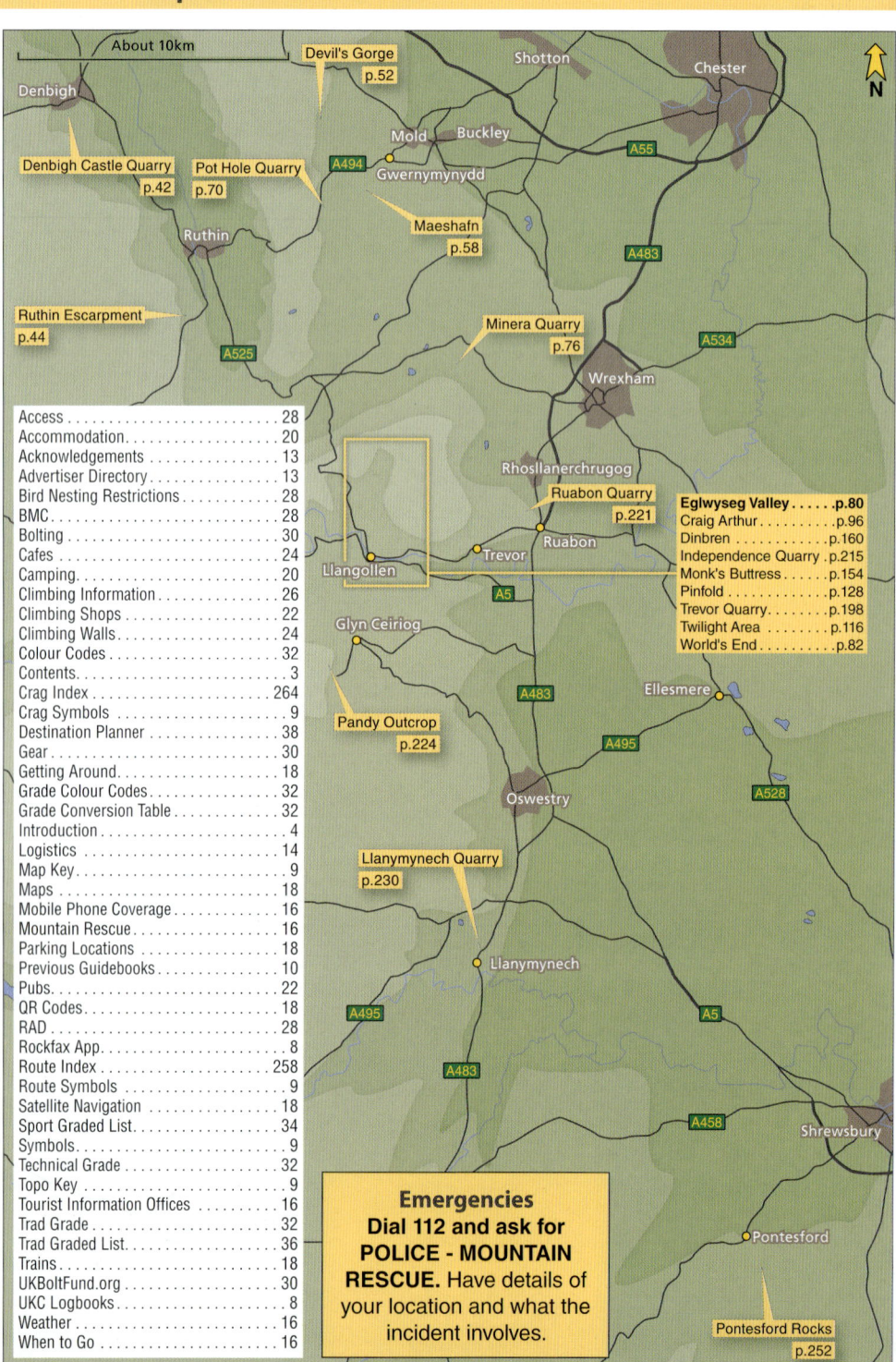

Access	28
Accommodation	20
Acknowledgements	13
Advertiser Directory	13
Bird Nesting Restrictions	28
BMC	28
Bolting	30
Cafes	24
Camping	20
Climbing Information	26
Climbing Shops	22
Climbing Walls	24
Colour Codes	32
Contents	3
Crag Index	264
Crag Symbols	9
Destination Planner	38
Gear	30
Getting Around	18
Grade Colour Codes	32
Grade Conversion Table	32
Introduction	4
Logistics	14
Map Key	9
Maps	18
Mobile Phone Coverage	16
Mountain Rescue	16
Parking Locations	18
Previous Guidebooks	10
Pubs	22
QR Codes	18
RAD	28
Rockfax App	8
Route Index	258
Route Symbols	9
Satellite Navigation	18
Sport Graded List	34
Symbols	9
Technical Grade	32
Topo Key	9
Tourist Information Offices	16
Trad Grade	32
Trad Graded List	36
Trains	18
UKBoltFund.org	30
UKC Logbooks	8
Weather	16
When to Go	16

Eglwyseg Valley p.80
Craig Arthur p.96
Dinbren p.160
Independence Quarry . p.215
Monk's Buttress p.154
Pinfold p.128
Trevor Quarry p.198
Twilight Area p.116
World's End p.82

Emergencies
Dial 112 and ask for
**POLICE - MOUNTAIN
RESCUE.** Have details of
your location and what the
incident involves.